D0090249

Second
Edition
German
in Review

Second
Edition

German in Review

Kimberly Sparks
Middlebury College

Van Horn Vail
Middlebury College

Harcourt Brace Jovanovich College Publishers
Fort Worth   Philadelphia   San Diego
New York   Orlando   Austin   San Antonio
Toronto   Montreal   London   Sydney   Tokyo

Copyright © 1986, 1967 by Holt, Rinehart and Winston, Inc.

All rights reserved. No part of this publication may be reproduced or transmitted
in any form or by any means, electronic or mechanical, including photocopy,
recording, or any information-storage and retrieval system, without permission in
writing from the publisher.

Requests for permission to make copies of any part of the work should be mailed
to: Copyrights and Permissions Department, Harcourt Brace Jovanovich, Publishers,
Orlando, Florida 32887.

Printed in the United States of America

Library of Congress Catalog Card Number: 85-80869

ISBN 0-15-529592-6
Second Edition

2 3   016   6 5 4 3

Preface

This book offers a systematic and comprehensive solution to one of the most difficult problems in foreign language teaching: providing a full and workable review of grammar and usage. At the college level, a review must accommodate students who have been taught by a variety of methods. Although instructors may assume a certain overall class achievement, they know very little about an individual student's knowledge of a given problem. For this reason we have begun each chapter with a basic review that allows students to reacquaint themselves with structural problems from the ground up. This in turn allows teachers to conduct review courses at a pace that challenges the whole class. Our method is predicated on fast-paced classroom drilling; the sequence of exercises ensures a lively tempo and guarantees mastery of the principles involved.

Each chapter proceeds from a step-by-step explanation of a particular grammatical principle to extensive exercises and drills that require students to apply that principle. Where the chapter subject requires a more detailed explanation, it is discussed in two or three stages, with corresponding exercises for each level. For example, the chapter on verbs is divided into three levels: "Present Tense"; "Past, Perfect, and Future Tenses"; and "Separable and Inseparable Prefixes." At each level students perform the accompanying exercises before going on to the next level.

Important features of the book include:

1. *A complete and systematic presentation of grammar.*

Grammar presentations are programmed to let the students prepare themselves fully *before* class; the instructor can use the entire hour for drill.

2. *A large number and variety of drills.*

Each explanation is followed by a *series of exercises* that drill the students on the different aspects of the problem at hand. Pattern drills, completion exercises, substitutions, transformations, and synthetic exercises (dehydrated sentences) lead up to the "Express-in-German" drills, which are the final group of exercises in each drill sequence. These drills use English sentences as *cues* (not as translation exercises), because the students have already dealt with the same sentences in the preceding German-German exercises. The "Express-in-German" drills demand *total performance* from the students, requiring them to confirm their knowledge of both grammar and vocabulary.

3. *Systematic introduction of vocabulary.*

Vocabulary is systematically introduced in the German-German exercises so that the students are familiar with all new vocabulary items before they reach the "Express-in-German" drills.

4. *An approach that can be used as a review and as a supplement.*

Besides serving as a review grammar, this book can supplement any basic college text that does not provide sufficient drills to ensure the students' mastery of a particular area. It can, in fact, be used to introduce, as well as reinforce, any grammatical area of college German instruction.

5. *Tapes.*

The students may use the tapes that accompany this book to prepare themselves more efficiently for fluent classroom performance.

KIMBERLY SPARKS
VAN HORN VAIL

Contents

Second
Edition
German
in Review

Verbs

1

LEVEL ONE

I. PRESENT TENSE

1. Infinitives and verb stems

The infinitive is the form of the verb found in dictionaries and word lists. Most German infinitives end in **–en.** Remove this ending and you have the *verb stem.*

INFINITIVE	STEM
sagen	sag–
finden	find–

2. Basic forms of the present tense

The present tense is formed by adding the following endings to the stem of the verb:

sagen to say						
ich	sag	e	wir	sag	en
du	sag	st	ihr	sag	t
er, sie, es	sag	t	sie, Sie	sag	en

If the stem of the verb ends in

$$-d \quad \text{or} \quad -t$$

all of the endings begin with **e.** Compare the endings of **sagen** and **finden** (whose stem ends in **–d**) in the following table.

ich	sag	e	wir	sag	en
	find	e		find	en
du	sag	st	ihr	sag	t
	find	est		find	et
er	sag	t	sie	sag	en
	find	et		find	en

The **e** in the 2nd and 3rd persons singular and in the 2nd person plural of **finden** makes the endings pronounceable.

NOTE: For a review of basic sentence structure see Chapter 14, Special Problem 1, p. 295.

3. Verb stems ending in –s, –ss, –ß, –tz, –z

Verbs of this type have a –**t** (instead of –**st**) ending in the *2nd person singular:*

heißen to be called		**lesen** to read		**sitzen** to sit	
ich	heiß e		les e		sitz e
du	heiß t		lies t		sitz t
er	heiß t		lies t		sitz t

4. Stem-vowel change: e → i or ie

Some (but not all) verbs with the stem vowel **e** change their stems in the 2nd and 3rd person singular.

e → i or ie

geben to give		sehen to see	
ich gebe	wir geben	ich sehe	wir sehen
du **gibst**	ihr gebt	du **siehst**	ihr seht
er **gibt**	sie geben	er **sieht**	sie sehen

e → i		e → ie	
essen	to eat	empfehlen	to recommend
geben	to give	geschehen	to happen
helfen	to help	lesen	to read
nehmen	to take	sehen	to see
sprechen	to speak	stehlen	to steal
sterben	to die		
treffen	to meet		
vergessen	to forget		
werfen	to throw		

EXCEPTIONS: These two verbs change a consonant as well as the stem vowel:

nehmen to take	treten to step
ich nehme	ich trete
du **nimmst**	du **trittst**
er **nimmt**	er **tritt**

5. *Stem-vowel change:* a → ä *and* au → äu

Some verbs with the stem vowels **a** and **au** change their stem vowels in the 2nd and 3rd person singular.

a → ä and au → äu

fahren to drive, travel		laufen to run	
ich fahre	wir fahren	ich laufe	wir laufen
du **fährst**	ihr fahrt	du **läufst**	ihr lauft
er **fährt**	sie fahren	er **läuft**	sie laufen

a → ä		**au → äu**	
fahren	to drive	laufen	to run
fallen	to fall	saufen	to drink (of animals); to booze
fangen	to catch		
halten	to stop		
laden	to load		
lassen	to leave		
raten	to advise		
schlafen	to sleep		
tragen	to carry		
waschen	to wash		

EXCEPTIONS: In addition to taking an umlaut, these verbs have unusual endings in the 2nd and 3rd persons singular:

halten to stop		**raten** to advise		**laden** to load	
ich	halt **e**		rat **e**		lad **e**
du	**hält st**		**rät st**		**läd st**
er	**hält**		**rät**		**läd t**
wir	halt en		rat en		lad en
ihr	halt et		rat et		lad et
sie	halt en		rat en		lad en

NOTE: Not all verbs with the stem vowels, **e, a,** and **au** undergo stem-vowel change. Those that do must be memorized.

6. *Infinitives ending in* –n (*rather than* –en)

Verbs of this type take an –n (rather than –en) ending in the *1st and 3rd persons plural:*

tun to do		**sammeln** to collect		**plaudern** to chat	
ich	tu **e**	samml	**e***	plauder	**e**
du	tu **st**	sammel	**st**	plauder	**st**
er	tu **t**	sammel	**t**	plauder	**t**
wir	tu **n**	sammel	**n**	plauder	**n**
ihr	tu **t**	sammel	**t**	plauder	**t**
sie	tu **n**	sammel	**n**	plauder	**n**

---

* The **ich**-form is **sammle** (not **sammele**). All verbs ending in **-eln** form the first person singular in this way.

The most common verbs of this type are:

ändern	to change	tun	to do
plaudern	to chat	wandern	to hike
sammeln	to collect		

7. *Exceptions:* **haben, sein, werden**

haben to have	**sein** to be	**werden** to become
ich habe	bin	werde
du hast	bist	wirst
er hat	ist	wird
wir haben	sind	werden
ihr habt	seid	werdet
sie haben	sind	werden

8. *Basic word order in simple sentences*

a. *Word order with statements*

When a simple sentence is a *statement* (rather than a question), the *verb* is the *second element* in the sentence. Look at the following example:

1	2	
Er	geht	nach Hause.
Der junge Mann	geht	nach Hause.

In both sentences, the verb is the *second element* (but not necessarily the *second word*). In the second sentence, the phrase **Der junge Mann** has simply been substituted for the word **Er.** As you can see by analogy to English, one could not break up the phrase **Der junge Mann.** Hence this entire phrase is the first element in the second sentence (as **Er** is in the first sentence), and the *verb is still the second element.*

b. *Word order with questions*

There are three ways of forming questions in German:

1. *inversion* (verb first, subject second)

1	2	
Gehen	Sie	jetzt nach Hause?

(Are you going home now?)

Both English and German can form questions by *inverting the normal word order* of the subject and the verb. In such a sentence, the *verb is the first element* (rather than the second element) and is immediately followed by the subject.

NOTE: In English questions the present tense verb form is composed of more than one word (*Are* you *going?*). In German however there is only one word (**Gehen** Sie?).

> **Verstehen** Sie ihn?
> (*Do* you *understand* him?)
>
> **Siehst** du ihn jetzt?
> (*Do* you *see* him now?)
>
> **Fahrt** ihr mit dem Schiff?
> (*Are* you *going* by ship?)

2. *question words*

A question can also be formed by using a *question word.* In this case

> the *question word* is the *first* element
> the *verb* is the *second* element
> the *subject* is the *third* element

> **Wer** ist das?
> (*Who* is that?)
>
> **Wo** ist Hans?
> (*Where* is Hans?)
>
> **Warum** geben Sie es mir nicht?
> (*Why* don't you give it to me?)
>
> **Wann** kommt er nach Hause?
> (*When* is he coming home?)

c. *Order of objects*

1. If the *direct object* is a *personal pronoun,* it comes *before* the indirect object.

> Gib es mir.   (Give it to me.)
> Gib es dem Chef.   (Give it to the boss.)

2. If the *direct object* is a *noun,* it comes *after* the indirect object.

> Gib mir den Brief. (Give me the letter.)
> Gib dem Chef den Brief. (Give the letter to the boss.)

alles, etwas and **nichts**

Alles (everything), **etwas** (something), and **nichts** (nothing) are *indefinite pronouns,* but as far as word order is concerned, they behave like *nouns.* They come after an indirect object.

> Ich zeige dir etwas. (I'll show you something.)
> Ich sage dir alles. (I'll tell you everything.)

d. *Order of adverbs*

When a German sentence contains two or more adverbial expressions, they occur in the following order:

	TIME	MANNER	PLACE
	wann (when)	wie (how)	wo (where)
ich fahre	immer	schnell	
ich fahre	sehr oft		nach München.
ich fahre		schnell	nach Hause.
ich fahre	immer	gern	nach München.

9. *Imperatives*

The imperative is the form of the verb used to give commands:

> Sagen Sie das nicht!
> (Don't say that!)

The imperative is not, however, restricted to commands in the military sense of the word. It can also be used to give instructions, to make suggestions, or even to wish someone well:

INSTRUCTION	Fahren Sie geradeaus, dann rechts.
	(Drive straight ahead, then to the right.)
SUGGESTION	Nehmen Sie das Wienerschnitzel.
	(Take the wienerschnitzel.)
WISH	Kommen Sie gut nach Hause.
	([I hope] you get home O.K.)

Commands (Sagen Sie das nicht!) commonly use an exclamation point. Instructions, suggestions, and wishes usually don't.

a. German imperative forms

In German, every verb has *three imperative forms,* corresponding to the **du-, ihr-,** and **Sie-**forms of address:

du-FORM	Sag	das nicht, Paul!
ihr-FORM	Sagt	das nicht, Kinder!
Sie-FORM	Sagen Sie	das nicht, Herr Busch!

1. The **du-**form is composed of:

verb stem + (e)

The ending **e** *must* be used if the verb stem ends in:

-t   (antworte)
-d   (finde)
-ig   (besichtige)

In most other cases, the -e ending is not used in colloquial German:

Sag das nicht!
Komm mit.
Geh nach Hause!

2. The **ihr-**form is the same as the regular 2nd person plural form of the verb. It is made up of:

verb stem + -t   (sagt, kommt)

or: *verb stem* + -et   (if the verb stem ends
in -d or -t: antwortet, findet)

3. The **Sie-**form of the imperative is also the same as the regular present tense form:

verb stem + -en

But the verb is immediately followed by **Sie:**

Folgen Sie mir, bitte!
(Follow me, please.)

b. Imperatives of verbs with stem-vowel change

1. e → i   or   ie

	e → i		e → ie	
du-FORM	**Gib**	es mir!	**Lies**	es, Thomas!
ihr-FORM	**Gebt**	es mir!	**Lest**	es, Thomas und Ulla!
Sie-FORM	**Geben Sie**	es mir!	**Lesen Sie**	es, Herr Huber!

Verbs that change their stem vowel from **e** to **i** or **ie** *use the changed stem* (**i** or **ie**) in the **du**-form of the imperative.

The **ihr**-form and the **Sie**-form use the regular infinitive stem.

2. Verbs that take an *umlaut* in the 2nd and 3rd persons singular (e.g., **ich schlafe, du schläfst, er schläft** and **ich laufe, du läufst, er läuft**) do NOT take an *umlaut* in forming the imperative:

du-FORM	**Schlaf** gut, Hans!	**Lauf** schneller!
ihr-FORM	**Schlaft** gut, Freunde!	**Lauft** schneller!
Sie-FORM	**Schlafen** Sie gut, Herr Lange!	**Laufen** Sie schneller!

Contrast: Du schläfst gut, Hans.   Schlaf gut, Hans!

c. Sein: *irregular imperative forms*

du-FORM	**Sei**	vorsichtig!
ihr-FORM	**Seid**	vorsichtig!
Sie-FORM	**Seien** Sie vorsichtig!	

d. First person plural imperative: **Gehen wir**! (*Let's go.*)

The **wir**-form of the imperative looks like the present tense of a question. The verb comes first and *is followed immediately by the pronoun* **wir.** (No stem-vowel change occurs.)

Gehen wir!   (Let's go.)
Essen wir zu Hause!   (Let's eat at home.)

■ DRILLS

Basic Forms of the Present Tense (No Stem Changes)

Replace the subjects of the following sentences with the words in parentheses, making all necessary changes in the verb forms.

1. Machst du das für mich? (er, Sie)
2. Warum antwortet er nicht? (du, sie [they])
3. Wir kaufen ein Haus. (sie [she], ich)
4. Ich gehe später nach Hause. (wir, er)
5. Er sagt das immer. (du)
6. Wir finden es später. (du, sie [she])
7. Ich bleibe hier. (du, er)
8. Wir trinken eine Cola. (er)
9. Was kosten die Krawatten? (die Krawatte)
10. Wir spielen Karten. (sie [she])
11. Ich kenne sie sehr gut. (er, wir)

Verb Stems Ending in –s, –ss, –ß, –tz, –z

Replace the subjects of the following sentences with the words in parentheses, making all necessary changes in the verb forms.

1. Wie heißen Sie? (du, sie [she])
2. Ich reise gern. (er, sie [they])
3. Wo sitzen sie? (du, ihr)
4. Reisen Sie oft nach Österreich? (du)
5. Warum sitzt er noch da? (du, Sie)

Verbs with Stem Vowels that Change from e to i or ie

Replace the subjects of the following sentences with the words in parentheses, making all necessary changes in the verb forms.

1. Wir geben es dir morgen. (sie [she])
2. Sehen Sie es? (er)
3. Sie sprechen zu schnell. (du)
4. Ich vergesse alles. (du)
5. Wir lesen es nicht. (sie [she])
6. Wann treffen Sie ihn? (du)
7. Ich nehme den Anzug. (er)

8. Sie werfen Tomaten. (er)
9. Ich empfehle das Schnitzel. (sie [she])
10. Helfen Sie ihm? (du)
11. Wo essen Sie heute abend? (er)
12. Sie stehlen den Wagen. (er)
13. Sehen Sie das Haus da drüben? (du)
14. Sie sterben bald. (er)
15. Ich lese die Zeitung. (sie [she])
16. Was empfiehlt sie? (ihr)
17. Wir geben es einem Freund. (sie [she])
18. Ich treffe ihn morgen. (wir, er)
19. Was essen Sie da? (du)
20. Nehmen Sie den Bus? (du, sie [she])

Verbs with Stems Vowels that Change from a to ä or au to äu

Replace the subjects of the following sentences with the words in parentheses, making all necessary changes in the verb forms.

1. Sie fahren bald nach Deutschland. (Erika)
2. Ich schlafe nicht genug. (Peter)
3. Was raten Sie mir? (du)
4. Tragen Sie nicht zuviel? (du)
5. Ich wasche den Wagen heute. (sie [she])
6. Ich lasse den Koffer hier. (er)
7. Warum laufen Sie weg? (er)
8. Wir laden die Koffer in den Wagen. (sie [she])
9. Wir fahren nach München. (er)
10. Katzen fangen Mäuse. (Unsere Katze)
11. Ich lade die Pistole. (er)
12. Alle Schnellzüge halten hier. (Der Schnellzug)
13. Schlafen Sie immer so lange? (ihr, du)
14. Wir waschen die Fenster heute. (er)
15. Ich trage das Gepäck für dich. (er, wir)

Verbs with Infinitives Ending in —n

1. Was tun Sie da? (du, wir)
2. Ich sammle Briefmarken. (wir, sie [she])
3. Wandert er in den Alpen? (ihr, du, Sie)
4. Ich plaudere mit ihr. (wir)
5. Er ändert nichts. (ich, wir)

Haben, sein, werden

1. Was haben Sie da? (er, du, ihr)
2. Die Kinder werden groß. (er, du, ihr)
3. Wann sind Sie zu Hause? (sie [she], du, ihr)
4. Haben Sie einen Wagen? (er, du, ihr)
5. Ich werde müde. (sie [she], wir, die Kinder)
6. Er ist nicht sicher. (wir, ich)
7. Ich habe es nicht. (sie [she], wir)
8. Sind Sie Amerikaner? (du, ihr)
9. Ich werde Arzt. (er)

Imperatives

Supply the suggested imperative form.

1. (kommen) _____ etwas früher, Herr Hammer.
   _____ etwas früher, Jürgen.

2. (helfen) _____ mir bitte, Dieter.
   _____ mir bitte, Herr Kafitz.

3. (fahren) _____ etwas langsamer, Konrad!
   _____ etwas langsamer, Frau Steltzer!

4. (werfen) _____ den Ball, Otto!

5. (arbeiten) _____ nicht so viel, Frau Hollandt.
   _____ nicht so viel, Gisela.

6. (laufen) _____ schneller, Hanna!
   _____ schneller, Herr Litz!

7. (geben) _____ es mir morgen, Frau Huber.
   _____ es mir morgen, Klaus.
   _____ es mir morgen, Jungens.

8. (essen) _____ nicht so schnell, Kai!
   _____ nicht so schnell, Kinder!

9. (sagen) _____ das nicht, Herr Lange!
   _____ das nicht, Viktor!

10. (schlafen) _____ gut, Herr Emrich.

_____ gut, Freunde.

_____ gut, Willi.

11. (vergessen) _____ die Adresse nicht, Hans.

_____ die Adresse nicht, Herr Brandt.

12. (empfehlen) _____ mir etwas, Wolf.

_____ mir etwas, Herr Ober.

13. (lassen) _____ die Pakete hier, Frau Müller.

_____ die Pakete hier, Christina.

14. (treffen) _____ uns später, Herr Kuhn.

_____ uns später, Kinder.

_____ uns später, Benno.

15. (sein) _____ vorsichtig, Frau Strauß.

_____ vorsichtig, Renate.

Mixed Drills

1. Ich kenne ihn sehr gut. (er)
2. Sie schlafen nicht genug. (Helga)
3. Wir finden es später. (du)
4. Sie sprechen zu schnell. (er)
5. Sehen Sie das Haus da drüben? (du)
6. Ich bleibe hier. (sie [she])
7. Tragen Sie nicht zuviel? (du)
8. Ich lese die Zeitung. (er)
9. Sie gehen später nach Hause. (ich)
10. Ich vergesse alles. (du)
11. Wir trinken eine Cola. (sie [she])
12. Wann treffen Sie ihn? (du)
13. Wir laden die Koffer in den Wagen. (er)
14. Sie trinken nicht, sie saufen. (er)
15. Wir geben es dir morgen. (sie [she])
16. Wie heißen Sie? (du)
17. Ich nehme den Anzug. (er)
18. Was tun Sie da? (du)
19. Machst du das für mich? (ihr)
20. Helfen Sie mir, bitte. (du-form)

21. Schlafen Sie gut. (du-form)
22. Die Kinder werden groß. (Karl)
23. Haben Sie einen Wagen? (du)
24. Warum antworten Sie nicht? (sie [she])
25. Helfen Sie ihm? (du)
26. Ich trage das Gepäck für dich. (er)
27. Fahren Sie nach München? (du)
28. Was essen Sie da? (du)
29. Er sammelt Briefmarken. (ich)
30. Warum lassen Sie den Koffer nicht hier? (du)
31. Sie werfen Tomaten. (sie [she])
32. Geben Sie es mir morgen. (du-form)
33. Iß nicht so schnell! (ihr-form)
34. Was raten Sie ihm? (du)
35. Wo sitzen Sie? (du)
36. Ich werde Arzt. (er)
37. Was kosten die Krawatten? (die Krawatte)
38. Sind Sie Amerikanerin? (sie [she])
39. Laufen Sie schneller! (du-form)
40. Ich empfehle das Schnitzel. (sie [she])
41. Wir spielen Karten. (er)
42. Alle Schnellzüge halten hier. (der Schnellzug)
43. Nehmen Sie den Bus? (du)
44. Ich werde müde. (er)
45. Kaufen Sie ein Haus? (du)
46. Wandert er in den Alpen? (Sie)
47. Sie fahren bald nach Deutschland. (Georg)
48. Was empfehlen Sie? (du)
49. Sei vorsichtig! (Sie-form)
50. Sind sie zu Hause? (Greta)

Express in German*

1. When are you meeting him, Hans?
2. He speaks too fast.
3. Are you (**du**) going to buy a house?
4. Is she an American?

---

* NOTE: German commonly uses the present tense to express future time. Although some of the English sentences in these drills are in the future tense, all of their German equivalents may be expressed by using the present tense.

5. Peter is going to Germany.
6. They're going home later.
7. He'll give it to you tomorrow.
8. Viktor forgets everything.
9. She's drinking a coke. (*use:* **Cola**)
10. Do you see the house over there, Karl?
11. What are you doing there, Mr. Huber?
12. Is Grete at home?
13. You'll find it later, Horst.
14. What is she carrying?
15. Kai is getting (is becoming) big.
16. Help me, Franz!
17. Are you taking the bus, Barbara?
18. Give it to me tomorrow, Mr. Binder.
19. They are hiking in the Alps.
20. He knows her very well.
21. Richard doesn't sleep enough.
22. What's her name?
23. Sleep well, Willi.
24. He collects stamps.
25. I'm staying here.
26. Why doesn't she answer me?
27. Are you helping him, Dieter?
28. We're meeting him tomorrow.
29. Don't eat so fast, Heinrich!
30. She's reading the newspaper.
31. Where are you (**du**) sitting?
32. He's loading the suitcases in the car.
33. What does she recommend?
34. The express train stops here.
35. He's playing cards.
36. She's getting tired.
37. Will you (**ihr**) do that for me?
38. Does he have a car?
39. Run faster, Hanna!
40. He's leaving the suitcase here.
41. She recommends the schnitzel.
42. What are you eating there, Albert?
43. We're carrying too much.
44. She's throwing tomatoes.
45. Be careful, Mrs. Strauß.

LEVEL TWO

I. PAST, PERFECT, AND FUTURE TENSES

A. Past tense and present perfect tense of weak [regular] verbs

1. Weak (regular) verbs = verbs with only one stem

Weak (regular) verbs are verbs which use the same stem in forming their present, past, and perfect tenses. Both English and German have verbs of this type. In English these verbs add the endings –ed or –d to form their past and perfect tenses. For example, the infinitive (to) *answer* is used to form:

PRESENT TENSE	they *answer*
PAST TENSE	they *answered*
PERFECT TENSE	they have *answered*

As you can see, the infinitive *answer* (which is also the stem in English) is present in every tense. By adding the appropriate endings (–ed or –d), you can form the past tense and present perfect tense of any verb of this type (e.g., they *work,* they *work*ed, they have *work*ed; they *place,* they *place*d, they have *place*d). Similarly, the past and perfect forms of German weak verbs are *predictable.*

2. Past tense

The past tense of a German *weak verb* is formed by adding *past tense endings* to its stem:

INFINITIVE	STEM
sagen	sag-
antworten	antwort-

sagen to say					
ich	sag	te	wir	sag	ten
du	sag	test	ihr	sag	tet
er	sag	te	sie	sag	ten

If the stem of the verb ends in **–d** or **–t,** an **e** is inserted before these endings to make the verb forms pronounceable:

ich	sag	te	wir	sag	ten
	antwort	ete		antwort	eten
du	sag	test	ihr	sag	tet
	antwort	etest		antwort	etet
er	sag	te	sie	sag	ten
	antwort	ete		antwort	eten

It should be noted that these are the past tense endings *for weak verbs only.*

3. Present perfect tense

a. Compound form

The present perfect is a *compound tense* (not a simple one-word form like the present or past tense). It is made up of:

AUXILIARY VERB   and   PAST PARTICIPLE
(the present tense
of **haben** or **sein***)
          Er   hat   gesagt
          (He   has   said)

b. Past participles of weak verbs

The past participles of weak (regular) verbs are formed by adding both the prefix **ge–** and the ending **–t** (or **–et** if the stem ends in **–d** or **–t**) to the verb stem:

          gesagt   (ge sag t)
          geantwortet   (ge antwort et)

NOTE: Verbs of foreign origin with infinitives ending in **–ieren** do not add a **ge–** prefix in forming their past participles:

          INFINITIVE   PAST PARTICIPLE
          reservieren   reserviert
          studieren   studiert

---

* The choice between the auxiliary verbs **haben** and **sein** is discussed on pp. 24–25.

c. *Tense formation*

In a compound tense it is the *auxiliary* that changes according to person and number (i.e., is conjugated); the past participle remains constant:

ich habe **gesagt**	wir haben **gesagt**
du hast **gesagt**	ihr habt **gesagt**
er hat **gesagt**	sie haben **gesagt**

d. *Word order*

The past participle is the *last element* in a simple sentence:

> Ich habe es ihm gestern gesagt.
> (I told him yesterday.)

The auxiliary verb (*here:* **habe**) is the second element in the sentence (i.e. is in the normal verb position).

4. *Usage*

Conversational German often uses the *present perfect* where English uses the past tense.

I said can be rendered by either

> Ich sagte or Ich habe gesagt.

He didn't answer is either

> Er antwortete nicht or Er hat nicht geantwortet.

The tendency is to use the present perfect in a give-and-take conversational situation and to use the past tense in narration. For this reason, the present perfect is often called the "conversational past" and the past tense is called the "narrative past." Many present perfect sentences in German have no present perfect equivalent in English.

> Ich habe es ihm gestern gesagt*

must be rendered in English by the past tense (I told him yesterday), since the perfect tense (I have told him yesterday) is not an English sentence.

---

* NOTE: **Sagen** *must* have a direct object in German: Ich habe **es** ihm gesagt.

5. Summary

Weak (regular) verbs are verbs that use the *same stem* to form all of their tenses. **Sagen** is a regular verb, and, as you have seen, the stem **sag–** occurs in the present, past, and perfect tenses. The forms of all verbs of this type are predictable; that is, they may be formed from the stem according to the rules just discussed. Given the infinitives **rauchen** (to smoke) and **stören** (to disturb), we know that the past tense forms (3rd person) are rauch**te** and stör**te** and that the past participles are **ge**rauch**t** and **ge**stör**t**.

B. Past tense and present perfect tense of strong [irregular] verbs

1. Strong (irregular) verbs = verbs with more than one stem

Many verbs use different stems in forming their present, past, and perfect tenses. Often only the stem vowel is affected, as in the following example in English:

PRESENT	PAST	PAST PARTICIPLE
sing	sang	sung

In other cases more radical changes are involved:

go	went	gone

2. Past tense

a. Tense formation

The past tense of strong verbs is formed by adding endings to a *past tense stem that differs from the present tense stem:*

INFINITIVE		PRESENT TENSE STEM (or *stems* where there is stem-vowel change in the present tense)	PAST TENSE STEM
singen	to sing	sing–	sang–
fahren	to ride, travel	fahr– (fähr–)	fuhr–
bitten	to ask, request	bitt–	bat–
lesen	to read	les– (lies–)	las–
nehmen	to take	nehm– (nimm–)	nahm–
kommen	to come	komm–	kam–
gehen	to go	geh–	ging–

The stem changes of irregular verbs are *not predictable* and must, therefore, be *memorized*. In most cases only the stem vowel is affected. There are, however, quite a few verbs that have double consonants in one stem and single consonants in another (e.g., kommen, kam; bitten, bat) and a few with even more radical changes (e.g., **gehen, ging**).

b. Past tense endings for strong verbs

Strong verbs have their own set of past tense endings (different from those used with weak verbs):

gehen to go					
ich	ging	—	wir	ging	en
du	ging	st	ihr	ging	t
er	ging	—	sie	ging	en

NOTE: The 1st and 3rd person singular forms have no ending.

EXCEPTIONS:

1. If the past tense stem ends in an **s**-sound (**–s, –ss, –ß, –z**), the past tense ending of the 2nd person singular is **–est** (e.g., **du lasest**).

2. If the past tense stem ends in **–t** or **–d**, the past tense ending of the 2nd person singular is **–est** (e.g., **du batest**) and the ending of the 2nd person plural is **–et** (e.g., **ihr batet**).

gehen (normal)			lesen (1) bitten (2)		
ich	ging	—	wir	ging	en
	las	—		las	en
	bat	—		bat	en
du	ging	st	ihr	ging	**t**
	las	est		las	**t**
	bat	est		bat	**et**
er	ging	—	sie	ging	en
	las	—		las	en
	bat	—		bat	en

The **e** before these endings makes the verb forms pronounceable.

3. Present perfect tense

a. Compound form

Like the present perfect tense of weak verbs, the present perfect of strong (irregular) verbs consists of:

AUXILIARY VERB	and	PAST PARTICIPLE
(the present tense		
of sein or haben)		
Er ist		gegangen.
(He has		gone)

As you can see from the example of gehen, ging, gegangen, the stem of the *past participle* of a strong (irregular) verb is *not predictable*. Thus the past participle, like the past tense stem, *must be memorized.*

b. Past participles of strong verbs

With the exception of a small group of verbs (which is discussed below), the past participles of strong verbs begin with a **ge–** prefix and take an **–en** ending:*

INFINITIVE	PAST TENSE	PAST PARTICIPLE
gehen	ging	gegangen
fahren	fuhr	gefahren
bitten	bat	gebeten
nehmen	nahm	genommen

c. Word order

A past participle is the *last element* in a simple sentence:

> Er hat es gestern genommen.
> (He took it yesterday.)

4. Mixed verbs (a sub-group of strong verbs)

There are eight verbs that follow a pattern of their own. *They change their stems* (as do all strong verbs), but, instead of adding the endings for strong

---

* Verbs with separable and inseparable prefixes behave differently. See pp. 39–44.

verbs, *they take the endings used with weak verbs:*

bringen to bring	
ich brach**te**	wir brach**ten**
du brach**test**	ihr brach**tet**
er brach**te**	sie brach**ten**

(PAST TENSE)

The past participles of these verbs, like those of weak verbs, begin with a **ge–** prefix and take the ending **–t:**

Ich habe gebrach**t**.

The six most common verbs that behave this way are:

INFINITIVE		PAST TENSE	PAST PARTICIPLE
brennen	to burn	brannte	gebrannt
bringen	to bring	brachte	gebracht
denken	to think	dachte	gedacht
kennen	to be acquainted with, know	kannte	gekannt
nennen	to call, name	nannte	genannt
rennen	to run	rannte	gerannt

NOTE: Each of these verbs uses the *same stem* to form its *past tense* and its *past participle*. In all six cases, the stem vowel for the past tense and the past participle is **a. Bringen** and **denken** have even more radical changes.

5. *Past and perfect tenses of* **haben, sein,** *and* **werden**

a. Haben

haben to have					
ich	hat	**te**	wir	hat	**ten**
du	hat	**test**	ihr	hat	**tet**
er	hat	**te**	sie	hat	**ten**

(PAST TENSE)

As you can see, the past tense of **haben** is formed by adding the *endings used with weak verbs* to a *new past tense stem* (**hat–**).

PRESENT PERFECT | Ich habe **gehabt,** etc. |

Gehabt takes the *weak* verb ending: **–t.** Its auxiliary verb is **haben.**

b. Sein

sein to be					
ich	war	—	wir	war	**en**
du	war	**st**	ihr	war	**t**
er	war	—	sie	war	**en**

PAST TENSE

The past tense of **sein** is formed by adding the *endings used with strong verbs* to a *new past tense stem* (**war–**).

PRESENT PERFECT | ich bin **gewesen,** etc. |

Gewesen takes the *strong* verb ending: **–en.** Its auxiliary verb is **sein.**

c. Werden

werden to become	
ich wurde	wir wurden
du wurdest	ihr wurdet
er wurde	sie wurden

PAST TENSE

The past tense of **werden** is unique.

PRESENT PERFECT | ich bin **geworden,** etc. |

Geworden takes the strong verb ending: **–en.** Its auxiliary verb is **sein.**

6. *Usage*

You will rarely hear the **du-** and **ihr-**forms of strong verbs in the simple past tense. The reason for this is that the **du-** and **ihr-**forms of address are used in *informal conversation*. When you use **du,** you also use the *conversational past,* that is, the *present perfect.* This is especially true when the sentence is a question, since questions are characteristic of the give and take of a conversation. There are rare exceptions; you will hear:

Wo warst du?

But other strong verb forms (e.g., "Wohin **flogst** du?") are never heard.

C. HABEN or SEIN as auxiliary verbs

Most German verbs use **haben** as their auxiliary in forming the present perfect tense. Certain verbs, however, require **sein.** **Sein** must be used when two conditions are met. (N.B. *Both* conditions must be satisfied.)

1. The verb is *intransitive* (i.e., *cannot* take a direct object)

2. The verb expresses *motion toward a destination* or it expresses a *change of condition.*

Thus:	Er hat Bier getrunken. (He drank beer.)	(Trinken is transitive.)
	Er hat gut geschlafen. (He slept well.)	(Schlafen is intransitive, but there is no motion or change of condition involved.)
	Er hat den Wagen geschoben. (He pushed the car.)	(Motion is involved, but schieben is transitive.)
	Er hat kräftig geschoben. (He pushed hard.)	(Schieben is still transitive, (i.e. it *can* take an object, even though it does not in this sentence.)
But:	Er ist schnell gelaufen. (He ran fast.)	(Laufen is an *intransitive* verb of *motion.*)

Es ist kalt geworden.	(Werden is an *intransitive**
(It's gotten cold.)	verb describing a *change of condition*.)
Er ist nach Frankfurt gefahren.	(Fahren is an *intransitive*
(He's driven to Frankfurt.)	verb of *motion*.)
Er ist gestorben.	(Sterben is an *intransitive*
(He died.)	verb describing a radical *change of condition*.)

The following three verbs don't obey these rules, but they *do use* **sein** as their perfect auxiliary nonetheless:

sein	to be	Er ist nie da gewesen.
bleiben	to stay, remain	Er ist hier geblieben.
geschehen	to happen	Was ist geschehen?

D. Past perfect tense of weak and strong verbs

a. Tense formation

The past perfect is formed like the present perfect; the only difference is that the *auxiliary verb* (**haben** or **sein**) *is in the past tense:*

PRESENT PERFECT	Ich habe es gesehen.	(I have seen it.)
PAST PERFECT	Ich hatte es gesehen	(I had seen it.)
PRESENT PERFECT	Er ist nicht gekommen.	(He hasn't come.)
PAST PERFECT	Er war nicht gekommen.	(He hadn't come.)
PRESENT PERFECT	Er ist hier gewesen.	(He's been here.)
PAST PERFECT	Er war hier gewesen.	(He'd been here.)

---

* **Werden** is always intransitive. In the sentence

Er ist Journalist geworden.
(He's become a journalist.)

Journalist is a *predicate nominative* (nominative case), not a *direct object* (accusative case). The accusative would be Journalist**en**. See weak nouns, pp. 313ff.

b. Word order

The past participle is the *last element* in a simple sentence:

> Er war sehr spät nach Hause gekommen.
> (He had come home very late.)

c. Usage

The past perfect has a special function. You use it when you want to show that something happened *before a point in past time*.

PAST	Ich wollte gestern ins Kino gehen.	(I wanted to go to the movies yesterday.)
PAST PERFECT	Aber ich hatte den Film schon gesehen.	(But I *had* already *seen* the picture; that is, I had seen it *before*.)

The past perfect is used to put past events in their proper sequence. "I wanted to go to the movies yesterday" refers to a past time. The next sentence ("But I had already seen the picture.") refers to an even earlier past time: a *past* past time. The past perfect is the tense used to make this distinction.

Look at the following example:

1ST PAST TIME	Bond *ging* in sein Zimmer. Seine geschulten Augen **sahen** es sofort.	Bond *went* into his room. His schooled eyes *saw* it immediately.
2ND PAST TIME	Ein Smersh-Agent **war** da **gewesen** und **hatte** sein Zimmer **durchsucht.**	A Smersh agent *had been* there and *had searched* his room.

The first two clauses relate something that took place in the past. The verbs, **ging** (*went*) and **sahen** (*saw*), are in the past tense. The action of the second pair of clauses also took place in the past; but it is *a period of past time prior to the past time of the first two clauses,* that is, a second, earlier period of past time.

2ND PAST TIME   1ST PAST TIME   PRESENT

X ⟵ X ⟵ X

The verbs, **war . . . gewesen** (*had been*) and **hatte . . . durchsucht** (*had searched*), are in the past perfect. The Smersh agent *had been* in Bond's room and *had searched* it (during a second period of past time).

E. Future tense = WERDEN and infinitive

a. Tense formation

The future tense is made up of the present tense of the auxiliary verb **werden** plus *an infinitive:*

Ich werde wohl kommen.	(I'll probably come.)
Du wirst wohl kommen.	(You'll probably come.)
Er wird wohl kommen.	(He'll probably come.)
Wir werden wohl kommen.	(We'll probably come.)
Ihr werdet wohl kommen.	(You'll probably come.)
Sie werden wohl kommen.	(They'll probably come.)

b. Word order

When the future tense is used, the infinitive is the *last element* in a simple sentence:

> Er wird wohl morgen kommen.
> (He will probably come tomorrow.)

As you can see from the examples, the *auxiliary* (**werden**) *changes* according to person and number (ich werde kommen, du wirst kommen, etc.), while the *infinitive remains constant.*

c. Usage

Look at the following example:

> Ich fahre nächstes Jahr nach Deutschland.
> (*I'm going* to Germany next year.)

As you can see, *future time* may be expressed by the *present tense* in both English and German. In fact, the future tense often sounds awkward. For instance, the sentence

> I will go to Germany next year

may be grammatically correct (i.e., it uses the future *tense* to express future *time*), but it sounds somewhat stilted. The same is even more often the case in German.

GENERALIZATION: Conversational German tends to use the *present tense to express future time.*

However, German uses the future tense in the following cases:

1. *in the absence of a time expression*

In the sentence

> Er reist nächstes Jahr durch ganz Europa.
> (He's going to travel all over Europe next year).*

the time expression **nächstes Jahr** clearly shows that the action is to take place in the *future* (next year). When the time expression is omitted, the action appears to be taking place in the present:

> Er reist durch ganz Europa.

In such a case, **werden** is used to avoid any confusion of time and to place the action clearly in the future:

> Er wird durch ganz Europa reisen.

2. **werden** *and* **wohl**

> Er wird wohl zu Hause bleiben.
> (He'll probably stay at home.)

Werden and **wohl** are used to indicate probability: a judgment or assumption on the part of the speaker.

3. **werden** *and present time*

> Das wird Ihre Schwester sein.
> (That will be your sister, i.e., I assume that is your sister.)

---

* English commonly uses the phrase *going to* to imply future time.

Werden can be used to indicate an assumption about something connected with the present time. This will occur in such contexts as:

Who is knocking at the door? *That'll be Peter.*
Wer klopft an die Tür? Das wird Peter sein .

DRILLS

Past Tense and Present Perfect Tense of Weak Verbs

Put the following sentences into the past tense and the present perfect tense.

1. Ich hole den Schlüssel.
2. Wir warten auf dich.
3. Sie kauft ein neues Sofa.
4. Wir sagen es ihm später.
5. Sie reservieren ein Zimmer für uns.
6. Das ändert nichts.
7. Wir wandern in den Alpen.
8. Ich lerne das nicht.
9. Großvater reist immer gern.
10. Zeigt er dir die Wohnung?
11. Wir fragen nach der Adresse.
12. Sie spielt Tennis.
13. Ich mache eine kurze Reise.
14. Sie tanzen den ganzen Abend.
15. Er studiert in Heidelberg.
16. Erich sammelt Briefmarken.
17. Sie antworten nicht auf meine Briefe.
18. Peter macht zu viele Fehler.
19. Wir suchen ihn den ganzen Tag.
20. Hanna plaudert mit ihrem Freund.

Past Tense and Present Perfect Tense of Strong Verbs

Although the stem changes of strong verbs are *not* predictable, certain recurring patterns should be noted.

a. **essen, geben, lesen, sehen, treten**

	INFINITIVE	(3RD PERSON)	PAST	PAST PARTICIPLE
	e	(i or ie)	a	e
to eat	essen	(ißt)	aß	gegessen
to give	geben	(gibt)	gab	gegeben
to read	lesen	(liest)	las	gelesen
to see	sehen	(sieht)	sah	gesehen
to step	treten	(tritt)	trat	ist getreten

b. **helfen, nehmen, sprechen, sterben, treffen, werfen**

	INFINITIVE	(3RD PERSON)	PAST	PAST PARTICIPLE
	e	(i)	a	o
to help	helfen	(hilft)	half	geholfen
to take	nehmen	(nimmt)	nahm	genommen
to speak	sprechen	(spricht)	sprach	gesprochen
to die	sterben	(stirbt)	starb	ist gestorben
to meet	treffen	(trifft)	traf	getroffen
to throw	werfen	(wirft)	warf	geworfen

Put the following sentences into the past tense and the present perfect tense unless otherwise indicated.

1. Wir geben es ihm Montag.
2. Er spricht zu schnell.
3. Ich nehme den braunen Anzug.
4. Wir essen immer zu Hause.
5. Er liest zu viel.
6. Sie wirft es aufs Sofa.
7. Wir sehen ihn sehr selten.
8. Ich treffe ihn um zehn Uhr.
9. Er tritt durch die Tür.
10. Er stirbt.
11. Hilft sie dir? (*present perfect* only)

c. **bleiben, heißen, schreiben, steigen**

	INFINITIVE	PAST	PAST PARTICIPLE
	ei	ie	ie
to stay	bleiben	blieb	ist geblieben
to be called	heißen	hieß	geheißen
to write	schreiben	schrieb	geschrieben
to climb	steigen	stieg	ist gestiegen

d. **fliegen, schieben, schließen**

	INFINITIVE	PAST	PAST PARTICIPLE
	ie	o	o
to fly	fliegen	flog	ist geflogen
to shove, push	schieben	schob	geschoben
to close	schließen	schloß	geschlossen

e. **finden, singen, trinken**

	INFINITIVE	PAST	PAST PARTICIPLE
	i	a	u
to find	finden	fand	gefunden
to sing	singen	sang	gesungen
to drink	trinken	trank	getrunken

Put the following sentences into the past tense and the present perfect tense.

1. Ich schreibe ihm einen langen Brief.
2. Sie trinkt eine Cola.
3. Herr Siebenmann fliegt nach Zürich.
4. Ich bleibe zu Hause.
5. Er schließt die Tür.
6. Ich finde seine Adresse nicht.

7. Sie steigt aus dem Wagen.
8. Er singt sehr laut.
9. Wie heißt der Film?
10. Ich schiebe den Brief unter die Tür.

f. **fahren, laden, schlagen, tragen, waschen**

	INFINITIVE	(3RD PERSON)	PAST	PAST PARTICIPLE
	a	(ä)	u	a
to drive	fahren	(fährt)	fuhr	ist (hat) gefahren
to load	laden	(lädt)	lud	geladen
to strike, hit	schlagen	(schlägt)	schlug	geschlagen
to carry; wear	tragen	(trägt)	trug	getragen
to wash	waschen	(wäscht)	wusch	gewaschen

g. **fallen, halten, lassen, raten, schlafen // laufen**

	INFINITIVE	(3RD PERSON)	PAST	PAST PARTICIPLE
	a	(ä)	ie	a
to fall	fallen	(fällt)	fiel	ist gefallen
to hold, think	halten	(hält)	hielt	gehalten
to leave	lassen	(läßt)	ließ	gelassen
to advise	raten	(rät)	riet	geraten
to sleep	schlafen	(schläft)	schlief	geschlafen
	au	(äu)	ie	au
to run	laufen	(läuft)	lief	ist gelaufen

Put the following sentences into the past tense and the present perfect tense.

1. Er trägt zu viele Pakete.
2. Sie fahren zu schnell.
3. Er schläft zuviel.
4. Jeden Samstag wäscht er den Wagen.
5. Ich halte nicht viel von ihm.

6. Sie fährt den Wagen nach München.
7. Was rät er ihm?
8. Es schlägt drei Uhr.
9. Er läuft sehr schnell.
10. Wir lassen die Koffer hier.
11. Sie fällt aus dem Bett.
12. Er lädt die Koffer in den Wagen.

h. bringen, denken, kennen

	INFINITIVE	PAST	PAST PARTICIPLE
	e / i	a	a
to bring	bringen	brachte	gebracht
to think	denken	dachte	gedacht
to know	kennen	kannte	gekannt

i. haben, sein, werden

	INFINITIVE	PAST	PAST PARTICIPLE
to have	haben	hatte	gehabt
to be	sein	war	ist gewesen
to become (get)	werden	wurde	ist geworden

Put the following sentences into the past tense and the present perfect tense.

1. Es ist nicht sicher.
2. Ich kenne ihn sehr gut.
3. Sie bringt es mir heute.
4. Er wird Arzt.
5. Wir sind zu Hause.
6. Ich denke an etwas anderes.
7. Sie hat Zeit.

j. Exceptions: bitten, gehen, kommen, rufen, sitzen, stehen

Except for **haben, sein,** and **werden,** the verbs you have drilled up until now have belonged to sets which can be expanded or added to. The verbs drilled below are not of that type. They are not members of a larger set or group and must therefore be memorized individually.

	INFINITIVE	PAST	PAST PARTICIPLE
to ask, request	bitten	bat	gebeten
to go	gehen	ging	ist gegangen
to come	kommen	kam	ist gekommen
to call	rufen	rief	gerufen
to sit	sitzen	saß	gesessen
to stand	stehen	stand	gestanden

Put the following sentences into the past tense and the present perfect tense.

1. Er kommt später.
2. Wir gehen nach Hause.
3. Wo steht er?
4. Sie ruft ein Taxi.
5. Sie sitzen auf der anderen Seite.
6. Er bittet mich um zehn Mark.

Mixed Drills: Past Tense and Present Perfect Tense of Strong Verbs

Put the following sentences into the past tense and the present perfect tense, unless otherwise indicated.

1. Wir geben es ihm Montag.
2. Sie hat Zeit.
3. Er spricht zu schnell.
4. Ich nehme den braunen Anzug.
5. Sie sitzen auf der anderen Seite.
6. Ich bleibe zu Hause.
7. Sie bringt es mir heute.
8. Hilft sie dir? (*present perfect* only)
9. Wir essen immer zu Hause.
10. Sie läuft sehr schnell.
11. Es ist nicht sicher.
12. Ich schreibe ihm einen langen Brief.
13. Sie wirft es aufs Sofa.
14. Er liest zuviel.
15. Sie trinkt eine Cola.

16. Wie heißt der Film?
17. Sie wird Ärztin.
18. Wir sind zu Hause.
19. Er ruft ein Taxi.
20. Er trägt zu viele Pakete.
21. Wir laden die Koffer in den Wagen.
22. Ich komme später.
23. Wo steht er?
24. Wir lassen die Koffer hier.
25. Er bittet mich um zehn Mark.
26. Wir gehen nach Hause.
27. Ich denke an etwas anderes.
28. Ich kenne ihn sehr gut.
29. Wir treffen ihn um zehn Uhr.
30. Sie steigt aus dem Wagen.
31. Mutti wird böse und wirft die Lampe durch das Fenster.
32. Er schläft zuviel.
33. Sie fahren zu schnell.
34. Er stirbt.
35. Es schlägt drei Uhr.
36. Ich schiebe den Brief unter die Tür.
37. Wir sehen ihn sehr selten.
38. Er tritt durch die Tür.
39. Ich halte nicht viel von ihm.
40. Ich finde seine Adresse nicht.
41. Herr Siebenmann fliegt nach Zürich.
42. Was rätst du ihm? (*present perfect* only)
43. Er schließt die Tür.
44. Jeden Samstag wäscht er den Wagen.
45. Sie singen und tanzen den ganzen Abend.
46. Sie fährt den Wagen nach München.
47. Sie essen und trinken sehr viel.

Present Perfect and Past Perfect Tenses of Weak and Strong Verbs

Put the following sentences into the present perfect tense and the past perfect tense.

1. Wir gehen nach Hause.
2. Ich komme später.
3. Wir suchen ihn den ganzen Tag.

4. Ich schreibe ihm einen langen Brief.
5. Er wird Arzt.
6. Wir geben es ihm Montag.
7. Ich lerne das nicht.
8. Herr Siebenmann fliegt nach Zürich.
9. Ich denke an etwas anderes.
10. Wir sind zu Hause.
11. Sie steigt aus dem Wagen.
12. Wir warten auf dich.
13. Er fährt nach München.
14. Ich bleibe zu Hause.
15. Er läuft sehr schnell.
16. Ich bringe es Ihnen.
17. Er zeigt uns die Bilder.

Future Tense

Put the following sentences into the future tense (using **werden**).

1. Sehen Sie ihn?
2. Wir sind zu Hause.
3. Was rätst du ihm?
4. Sie hat wohl Zeit.
5. Helft ihr ihm?
6. Das lesen wir wohl nicht.
7. Ich bringe es dir.
8. Sie tun es nicht.
9. Wir spielen Karten.
10. Siehst du ihn?

Mixed Drills

Put the following sentences into the past tense and the present perfect tense, unless otherwise indicated. Both weak and strong verbs are included.

1. Wir warten auf dich.
2. Er spricht zu schnell.
3. Es ist nicht sicher.
4. Peter macht zu viele Fehler.
5. Ich komme später.
6. Wo steht er?
7. Ich hole den Schlüssel.

8. Sie ruft ein Taxi.
9. Er reist nach Süddeutschland.
10. Wie heißt der Film?
11. Wir sehen ihn sehr oft.
12. Wir tanzen den ganzen Abend.
13. Sie gibt es ihm Montag.
14. Wir essen immer zu Hause.
15. Er schließt die Tür.
16. Ich treffe ihn um zehn Uhr.
17. Erich sammelt Briefmarken.
18. Das ändert nichts.
19. Sie hat Zeit.
20. Sie sitzen auf der anderen Seite.
21. Ich lerne das nicht.
22. Er schläft zuviel.
23. Ich finde seine Adresse nicht.
24. Herr Siebenmann fliegt nach Zürich.
25. Er stirbt.
26. Sie fahren zu schnell.
27. Sie steigt aus dem Wagen.
28. Wir spielen Tennis.
29. Er wird Arzt.
30. Er trägt zu viele Pakete.
31. Wir suchen ihn den ganzen Tag.
32. Hilft er dir? (*present perfect* only)
33. Ich bleibe zu Hause.
34. Ich mache eine kurze Reise.
35. Er bittet mich um zehn Mark.
36. Ich denke an etwas anderes.
37. Wir laden die Koffer in den Wagen.
38. Wir kaufen ein neues Sofa.
39. Sie trinkt eine Cola.
40. Wir gehen nach Hause.
41. Es schlägt drei Uhr.
42. Sie fragt ihn nach der Adresse.
43. Wir wandern in den Alpen.
44. Ich nehme den braunen Anzug.
45. Sie bringt es mir heute.
46. Er liest zuviel.
47. Sie antworten nicht auf meine Briefe.
48. Er läuft sehr schnell.
49. Ich schreibe ihm einen langen Brief.

50. Sie wirft es aufs Sofa.
51. Hanna plaudert mit ihrem Freund.
52. Wir sind zu Hause.
53. Ich kenne ihn sehr gut.
54. Ich lasse den Koffer hier.
55. Er fährt meinen Wagen nach München.
56. Sie essen und trinken sehr viel.
57. Was raten Sie? (*present perfect* only)

Express in German

Express each sentence in the past tense and the present perfect tense, unless otherwise indicated.

1. He came later.
2. He slept too much.
3. I gave it to him Monday.
4. We bought a new sofa.
5. Where was he standing?
6. I stayed home.
7. She brought it to me yesterday.
8. I took (**machen**) a short trip.
9. We went home.
10. He became a doctor.
11. I was thinking of (**denken an** + *acc.*) something else.
12. She called a taxi.
13. He spoke too fast.
14. I met him at ten o'clock.
15. We danced all evening.
16. She had time.
17. It wasn't certain.
18. He carried too many packages.
19. I didn't learn that.
20. She got out of the car.
21. I knew him very well.
22. What did you advise? (*present perfect* only)
23. He ran very fast.
24. We played tennis.
25. It struck three o'clock.
26. I wrote him a long letter.
27. We were at home.

28. I took the brown suit.
29. She drank a coke. (**eine Cola**).
30. Did he help you? (*present perfect* only)
31. I left the suitcase here.
32. He read too much.
33. I didn't find his address.
34. Peter made too many mistakes.
35. We always ate at home.
36. We waited for (**warten auf** + *acc.*) you.
37. They didn't answer (**antworten auf** + *acc.*) my letters.
38. We saw him very often.
39. She closed the door.
40. We were hiking (**wandern**) in the Alps.
41. He loaded the suitcases in the car.
42. He asked me for (**bitten um** + *acc.*) ten marks.
43. They were driving too fast.
44. She traveled to South Germany.
45. Mr. Siebenmann flew to Zürich.
46. What was the film called?
47. That didn't change anything.
48. We asked him for (**fragen nach** + *dat.*) the address.
49. He drove my car to Munich.

LEVEL THREE

I. SEPARABLE AND INSEPARABLE PREFIXES

A. Verbs with inseparable prefixes

1. Introduction

A verb prefix is a syllable or a word that changes the meaning of the verb it is attached to. Look at the following examples:

stehen	to stand	verstehen	to understand
kommen	to come	bekommen	to receive, get
stellen	to put	bestellen	to order

The addition of a prefix can alter the meaning of a verb considerably.

2. Inseparable prefixes

The prefixes you have just seen are called *inseparable prefixes* because they remain *permanently attached to the basic verb*. Look at the following examples:

a. A weak verb: **bezahlen** (*to pay*)

PRESENT   Ich bezahle die Rechnung.   (I'll pay the bill.)
PAST   Ich bezahlte die Rechnung.   (I paid the bill.)
PRES. PERF. Ich habe die Rechnung bezahlt.   (I've paid the bill.)

b. A strong verb: **verstehen** (*to understand*)

PRESENT   Ich verstehe es nicht.   (I don't understand it.)
PAST   Ich verstand es nicht.   (I didn't understand it.)
PRES. PERF. Ich habe es nicht verstanden.   (I haven't understood it.)

NOTE 1: Adding an inseparable prefix to a verb doesn't affect the basic conjugation of the verb. If the basic verb is strong, the prefixed verb is also strong; if the basic verb is weak, the prefixed verb is also weak.

NOTE 2: Verbs with inseparable prefixes do not take a **ge–** prefix in forming their past participles:

Ich habe die Rechnung bezahlt.
Er hat es nicht verstanden.

	INFINITIVE	PAST	PAST PARTICIPLE	3RD PERSON PRESENT
STRONG VERB	**verstehen**	verstand	verstanden	versteht
WEAK VERB	**bezahlen**	bezahlte	bezahlt	bezahlt

3. Sein *or* haben

To take the auxiliary **sein,** a verb must satisfy two conditions.

1. It must be intransitive (that is, not take a direct object).

2. It must express *motion toward a destination* or a *change of condition*.

Otherwise the verb uses the auxiliary **haben.** (See p. 24.)

The addition of a prefix gives the basic verb a new meaning that determines whether the prefixed verb takes **sein** or **haben.** For example, the verb **kommen** is intransitive and it expresses motion toward a destination. **Kommen** therefore satisfies both conditions for taking **sein** as its auxiliary.

On the other hand, the prefixed verb **bekommen** (to get, receive) is *transitive* (it takes a direct object). Its auxiliary is therefore **haben.**

      Er ist gestern gekommen.   (He came yesterday.)

but   Er hat den Brief gestern bekommen.   (He got the letter yesterday.)

You have to decide in each individual case whether the prefixed verb takes **sein** or **haben.**

4. Stress

Inseparable prefixes are not stressed: **bezáhlen, verstéhen**

5. A list of common inseparable prefixes

        be–   ge–
        emp–   miß–
        ent–   ver–
        er–   zer–

6. Unter- and über- as inseparable prefixes

The prepositions **unter** and **über** normally function as inseparable prefixes. They are not stressed:

        unterschréiben   to sign
        übersétzen   to translate

The principal parts of these verbs are:

INFINITIVE	PAST	PAST PARTICIPLE	3RD PERSON PRESENT
unterschreiben	unterschrieb	unterschrieben	unterschreibt
übersetzen	übersetzte	übersetzt	übersetzt

B. Verbs with separable prefixes

1. Introduction

Separable prefixes are normally prepositions or adverbs. That is, they are complete words in their own right.

mit · kommen   to come along
weg · gehen   to go away

2. Word order

Look at the following examples:

a. A weak verb: **aufmachen** (*to open*)

PRESENT	Sie macht die Tür auf.	(She's opening the door.)
PAST	Sie machte die Tür auf.	(She opened the door.)
PRES. PERF.	Sie hat die Tür aufgemacht.	(She has opened the door.)

b. A strong verb: **mitkommen** (*to come along*)

PRESENT	Er kommt nicht mit.	(He's not coming along.)
PAST	Er kam nicht mit.	(He didn't come along.)
PRES. PERF.	Er ist nicht mitgekommen.	(He hasn't come along.)

Notice two things:

1. The separable prefix always comes at the end of the sentence.

2. Unlike inseparable prefixes, separable prefixes *do* use the normal **ge**– prefix in forming their past participles. Compare these two sentences:

Er ist nicht gekommen.   (He didn't [hasn't] come.)
Er ist nicht mitgekommen.   (He didn't [hasn't] come along.)

In both examples, the past participle is formed in essentially the same way: **gekommen** and mit**gekommen**. When a separable prefix is present, it immediately precedes the basic past participle. The two parts are written as one word:

mitgekommen

	INFINITIVE	PAST	PAST PARTICIPLE	3RD PERSON PRESENT
STRONG VERB	**mitkommen**	kam mit	mitgekommen	kommt mit
WEAK VERB	**aufmachen**	machte auf	aufgemacht	macht auf

3. sein *or* haben

As with inseparable prefixes, the meaning of the prefixed verb determines whether the auxiliary will be **sein** or **haben**. For example, **stehen** (to stand) is intransitive (meeting one condition for **sein**), but it clearly doesn't express motion of any kind. Therefore, it takes **haben**. But **aufstehen** (to stand up, get up) fulfills both conditions—it is intransitive and it expresses motion—so it takes sein as its auxiliary.

Wir sind sehr früh aufgestanden.   (We got up very early.)

4. Stress

Separable prefixes—rather than the stem of the basic verb—receive the primary stress: **ánkommen, aúfmachen.**

5. Common separable prefixes

ab–	ein–	vorbei–
an–	los–	weg–
auf–	mit–	zu–*
aus–	nach–*	zurück–
bei–*	vor–	zusammen–

---

* The objects of verbs with these prefixes are often in the dative case:

Du hörst mir nicht zu. (You're not listening to me.)

C. Summary table

Compare the principal parts of **ankommen** (**kommen** plus a separable prefix) and **bekommen** (**kommen** plus an inseparable prefix):

	INFINITIVE	PAST	PAST PARTICIPLE	3RD PERS. PRESENT
SEPARABLE	**mítkommen**	kam . . . mít	ist mítgekommen	kommt . . . mít
INSEPARABLE	**bekómmen**	bekám	hat bekómmen	bekómmt

NOTE: *Separable* prefixes are *stressed:* **ánkommen.** *Inseparable* prefixes are *unstressed:* **bekómmen.**

 DRILLS

Inseparable Prefixes

Use the following words to make complete sentences in the present, past, and present perfect tenses, unless otherwise indicated.

1. Ich / bezahlen / Rechnung
2. Wir / bestellen / Buch / für Sie
3. Sie (she) / empfehlen / Schnitzel
4. Ich / verstehen / ihn einfach nicht
5. Erkennen / du / mich nicht / ? (*present* and *present perfect* only)
6. Sie (they) / verkaufen / ihr Haus
7. Übersetzen / er / Brief / für dich / ?
8. Wir / bekommen / unseren Computer heute
9. Ich / erzählen / ihnen alles
10. Sie (she) / unterschreiben / Scheck / nicht

Separable Prefixes

Make complete sentences in the present, past, and present perfect tenses, unless otherwise indicated.

1. Wir / zurückbringen / Wagen
2. Er / ausgeben / zu viel Geld

3. Ich / einschlafen / früh
4. Wann / ankommen / Sie / ?
5. Ich / abholen / Wagen / später
6. Wir / vorbeikommen / um acht Uhr
7. Anna / aussehen / sehr gut
8. Wir / ausmachen / Licht
9. Er / aufwachen / plötzlich
10. Ich / anmachen / Fernseher
11. Warum / weggehen / Sie / ?
12. Ich / anziehen / Jacke
13. Sie (she) / ausziehen / Mantel
14. Zumachen / Sie / Fenster / ?
15. Du / zuhören / mir nicht (*present* and *present perfect* only)
16. Ich / einladen / ihn
17. Zug / abfahren / um zwanzig Uhr
18. Sie (she) / aufmachen / Tür
19. Kurt / anrufen / mich heute
20. Er / mitnehmen / seine Freundin

Mixed Drills

Make complete sentences in the present, past, and present perfect tenses, unless otherwise indicated.

1. Wir / ausmachen / Licht
2. Anna / aussehen / sehr gut
3. Ich / bezahlen / Rechnung
4. Wann / ankommen / Sie / ?
5. Ich / anmachen / Fernseher
6. Sie (she) / unterschreiben / Scheck / nicht
7. Wir / vorbeikommen / um acht Uhr
8. Kurt / anrufen / mich heute
9. Ich / verstehen / ihn einfach nicht
10. Warum / weggehen / Sie / ?
11. Er / ausgeben / zu viel Geld
12. Wir / bestellen / Buch / für Sie
13. Zumachen / Sie / Fenster / ?
14. Ich / abholen / Wagen / später
15. Sie (she) / ausziehen / Mantel
16. Wir / bekommen / unseren Computer / heute
17. Ich / einschlafen / früh

18. Sie (she) / aufmachen / Tür
19. Übersetzen / er / Brief / für dich / ?
20. Ich / anziehen / Jacke
21. Zug / abfahren / um zwanzig Uhr
22. Sie (they) / verkaufen / ihr Haus
23. Wir / zurückbringen / Wagen
24. Ich / erzählen / ihnen alles
25. Du / zuhören / mir nicht (*present* and *present perfect* only)
26. Er / mitnehmen / seine Freundin
27. Sie (she) / empfehlen / Schnitzel
28. Ich / einladen / ihn
29. Er / aufwachen / plötzlich
30. Erkennen / du / mich nicht / ? (*present* and *present perfect* only)

Express in German

1. We brought the car back. (*past*)
2. Anna is looking very well.
3. I paid the bill. (*present perfect*)
4. She opened the door. (*past*)
5. I'll pick the car up later.
6. Did he translate the letter for you? (*present perfect*)
7. When did you (**Sie**) arrive? (*present perfect*)
8. I'm putting on a sportscoat (jacket).
9. Did you (**Sie**) close the window? (*present perfect*)
10. They sold their house. (*past*)
11. I fell asleep early. (*present perfect*)
12. We'll order the book for you.
13. She took off her coat. (*past*)
14. Kurt called me up today. (*present perfect*)
15. I told them everything. (*present perfect*)
16. We turned out the light. (*past*)
17. Don't you (**du**) recognize me?
18. I turned on the television. (*present perfect*)
19. She recommended the schnitzel. (*present perfect*)
20. He spent too much money. (*past*)
21. I just don't understand him.
22. We came by at eight o'clock. (*present perfect*)
23. He woke up suddenly. (*past*)
24. You (**du**) aren't listening to me.

25. We got our computer today. (*present perfect*)
26. The train leaves at eight o'clock in the evening. (*lit.* "twenty o'clock")
27. I invited them. (*present perfect*)
28. She didn't sign the check. (*past*)
29. Why did you (**Sie**) leave? (*present perfect*)
30. He's taking his girlfriend along.

Adjective
Endings

2

LEVEL ONE

I. STRONG DECLENSION OF ADJECTIVES

The simplest sort of adjective-noun combination is a two-word phrase consisting of a single noun preceded by a single adjective:

> dieser Tisch
> dieses Sofa
> diese Lampe

In phrases of this sort the adjective takes a set of endings called *strong endings*. These are the fullest, most explicit adjective endings in German: *they show as much as the language can show about the gender, case and number.* The following table summarizes the strong endings:

	Singular		
	MASCULINE	NEUTER	FEMININE
NOMINATIVE	dieser Tisch	dieses Sofa	diese Lampe
ACCUSATIVE	diesen Tisch	dieses Sofa	diese Lampe
DATIVE	diesem Tisch	diesem Sofa	dieser Lampe
GENITIVE	dieses Tisches	dieses Sofas	dieser Lampe

	Plural		
	ALL GENDERS		
NOMINATIVE	diese	Tische, Sofas, Lampen	
ACCUSATIVE	diese	Tische, Sofas, Lampen	
DATIVE	diesen	Tischen, Sofas, Lampen	
GENITIVE	dieser	Tische, Sofas, Lampen	

Notice how much the strong adjective endings look like the endings of the definite article:

	MASCULINE	NEUTER	FEMININE	PLURAL
NOMINATIVE	der	das	die	die
	dieser	dieses	diese	diese
ACCUSATIVE	den	das	die	die
	diesen	dieses	diese	diese
DATIVE	dem	dem	der	den
	diesem	diesem	dieser	diesen
GENITIVE	des	des	der	der
	dieses	dieses	dieser	dieser

II. THE DER-WORDS

The following adjectives *always take strong endings.* They are called **der-words.**

der	the *or* that
dieser	this
jeder	each *or* every
welcher	which (the question word)

DRILLS

Masculine Singular Strong Endings

Supply the required endings.

NOM.	dieser	der
ACC.	diesen	den
DAT.	diesem	dem

NOMINATIVE
1. Dies___ Film ist sehr gut.
2. D___ Brief ist schon da.
3. Was kostet dies___ Wein?
4. Welch___ Zug ist das?
5. Dies___ Tisch ist zu klein.

ACCUSATIVE
1. Ich sehe d___ Film morgen.
2. Kennst du dies___ Mann?
3. Welch___ Wein trinkst du?
4. Ich nehme d___ Bus.
5. Ich kaufe dies___ Wein nicht.

DATIVE
1. Ich fahre mit d___ Zug.
2. Was machen Sie mit dies___ Tisch?
3. Antworten Sie d___ Mann!
4. Mit welch___ Zug fährst du?
5. Es ist auf d___ Tisch.

MIXED CASES
1. Welch___ Zug ist das?
2. Kaufst du d___ Tisch?
3. Was kostet dies___ Wein?
4. Was machen Sie mit dies___ Tisch?
5. Ich nehme d___ Bus.
6. Dies___ Film ist sehr gut.
7. Er fährt mit d___ Zug.
8. Kennst du dies___ Mann?

9. Antworten Sie d__ Mann!
10. Welch____ Wein trinkst du?

Neuter Singular Strong Endings

NOM.	dieser	das
ACC.	dieses	das
DAT.	diesem	dem

NOMINATIVE
1. D____ Bild kostet nur fünfzig Mark.
2. Dies____ Bier ist sehr gut.
3. Welch____ Haus ist das?
4. Was kostet dies____ Buch?
5. Jed____ Kind liebt Schokolade.

ACCUSATIVE
1. Liest du dies____ Buch?
2. Ich finde d____ Bier nicht gut.
3. Lesen Sie jed____ Wort!
4. Ich nehme dies____ Sofa.
5. Welch____ Haus kauft er?

DATIVE
1. Sie kommt gerade aus d____ Haus.
2. In welch____ Hotel bist du?
3. Was machst du mit dies____ Bild?
4. Er sitzt auf d____ Sofa.
5. Warum antwortest du d____ Mädchen nicht?

MIXED CASES
1. Dies____ Bier ist sehr gut.
2. Welch____ Haus kauft er?
3. Was machen Sie mit dies____ Bild?
4. Ich nehme dies____ Sofa.
5. Liest du d____ Buch?
6. In welch____ Hotel bist du?
7. D____ Bild kostet nur fünfzig Mark.
8. Welch____ Haus ist das?

9. Sie kommt gerade aus d____ Haus.
10. Warum antwortest du d____ Mädchen nicht?

Feminine Singular Strong Endings

NOM.	diese	die
ACC.	diese	die
DAT.	dieser	der

NOMINATIVE
1. Ich nehme dies____ Jacke.
2. Welch____ Zeitung ist das?
3. Was kostet dies____ Lampe?
4. D____ Adresse ist nicht richtig.
5. Dies____ Krawatte ist zu teuer.

ACCUSATIVE
1. Siehst du d____ Frau da drüben?
2. Welch____ Zeitung lesen Sie?
3. Er kennt jed____ Straße in Berlin.
4. Welch____ Krawatte nehmen Sie?
5. Ich kenne dies____ Stadt nicht sehr gut.

DATIVE
1. In welch____ Stadt wohnt er?
2. Was machen wir mit dies____ Lampe?
3. Helfen Sie d____ Frau!
4. Aus welch____ Stadt kommt sie?
5. Das kommt mit d____ Zeit.

MIXED CASES
1. D____ Adresse ist nicht richtig.
2. Welch____ Krawatte nehmen Sie?
3. Was machen wir mit dies____ Lampe?
4. Ich kenne dies____ Stadt nicht sehr gut.
5. Ich nehme dies____ Jacke.
6. Aus welch____ Stadt kommt sie?
7. Er kennt jed____ Straße in Berlin.
8. Was kostet dies____ Lampe?

9. Helfen Sie d____ Frau!
10. Welch____ Zeitung liest du?

Plural Strong Endings (All Genders)

NOM.	diese	die
ACC.	diese	die
DAT.	diesen	den

NOMINATIVE

1. D____ Bücher sind hier.
2. Dies____ Tische sind zu klein.
3. Welch____ Züge fahren nach Berlin?
4. Was kosten d____ Lampen?
5. Dies____ Adressen sind nicht richtig.

ACCUSATIVE

1. Dies____ Bücher lesen wir nicht.
2. Siehst du d____ Häuser da drüben?
3. Welch____ Zeitungen meinst du?
4. Ich finde dies____ Hotels zu teuer.
5. Liest du d____ Bücher?

DATIVE

1. Was geben wir d____ Kinder____?*
2. Wer wohnt in dies____ Häuser____?

---

* NOTE: *Dative plural (−n)*
   The plural form of the noun adds an −n in the dative case:

   NOM. die Männer
   ACC. die Männer
   DAT. den Männern

EXCEPTIONS: If the plural form of the noun ends in

   −n or −s

   the dative plural −n is *not* added.

EXAMPLES: NOM. die Hotels   die Lampen
         ACC. die Hotels   die Lampen
         DAT. den Hotels   den Lampen.

3. Was sagen wir d___ Eltern?
4. Was machen wir mit dies___ Bilder___?
5. Er spielt mit d___ Kinder___.

MIXED CASES

1. Dies___ Adressen sind nicht richtig.
2. Siehst du d___ Häuser da drüben?
3. Was machen wir mit dies___ Bilder___?
4. Welch___ Züge fahren nach Berlin?
5. Dies___ Krawatten sind zu teuer.
6. Was geben wir d___ Kinder___?
7. Welch___ Zeitungen meinst du?
8. Was kosten d___ Lampen?
9. Wer wohnt in dies___ Häuser___?
10. Dies___ Tische sind zu klein.

Mixed Drills (All Genders; Nominative, Accusative, and Dative Cases; Singular and Plural)

1. Dies___ Bier ist sehr gut.
2. Welch___ Zeitung lesen Sie?
3. Er nimmt d___ Bus.
4. Was machen Sie mit dies___ Tisch?
5. Dies___ Adressen sind nicht richtig.
6. Er kennt jed___ Straße in Berlin.
7. Sie kommt gerade aus d___ Haus.
8. Aus welch___ Stadt kommt sie?
9. Dies___ Tische sind zu klein.
10. Was kostet dies___ Wein?
11. Wir geben es d___ Kinder___.
12. Welch___ Wein trinkst du?
13. Ich nehme dies___ Jacke.
14. Liest du d___ Buch?
15. Warum antwortest du d___ Mädchen nicht?
16. Welch___ Briefe meinst du?
17. Dies___ Krawatte ist zu teuer.
18. Kaufst du d___ Tisch?
19. In welch___ Hotel bist du?
20. Wir nehmen dies___ Sofa.
21. D___ Bild kostet nur fünfzig Mark.
22. Was machen wir mit dies___ Lampe?

23. Dies____ Film ist sehr gut.
24. Welch____ Züge fahren nach Frankfurt?
25. Helfen Sie d____ Frau!
26. Welch____ Haus kauft er?
27. Wer wohnt in dies____ Häuser____?
28. Ich kenne dies____ Stadt nicht sehr gut.
29. Welch____ Zug ist das?
30. Was kostet dies____ Lampe?

Express in German

1. What does this lamp cost?
2. I'm taking the bus.
3. This beer is very good.
4. She's just coming out of the house.
5. These addresses aren't correct.
6. Which newspaper is he reading?
7. What does this wine cost?
8. We'll take the sofa.
9. Which letters do you mean?
10. What'll we do with this lamp?
11. This picture (film) is very good.
12. He knows every street in Berlin.
13. What'll we give the children?
14. Why don't you (du) answer the girl?
15. I'll take this sportscoat (jacket).
16. Which wine are you drinking?
17. The picture only costs fifty marks.
18. Who lives in these houses?
19. I don't know this city very well.
20. Which hotel are you in?*

---

* English sentences often end with a *preposition*, especially when a question is involved:

> Which hotel are you *in*?
> Which city does she come *from*?

But in German, the preposition must *always be the first element* in a prepositional phrase. The literal English counterparts of the corresponding German sentences would look like this:

> *In* which hotel are you?
> *From* which city does she come?

21. Which trains go to Berlin?
22. This tie is too expensive.
23. Which house are you going to buy?
24. What'll we do with this table?

Genitive Strong Endings

MASCULINE	NEUTER	FEMININE	PLURAL
dieses Tisches des Tisches	dieses Sofas des Sofas	dieser Lampe der Lampe	dieser Tische der Tische

MASCULINE

1. Er kommt am Ende d____ Monat____.*
2. Es ist am Ende dies____ Korridor____.
3. Wer ist der Fahrer d____ Wagens?
4. Das Ende dies____ Film____ ist schlecht.
5. Die Farbe d____ Wagen____ ist hübsch.

NEUTER

1. Der Anfang d____ Semester____ ist immer schwer.
2. Er kommt am Ende d____ Jahr____.
3. Die Farbe dies____ Sofa____ ist sehr hübsch.
4. Lesen Sie das Ende d____ Buch____!
5. Weißt du die Adresse d____ Hotels?

FEMININE

1. Der Anfang d____ Reise ist interessant.
2. Es ist auf dieser Seite d____ Straße.
3. Sie kommt am Anfang d____ Woche.

---

* NOTE: Masculine and neuter nouns take an –(e)s ending in the genitive singular. Generally, the ending –es is used with nouns of one syllable (**Waldes, Brotes**) and all nouns ending in an s-sound (**Gesetzes**). Otherwise, the ending –s is used. (In *spoken* German the –s ending is also found with nouns of one syllable, e.g. **Weins**.)

4. Sein Haus ist am Ende dies____ Straße.
5. Hast du die Adresse d____ Firma?

PLURAL

1. Hast du eine List d____ Adressen?
2. Die Resultate d____ Experimente sind gut.
3. Hast du die Adressen dies____ Leute?
4. Ich habe eine Liste d____ Bücher.

Mixed Drills on the Genitive (All Three Genders, Singular and Plural)

1. Er kommt am Ende d____ Monat____.
2. Der Anfang d____ Reise ist interessant.
3. Wer ist der Fahrer d____ Wagen____?
4. Sein Haus ist am Ende dies____ Straße.
5. Hast du eine Liste d____ Adressen?
6. Das Ende dies____ Film____ ist schlecht.
7. Die Resultate d____ Experimente sind gut.
8. Der Anfang d____ Semester____ ist immer schwer.
9. Die Farbe dies____ Sofa____ ist sehr hübsch.
10. Hast du die Adresse d____ Firma?
11. Es ist am Ende dies____ Korridor____.
12. Ich habe eine Liste d____ Bücher.

Express in German

1. He's coming at the end of the month.
2. Do you have the address of the firm?
3. The end of this film is bad.
4. I have a list of the books.
5. The beginning of the semester is always hard.
6. His house is at the end of this street.
7. The color of this sofa is very pretty.
8. Who is the driver of the car?
9. The results of the experiments are good.
10. It's at the end of this hall (corridor).
11. The beginning of the trip is interesting.
12. Do you have a list of the addresses?

LEVEL TWO

I. THE DER-WORDS AS LIMITING WORDS: THE WEAK DECLENSION OF ADJECTIVES FOLLOWING DER-WORDS

A. Comparison of strong and weak endings

So far you have seen nothing but two-word phrases made up of a **der**-word and a noun:

dieser Tisch
diesen Tisch
diesem Tisch
dieses Tisches

As you have seen, the **der**-word always takes strong endings. But now look at some *three*-word phrases made up of a **der**-word *plus another adjective* plus a noun:

dieser neue Tisch
diesen neuen Tisch
diesem neuen Tisch
dieses neuen Tisches

In these phrases, **dieser** has full *strong endings*, but the endings of the adjective **neu** are less explicit. These less explicit endings are called *weak endings*.

B. Forms

Weak endings occur in the following pattern:

	Singular			*Plural*
	MASC.	NEUT.	FEM.	ALL GENDERS
NOM.	–e	–e	–e	–en
ACC.	–en	–e	–e	–en
DAT.	–en	–en	–en	–en
GEN.	–en	–en	–en	–en

NOTE: The weak ending –**e** is used in the

MASCULINE	nominative
NEUTER	nominative and accusative
FEMININE	nominative and accusative

Everywhere else the weak ending is –**en.**

C. Usage

1. Two different kinds of adjectives

a. Limiting adjectives (the **der**-words)

All of the **der**-words are limiting words; that is to say, they place a specific limit on the nouns they modify:

der Tisch	the or that table (not any old table)
dieser Tisch	this table (not that one or any other)
welcher Tisch	which table (which particular one)
jeder Tisch	every table (each individual one)

In all of these examples the **der**-word limits the table in question to a particular one: *this one, that one, which one, each one, every one.*

b. Descriptive adjectives

Descriptive adjectives answer the question "*what kind of . . . ?*" If someone asks you "*What kind of* table are you looking for?" you will probably try to *describe* the sort of table you're looking for (not specify *which* particular *one*). To do this you use descriptive adjectives: *old, cheap, long,* etc.

2. The effect of limiting words on adjective endings

As you have seen, there is an essential difference in meaning between limiting adjectives and descriptive adjectives. Still more important, however, is the difference in the way they affect adjective endings.

GENERAL RULE: When a limiting word takes a strong ending, the adjectives that follow it take weak endings.

| STRONG ENDING | WEAK ENDING | |
| dies**er** | neu**e** | Tisch |

SPECIFIC RULE: **Der**-words are limiting words that *always* take *strong endings*.

CONCLUSION: Therefore, *all* adjectives that follow **der**-words must take *weak endings*.

The following table shows the **der**-word **dieser** preceding a descriptive adjective and a noun:

	Singular		
	MASCULINE	NEUTER	FEMININE
NOM.	dieser neue Tisch	dieses neue Sofa	diese neue Lampe
ACC.	diesen neuen Tisch	dieses neue Sofa	diese neue Lampe
DAT.	diesem neuen Tisch	diesem neuen Sofa	dieser neuen Lampe
GEN.	dieses neuen Tisches	dieses neuen Sofas	dieser neuen Lampe

	Plural
	ALL GENDERS
NOM.	diese neuen Tische (Sofas, Lampen)
ACC.	diese neuen Tische
DAT.	diesen neuen Tischen
GEN.	dieser neuen Tische

You can see from the table that:

1. The **der**-word (**dieser**) always takes strong endings.
2. The adjective following the **der**-word takes weak endings (−e or −en).

The same pattern holds for any number of adjectives following a **der**-word:

> der neue grüne Wagen (masc.: nom.)
> das gute frische Brot (neut.: nom. & acc.)
> die guten alten Zeiten (plural: nom. & acc.)

II. ANOTHER SET OF LIMITING WORDS: THE EIN-WORDS

A. The EIN-words

Another group of words limits adjectives in almost the same way as the **der**-words do. This second group is made up of the **ein-** or **kein**-words, so called because they are all declined like **ein,** or better yet like **kein**—since **ein** lacks a plural. The **ein**-words are:

ein   a, an
kein   not a, no

and *all the possessive adjectives:*

mein	my	unser	our
dein	your	euer	your
sein	his	ihr	their
ihr	her	Ihr	your (polite form)
sein	its		

NOTE: The **er** at the end of **unser** and **euer** is *part of the stem*. It is NOT *an ending*! **Euer** becomes **eur-** when it takes an ending: **euer** but **eure.**

B. Comparison of DIESER and KEIN

There is an *important difference* between **der**-words and **ein**-words. Compare the endings of **dieser** (a **der**-word) with those of **kein** (an **ein**-word):

	Singular				
	MASCULINE		NEUTER		FEMININE
NOM.	dieser	kein☐	dieses	kein☐	diese	keine
ACC.	diesen	keinen	dieses	kein☐	diese	keine
DAT.	diesem	keinem	diesem	keinem	dieser	keiner
GEN.	dieses	keines	dieses	keines	dieser	keiner

	Plural	
	ALL GENDERS	
NOM.	diese	keine
ACC.	diese	keine
DAT.	diesen	keinen
GEN.	dieser	keiner

The table above shows the following:

1. **Der**-words: **der**-words *always* take *strong* endings.

2. **Ein**-words:

  a. **Ein**-words (such as **kein**) use only their stems, with *no ending,* in the

> masculine: nominative
> neuter: nominative and accusative

  b. In all *other instances,* **ein**-words take *strong endings.*

To summarize: **Der**-words and **ein**-words take the *same* (strong) *endings,* EXCEPT in those three instances where **ein**-words take no endings at all:

	MASCULINE		NEUTER	
NOM.	dieser	kein☐	dieses	kein☐
ACC.			dieses	kein☐

C. Endings on adjectives that follow EIN-words

The same general rule applies to **ein**-words as well as to **der**-words:

1. *When a limiting word takes a strong ending, the adjectives that follow it take weak endings.* Thus, whenever an **ein**-word takes a strong ending, the adjectives following it must take weak endings.

As you have just seen, however, there are three instances where a limiting word takes no ending at all. **Ein**-words take no endings in the

> masculine: nominative
> neuter: nominative and accusative

A specific rule governs this situation:

2. *In those three instances where a limiting word uses only its stem (i.e. has no ending), the adjectives that follow will take* STRONG *endings:*

NOM.	ein	alter Freund		NOM.	ein	altes Haus
	sein	alter Freund			sein	altes Haus
	unser	alter Freund			unser	altes Haus
				ACC.	ein	altes Haus
					sein	altes Haus
					unser	altes Haus

III. ADJECTIVE-NOUN PHRASES WITHOUT LIMITING WORDS

Although most adjective-noun phrases begin with a limiting word (a **der-**word or an **ein-**word), some do not:

> Frisches Brot ist sehr gut.
> (Fresh bread is very good.)

> Thomas Mann schreibt lange Sätze.
> (Thomas Mann writes long sentences.)

When the phrase doesn't start with a limiting word, all adjectives preceding a noun take *strong endings*. This also holds for adjectives in a series:

> Guter, alter, treuer Franz!
> (Good, old, faithful Franz!)

IV. VIELE, WENIGE, ANDERE, EINIGE, MEHRERE

Viele (many), **wenige** (few), **andere** (other), **einige** (some), and **mehrere** (several) are all plural expressions that suggest indefinite quantities. *They do not act as limiting words,* which means that adjectives that follow them take *strong endings:*

> Er hat viele gute Ideen.
> (He has a lot of good ideas.)

> Ich habe mehrere gute Freunde in Berlin.
> (I have several good friends in Berlin.)

The result is a string of strong adjective endings:

> viele gute alte Weine

Alle, however, *does* act as a limiting word:

> Nicht alle guten Dinge sind teuer.
> (Not all good things are expensive.)

The following scale, which proceeds from *none* to *all,* will help you keep these straight.

keine no, not a	*a limiting word*	keine guten Freunde
wenige few		wenige gute Freunde
einige some		einige gute Freunde
andere other	— *not limiting words* —	andere gute Freunde
mehrere several		mehrere gute Freunde
viele many		viele gute Freunde
alle all	*a limiting word*	alle guten Freunde

The extremes **alle** and **keine** indicate a definite number (*all* of a certain group or *none* of a certain group) and are limiting words. The words indicating an indefinite number or an approximation between these definite extremes (*few, some, other, several, many*) are *not* limiting words.

V. NOTES ON SPECIAL CONSTRUCTIONS

A. SOLCHER and MANCHER: two more limiting words

In the plural, these two adjectives function as normal limiting words:

> Solche langen Bücher lese ich nicht gern.
> (I don't like to read such long books.)

> Manche alten Leute verbringen den Winter in Florida.
> (Many old people spend the winter in Florida.)

In the singular, **mancher** means *many a* and uses the *strong* endings of a **der**-word:

> mancher Mann   many a man
> manche Frau   many a woman
> manches Kind   many a child

and **solcher** means *such* and takes the same (strong) endings:

> solcher Unsinn   such nonsense

When used with another adjective in the singular, however, **mancher** becomes **manch ein** (many a) and **solcher** becomes **so ein** (such a). They decline like this:

NOM.	so ein langes Buch	manch ein guter Mann
ACC.	so ein langes Buch	manch einen guten Mann
DAT.	so einem langen Buch	manch einem guten Mann

So and **manch** remain constant and the rest of the expression behaves just like an ein-phrase. **Solcher** and **so ein** are common and useful; **mancher** and **manch ein,** however, have an archaic ring.

B. Masculine and neuter genitive singular

Any adjective-noun phrase that begins with a limiting word is completely regular. Look at the following example:

Ende des vorigen Monats
(the end of [the] last month)

When there is no limiting word, however, you will find the adjective with a weak genitive ending where—according to the "rules"—you would expect a strong genitive ending:

Ende vorigen Monats
(the end of last month)

not: Ende voriges Monats

NOTE: This exceptional construction applies only to the *genitive singular of masculine and neuter nouns.* Since it is a fairly uncommon construction, it is best to learn these expressions as *idioms* when they crop up, rather than as basic structural problems.

VI. PREDICATE ADJECTIVES

The words in color are *predicate adjectives.* A predicate adjective is an adjective that *does not immediately precede the noun it modifies.*

Der Wein ist gut.
(The wine is good.)

Deine Suppe wird kalt.
(Your soup is getting cold.)

Ich finde das Buch interessant.
(I find the book interesting.)

As the examples show, predicate adjectives take *no endings:* they consist only of the adjective stem.

VII. SUMMARY

1. There are two types of limiting words:

der-words	and	**ein**-words
der		ein
dieser		kein
jeder		and all posses-
welcher		sive adjectives

2. *Limiting words* take   (*a*) strong endings

        or   (*b*) no endings at all (in only 3 instances)

   a. When a limiting word has a strong ending, the adjectives that follow it take *weak endings:*

	Singular			Plural
	MASC.	NEUT.	FEM.	ALL GENDERS
NOM.	–e	–e	–e	–en
ACC.	–en	–e	–e	–en
DAT.	–en	–en	–en	–en
GEN.	–en	–en	–en	–en

   b. When a limiting word has no ending at all, the adjectives that follow it must take *strong endings.* There are only 3 instances where a limiting word takes no ending: **ein**-words in the

            masculine nominative   (ein alter Wein)
            neuter nominative   (ein gutes Bier)
            neuter accusative   (ein gutes Bier)

In all other instances, limiting words take strong endings and are therefore followed by adjectives with weak endings.

3. *No limiting word*

When an adjective-noun combination does *not* begin with a limiting word the adjectives take strong endings. Such combinations are of the following two types:

   a. combinations beginning with a descriptive adjective:

            gute alte Weine
            armer Hans!

b. combinations beginning with **viele, wenige, andere, einige,** or **mehrere:**

viel e alt e Weine

4. *Predicate adjectives* do not take adjective endings.

VIII. SUMMARY TABLES FOR VARIOUS ADJECTIVE-NOUN COMBINATIONS

MASCULINE

	with **der**-words	with **ein**-words
NOM.	dies er alt e Wein	ein alt er Wein
ACC.	dies en alt en Wein	ein en alt en Wein
DAT.	dies em alt en Wein	ein em alt en Wein
GEN.	dies es alt en Wein(e)s	ein es alt en Wein(e)s

	with NO limiting word
NOM.	alt er Wein
ACC.	alt en Wein
DAT.	alt em Wein
GEN.	alt en Wein(e)s (See p. 65.)

NEUTER

	with **der**-words	with **ein**-words
NOM.	dies es gut e Bier	ein gut es Bier
ACC.	dies es gut e Bier	ein gut es Bier
DAT.	dies em gut en Bier	ein em gut en Bier
GEN.	dies es gut en Bier(e)s	ein es gut en Bier(e)s

	with NO limiting word
NOM.	gut es Bier
ACC.	gut es Bier
DAT.	gut em Bier
GEN.	gut en Bier(e)s (See p. 65.)

FEMININE

	with **der**-words		with **ein**-words
NOM.	diese gute Suppe		eine gute Suppe
ACC.	diese gute Suppe		eine gute Suppe
DAT.	dieser guten Suppe		einer guten Suppe
GEN.	dieser guten Suppe		einer guten Suppe

with NO limiting word

NOM.	gute Suppe
ACC.	gute Suppe
DAT.	guter Suppe
GEN.	guter Suppe

PLURAL
(all three genders)

	with **der-** or **ein**-words	after **viele, wenige, andere, einige, mehrere**
NOM.	diese alten Leute keine alten Leute	viele alte Leute
ACC.	diese alten Leute keine alten Leute	viele alte Leute
DAT.	diesen alten Leuten keinen alten Leuten	vielen alten Leuten
GEN.	dieser alten Leute keiner alten Leute	vieler alter Leute

with NO limiting word

NOM.	alte Leute
ACC.	alte Leute
DAT.	alten Leuten
GEN.	alter Leute

■ DRILLS

NOTE: Genitive patterns will be drilled separately at the end of this section.

Masculine Singular with **der**-words

Supply the correct endings

	Strong Endings	Weak Endings	
NOM.	dieser	kleine	Tisch
ACC.	diesen	kleinen	Tisch
DAT.	diesem	kleinen	Tisch

NOMINATIVE
1. D____ neu____ Laden ist viel besser.
2. Wo ist d____ letzt____ Brief von Hans?
3. Dies____ klein____ Tisch ist hübsch.
4. Was kostet d____ ander____ Wein?
5. Wann kommt d____ nächst____ Zug?

ACCUSATIVE
1. Er nimmt d____ letzt____ Bus.
2. Nehmen Sie dies____ grau____ Anzug?
3. Ich meine d____ ander____ Brief.
4. Welch____ alt____ Mann meinst du?
5. Ich kaufe d____ braun____ Tisch.

DATIVE
1. Er kommt mit d____ letzt____ Zug.
2. Es ist auf d____ ander____ Tisch.
3. Gehen wir zu d____ ander____ Laden!

Masculine Singular with **ein**-words

NOM.	ein	kleiner	Tisch
ACC.	einen	kleinen	Tisch
DAT.	einem	kleinen	Tisch

NOMINATIVE
1. Das ist ein hübsch____ Wagen.
2. Dein braun____ Mantel ist da drüben.
3. Wo ist mein neu____ Anzug?

4. Das ist sein letzt____ Brief.
5. Das ist kein billig____ Wein.

ACCUSATIVE
1. Ich kaufe ein____ neu____ Anzug.
2. Meinst du sein____ erst____ Film?
3. Ich zeige dir sein____ letzt____ Brief.
4. Wir brauchen ein____ groß____ Tisch.
5. Kennst du ihr____ neu____ Mann?

DATIVE
1. Er geht zu ein____ gut____ Arzt.
2. Ich gebe es mein____ klein____ Bruder.
3. Der Brief ist von ein____ alt____ Freund.

Masculine Singular (Mixed Drills)

1. Ich meine d____ ander____ Brief.
2. Das ist kein billig____ Wein.
3. Ich kaufe ein____ neu____ Anzug.
4. Es ist auf d____ ander____ Tisch.
5. Wann kommt d____ nächst____ Zug?
6. Ich zeige dir sein____ letzt____ Brief.
7. Wo ist mein neu____ Anzug?
8. Was kostet d____ ander____ Wein?
9. Ich gebe es mein____ klein____ Bruder.
10. Nehmen Sie dies____ grau____ Anzug?
11. Das ist ein hübsch____ Wagen.
12. Er kommt mit d____ letzt____ Zug.
13. Wir brauchen ein____ groß____ Tisch.
14. D____ neu____ Laden ist viel besser.
15. Der Brief ist von ein____ alt____ Freund.

Neuter Singular with **der**-words

	Strong Endings	Weak Endings	
NOM.	dieses	neue	Sofa
ACC.	dieses	neue	Sofa
DAT.	diesem	neuen	Sofa

NOMINATIVE
1. Es ist d____ best____ Restaurant in München.
2. Dies____ blau____ Kleid ist sehr hübsch.
3. Welch____ neu____ Auto?
4. D____ alt____ Sofa ist kaputt.
5. D____ ander____ Buch ist besser.

ACCUSATIVE
1. Welch____ neu____ Restaurant meinst du?
2. Kennst du d____ ander____ Mädchen?
3. Ich nehme d____ grün____ Kleid.
4. Welch____ alt____ Buch meinen Sie?

DATIVE
1. Was machen Sie mit dies____ alt____ Sofa?
2. Ich bin in d____ ander____ Hotel.
3. Gehen Sie zu d____ nächst____ Büro.

Neuter Singular with ein-words

NOM.	ein	neues	Sofa
ACC.	ein	neues	Sofa
DAT.	einem	neuen	Sofa

NOMINATIVE
1. Das ist sein best____ Buch.
2. Wo ist Ihr neu____ Büro?
3. Unser alt____ Sofa ist kaputt.
4. Das ist kein schlecht____ Bier.
5. Wo ist dein neu____ Auto?

ACCUSATIVE
1. Sie hat ein groß____ Zimmer.
2. Ich gebe dir ein gut____ Beispiel.
3. Wir verkaufen unser alt____ Auto.
4. Wir kaufen ein neu____ Sofa.
5. Kennst du ein gut____ Restaurant?

DATIVE
1. Ich gehe zu ein____ ander____ Hotel.
2. Wir essen heute in ein____ gut____ Restaurant.
3. Sie arbeitet in ein____ ander____ Büro.

Neuter Singular (Mixed Drills)

1. Das ist sein best____ Buch.
2. Ich nehme d____ grün____ Kleid.
3. Sie hat ein groß____ Zimmer.
4. Was machen Sie mit dies____ alt____ Sofa?
5. Es ist d____ best____ Restaurant in München.
6. Wo ist dein neu____ Auto?
7. Ich gehe zu ein____ ander____ Hotel.
8. Kennst du d____ ander____ Mädchen?
9. Das ist kein schlecht____ Bier.
10. Welch____ neu____ Auto?
11. Ich gebe dir ein gut____ Beispiel.
12. Sie arbeitet in ein____ ander____ Büro.
13. Dies____ blau____ Kleid ist sehr hübsch.
14. Kennst du ein gut____ Restaurant?
15. Gehen Sie zu d____ nächst____ Büro.

Feminine Singular with **der**-words

	Strong Endings	*Weak Endings*	
NOM.	diese	alte	Lampe
ACC.	diese	alte	Lampe
DAT.	dieser	alten	Lampe

NOMINATIVE

1. D____ neu____ Speisekarte ist viel interessanter.
2. Dies____ alt____ Adresse ist nicht richtig.
3. Welch____ alt____ Adresse?
4. Wo ist d____ nächst____ Tankstelle?
5. Was kostet dies____ klein____ Lampe?

ACCUSATIVE

1. Kennst du d____ neu____ Buchhandlung?
2. Ich nehme dies____ braun____ Jacke.
3. Welch____ deutsch____ Zeitung meinen Sie?
4. Hast du d____ neu____ Adresse?

DATIVE
1. Es steht* auf d____ nächst____ Seite.
2. Ich gehe zu d____ ander____ Buchhandlung.
3. Es steht* auf d____ neu____ Speisekarte.

Feminine Singular with ein-words

NOM.	eine	neue	Lampe
ACC.	eine	neue	Lampe
DAT.	einer	neuen	Lampe

NOMINATIVE
1. Das ist ein____ hübsch____ Farbe.
2. München ist ein____ interessant____ Stadt.
3. Das ist kein____ schlecht____ Idee.
4. Das ist ein____ gut____ Frage.

ACCUSATIVE
1. Ich nehme mein____ klein____ Schwester mit.
2. Hast du ihr____ neu____ Adresse?
3. Sie haben ein____ neu____ Speisekarte.
4. Ich habe ein____ gut____ Idee.

DATIVE
1. Ich gehe zu ein____ ander____ Bank.
2. Er kommt aus ein____ klein____ Stadt in Bayern.
3. Der Brief ist von mein____ klein____ Schwester.

Feminine Singular (Mixed Drills)

1. Das ist ein____ gut____ Frage.
2. Ich nehme dies____ braun____ Jacke.
3. Wo ist d____ nächst____ Tankstelle?

---

* NOTE: German commonly uses **stehen** (rather than **sein**) when referring to printed matter, e.g.

> Es **steht** in der Zeitung.
> It **is** in the newspaper.

4. Es steht auf d⎯⎯ neu⎯⎯ Speisekarte.
5. Das ist kein⎯⎯ schlecht⎯⎯ Idee.
6. Welch⎯⎯ alt⎯⎯ Adresse?
7. München ist ein⎯⎯ interessant⎯⎯ Stadt.
8. Es steht auf d⎯⎯ nächst⎯⎯ Seite.
9. Ich habe ein⎯⎯ gut⎯⎯ Idee.
10. Welch⎯⎯ deutsch⎯⎯ Zeitung meinst du?
11. Dies⎯⎯ alt⎯⎯ Adresse ist nicht richtig.
12. Er kommt aus ein⎯⎯ klein⎯⎯ Stadt in Bayern.
13. Kennst du d⎯⎯ neu⎯⎯ Buchhandlung?
14. Ich gehe zu ein⎯⎯ ander⎯⎯ Bank.
15. Hast du ihr⎯⎯ neu⎯⎯ Adresse?

Plural Forms with ein- and der-words

	Strong Endings	*Weak Endings*	
NOM.	diese meine	neuen	Bücher
ACC.	diese meine	neuen	Bücher
DAT.	diesen meinen	neuen	Büchern

NOMINATIVE
1. Unser⎯⎯ neu⎯⎯ Bücher sind hier.
2. D⎯⎯ erst⎯⎯ Seiten sind schwer.
3. Dies⎯⎯ alt⎯⎯ Bilder sind hübsch.
4. Sie sind unser⎯⎯ best⎯⎯ Freunde.
5. D⎯⎯ neu⎯⎯ Lampen sind hier.

ACCUSATIVE
1. Geben Sie mir d⎯⎯ neu⎯⎯ Adressen.
2. Er hat kein⎯⎯ gut⎯⎯ Ideen.
3. Ich meine d⎯⎯ ander⎯⎯ Briefe.
4. Zeigen Sie mir ihr⎯⎯ best⎯⎯ Anzüge!

DATIVE
1. Was machen wir mit dies⎯⎯ alt⎯⎯ Bücher⎯⎯?
2. Das findet man nur in d⎯⎯ best⎯⎯ Restaurants.
3. Der Brief ist von unser⎯⎯ alt⎯⎯ Freunde⎯⎯.

Plural Forms with **ein-** and **der-**words (Mixed Drills)

1. Geben Sie mir d___ neu___ Adressen.
2. Unser___ neu___ Bücher sind hier.
3. Der Brief ist von unser___ alt___ Freunde___.
4. Er hat kein___ gut___ Ideen.
5. Dies___ alt___ Bilder sind hübsch.
6. Zeigen Sie mir Ihr___ best___ Anzüge!
7. Das findet man nur in d___ best___ Restaurants.
8. D___ erst___ Seiten sind schwer.
9. D___ neu___ Lampen sind hier.
10. Was machen wir mit dies___ alt___ Bücher___?
11. Sie sind unser___ best___ Freunde.
12. Ich meine d___ ander___ Briefe.

Adjective-Noun Combinations *Without* **der-** or **ein-**words
(i.e., without limiting words)

There are two types:

   1. combinations beginning with descriptive adjectives:

> Das ist gut**es** Bier.
> Gut**er**, alter Franz!
> Sie schreibt nett**e** Briefe.

   2. combinations beginning with **viele, wenige, andere, einige, mehrere:**

> Er hat viel**e** gute Ideen.

NOMINATIVE
1. Arm___ Frau Heller!
2. Gut___ Hotels sind sehr teuer.
3. Das ist gut___ Bier.
4. Viel___ amerikanisch___ Studenten fahren nach Deutschland.
5. Lieb___ Dieter,

ACCUSATIVE
1. Er kennt einig___ gut___ Restaurants in dieser Stadt.
2. Sie schreibt nett___ Briefe.
3. Er hat viel___ gut___ Ideen.
4. Sie haben einig___ interessant___ Bilder.
5. Hat er gut___ Wein?

DATIVE
1. Sie schreibt mit rot____ Tinte.
2. Ich esse gern in klein____ Restaurants.
3. Wir haben es auch in ander____ Farben.

Adjective-Noun Combinations Without Limiting Words (Mixed Drills)

1. Das ist gut____ Bier.
2. Sie schreibt nett____ Briefe.
3. Sie hat viel____ gut____ Ideen.
4. Ich esse gern in klein____ Restaurants.
5. Lieb____ Dieter,
6. Gut____ Hotels sind teuer.
7. Arm____ Herr Schmidt!
8. Viel____ amerikanisch____ Studenten fahren nach Deutschland.
9. Sie schreibt mit rot____ Tinte.
10. Er kennt einig____ gut____ Restaurants in dieser Stadt.
11. Wir habe es auch in ander____ Farben.
12. Hat er gut____ Wein?

Mixed Drills

Gender, number, case, and type of limitation are mixed.

1. Wann kommt d____ nächst____ Zug?
2. Ich habe ein____ gut____ Idee.
3. Das ist kein schlecht____ Bier.
4. D____ erst____ Seiten sind schwer.
5. Das ist ein hübsch____ Wagen.
6. Sie arbeitet in ein____ ander____ Büro.
7. Tübingen ist ein____ schön____ alt____ Stadt.
8. Ich gebe dir ein gut____ Beispiel.
9. Lieb____ Dieter,
10. Ich esse gern in klein____ Restaurants.
11. Es steht auf d____ erst____ Seite.
12. Der Brief ist von ein____ gut____ Freund.
13. Er kennt einig____ gut____ Restaurants in dieser Stadt.
14. Das ist gut____ Bier.
15. Wo ist d____ nächst____ Tankstelle?
16. Geben Sie mir d____ neu____ Adressen.

17. Ich zeige dir sein＿＿ letzt＿＿ Brief.
18. Es ist auf d＿＿ ander＿＿ Tisch.
19. Es ist d＿＿ best＿＿ Restaurant in München.
20. Kennst du d＿＿ neu＿＿ Buchhandlung?
21. Wo ist dein alt＿＿ Auto?
22. Sie hat viel＿＿ gut＿＿ Ideen.
23. Er kommt aus ein＿＿ klein＿＿ Stadt in Bayern.
24. Ich meine d＿＿ ander＿＿ Brief.
25. Sie hat ein groß＿＿ Zimmer.
26. Dies＿＿ alt＿＿ Adressen sind nicht richtig.
27. Arm＿＿ Frau Heller!
28. Wo ist mein neu＿＿ Anzug?
29. Gehen Sie zu d＿＿ nächst＿＿ Büro!
30. Das ist kein＿＿ schlecht＿＿ Idee.
31. Sie schreibt nett＿＿ Briefe.
32. Er kommt mit d＿＿ letzt＿＿ Zug.
33. Kennst du d＿＿ ander＿＿ Mädchen?
34. Das ist sein best＿＿ Buch.
35. Das findet man nur in d＿＿ best＿＿ Restaurants.
36. München ist ein＿＿ interessant＿＿ Stadt.
37. Was kostet d＿＿ ander＿＿ Wein?
38. Ich nehme dies＿＿ braun＿＿ Jacke.
39. Dies＿＿ blau＿＿ Kleid ist sehr hübsch.
40. Gut＿＿ Hotels sind teuer.

Express in German

1. Tübingen is a pretty old city.
2. She has a large room.
3. When is the next train coming?
4. She writes nice letters.
5. Do you know the new bookstore?
6. He works in another office.
7. Where is my new suit?
8. I mean the other letter.
9. That's not a bad idea.
10. Give me the new addresses.
11. It's the best restaurant in Munich.
12. Dear Dieter,
13. The letter is from an old friend.

14. That's his best book.
15. Where is the next gas station?
16. It's on the other table.
17. That's good beer.
18. I'll show you his last letter.
19. The first pages are difficult.
20. I'll give you a good example.
21. What does the other wine cost?
22. It's on the next page. (use: **stehen**)
23. She has a lot of (many) good ideas.
24. This blue dress is pretty.
25. He comes from a small city in Bavaria.
26. Poor Mrs. Heller.
27. Go to the next office.
28. That's a pretty car.
29. Do you know the other girl?
30. Munich is an interesting city.
31. These old addresses aren't correct.
32. I have a good idea.
33. Where is your new car?
34. He knows some good restaurants in this city.
35. Good hotels are expensive.
36. I like to eat in small restaurants.

▮ DRILLS ON GENITIVE PATTERNS

Adjective-Noun Combinations Introduced by **der-** and **ein**-words

	Strong Endings	*Weak Endings*	
NOM.	des	anderen	Tisches
	eines	anderen	Tisches
NEUT.	des	neuen	Sofas
	eines	neuen	Sofas
FEM.	der	anderen	Lampe
	einer	anderen	Lampe
PLURAL	der	neuen	Bücher
	meiner	neuen	Bücher

MASCULINE and NEUTER
1. Wer war der Fahrer d____ ander____ Wagen____?
2. Der Anfang ein____ neu____ Semester____ ist immer schwer.
3. Die Farbe ein____ gut____ Wein____ ist auch wichtig.
4. Hast du die Adresse sein____ neu____ Büro____?
5. Das Ende sein____ letzt____ Film____ war schlecht.
6. Die Farbe dein____ neu____ Sofa____ ist hübsch.

FEMININE and PLURAL
1. Hast du die Adresse d____ ander____ Buchhandlung?
2. Die Resultate sein____ neu____ Experimente sind gut.
3. Haben Sie eine Liste d____ neu____ Adressen?
4. Heißt das Stück „Der Besuch ein____alt____Dame" oder „Der Besuch
   d____ alt____ Dame"?
5. Sein Haus ist am Ende d____ nächst____ Straße.
6. Hast du die Adressen d____ ander____ Firmen?

Adjective-Noun Combinations Beginning with Adjectives
Other Than Limiting Words (see pp. 63 and 65)

MASCULINE and NEUTER (weak endings)
1. Er kommt Ende nächst____ Monat____.
2. Anfang letzt____ Jahr____ war er in Deutschland.

FEMININE and PLURAL (strong endings)
1. Wann war das? Anfang vorig____ Woche.
2. Er ist ein Liebhaber klassisch____ Musik.

Genitive (Mixed Drills)

1. Wer war der Fahrer d____ ander____ Wagen____?
2. Sein Haus ist am Ende d____ nächst____ Straße.
3. Hast du die Adresse sein____ neu____ Büro____?
4. Die Resultate sein____ neu____ Experimente sind gut.
5. Er kommt Ende nächst____ Monat____.
6. Heißt das Stück „Der Besuch ein____alt____Dame" oder „Der Besuch
   d____ alt____ Dame"?
7. Der Anfang ein____ neu____ Semester____ ist immer schwer.
8. Er ist ein Liebhaber klassisch____ Musik.
9. Haben Sie eine Liste d____ neu____ Adressen?
10. Die Farbe ein____ gut____ Wein____ ist auch wichtig.

11. Wann war das? Anfang vorig____ Woche.
12. Hast du die Adresse d____ ander____ Buchhandlung?

Express in German (Genitive)

1. His house is at the end of the next street.
2. The beginning of a new semester is always hard.
3. Do you have a list of the new addresses?
4. He's coming (at the) end of next month.
5. Do you have the address of the other bookstore?
6. Who was the driver of the other car?
7. When was that? (The) Beginning of last week.
8. The color of a good wine is important too.
9. Is the play called "The Visit of an Old Lady" or "The Visit of the Old Lady"?
10. The results of his new experiments are good.
11. He's a lover of classical music.
12. Do you have the address of his new office?

Comparison of Adjectives and Adverbs

3

I. PREDICATE ADJECTIVES AND ADVERBS

A. Forms and functions

1. *Predicate adjectives.* A predicate adjective is an adjective that doesn't immediately precede the noun it modifies.

> Dieser Wagen ist schnell. This car is fast.
> Seine Arbeit ist gut. His paper is good.

Predicate adjectives occur only in the basic form; they do not take endings that show gender, number or case:

> Dieser Anzug ist hübsch.
> Dieses Hemd ist hübsch.
> Diese Bluse ist hübsch.
> Diese Schuhe sind hübsch.

The basic form **hübsch** remains constant even though the gender and number of the nouns change.

2. *Adverbs.* In German, the forms of the *adverb* are normally the same as the forms of the *predicate adjective.* The difference between an adverb and a predicate adjective is one of *function,* not *form.* Look at the following two examples:

PREDICATE ADJECTIVE	Der Porsche ist schnell.	(The Porsche is fast.)
ADVERB	Erich fährt schnell.	(Erich drives fast.)

The predicate adjective **schnell** *describes the Porsche.* The adverb **schnell** shows *how Erich drives.* Both the adjective and the adverb occur in the basic form **schnell.**

B. Comparative forms of adverbs and predicate adjectives

German adverbs and predicate adjectives actually have three basic forms:

POSITIVE	schnell	fast
COMPARATIVE	schneller	faster
SUPERLATIVE	schnellst-	fastest

1. The *positive* is the form you already know. It is the basic form of the adjective or adverb that you find in word lists or dictionaries.

2. The *comparative* is made by adding –**er** to the positive form.

3. The *superlative* is made by adding –**st** to the positive form. Here the result is a new stem that can't stand alone. When used as an adverb or predicative adjective, the superlative stem always occurs in the following matrix:

$$\text{am} \underline{\hspace{2cm}} \text{en}$$
am schnellsten

Dieser Wagen ist am schnellsten.

C. English predicate adjectives and adverbs

1. *Predicate adjectives.* English has two ways of forming the comparative and superlative of predicate adjectives.

a. slow, slow**er,** slow**est**

The suffixes *–er* and *est* are added to the positive form of all one-syllable and some two-syllable adjectives. This is similar to the way German forms the comparative and superlative of predicate adjectives.

 b. interesting, *more* interesting, *most* interesting

The words *more* and *most* are used to form the comparative and superlative of most longer adjectives.

 2. *Adverbs.* Most (but not all) English adverbs use the suffix *-ly* to distinguish adverbs from predicate adjectives:

<table>
<tr><td>PREDICATE ADJECTIVE</td><td>He is *careful.*</td></tr>
<tr><td>ADVERB</td><td>He works *carefully.*</td></tr>
</table>

As you have already seen, German doesn't make this distinction in form.

D. German forms: a summary

German forms the comparative and superlative of adverbs and predicate adjectives in only *one* basic way: by the use of suffixes. Note again that there is no distinction in form between German adverbs and predicate adjectives.

<table>
<tr><td>POSITIVE</td><td>Der VW ist schnell.</td><td>(pred. adj.)</td></tr>
<tr><td></td><td>Dieter fährt schnell.</td><td>(adverb)</td></tr>
<tr><td>COMPARATIVE</td><td>Der Mercedes ist schneller.</td><td>(pred. adj.)</td></tr>
<tr><td></td><td>Hans fährt schneller.</td><td>(adverb)</td></tr>
<tr><td>SUPERLATIVE</td><td>Der Porsche ist am schnellsten.</td><td>(pred. adj.)</td></tr>
<tr><td></td><td>Klaus fährt am schnellsten.</td><td>(adverb)</td></tr>
</table>

E. Predictable variations in the basic pattern

 1. *The Suffixes* –er *and* –(e)st

 a. Positive forms ending in **–d, –t,** or any "s" sound (**–s, –ss, –ß –z, –sch**) add **–est** (rather than just **–st**) to form the superlative:

<table>
<tr><td>interessant</td><td>heiß</td><td>hübsch</td></tr>
<tr><td>interessanter</td><td>heißer</td><td>hübscher</td></tr>
<tr><td>am interessantesten</td><td>am heißesten</td><td>am hübschesten</td></tr>
</table>

   b. Positive forms ending in –e add only –r (rather than –er) to form the comparative:

> leise
> leiser
> am leisesten

   c. Positive forms ending in –el drop the e in the comparative:

> dunkel
> dunkler (*not* dunkeler)
> am dunkelsten

   d. Positive forms ending in –euer drop the second e in the comparative:

> teuer
> teurer (*not* teuerer)
> am teuersten

F. Umlaut

Most *one-syllable* adjectives with the stem vowels **a** and **u** take an umlaut in their comparative and superlative forms. The stem vowel **o** is only occasionally umlauted.

POSITIVE	alt	lang	jung	kurz	grob
COMPARATIVE	älter	länger	jünger	kürzer	gröber
SUPERLATIVE	ältest–	längst–	jüngst–	kürzest–	gröbst–

The following lists show some commonly used adjectives that *must* take an umlaut in the comparative and superlative, and some others that *do not* take an umlaut:

MANDATORY UMLAUT				NO UMLAUT	
alt	(old)	arm	(poor)	flach	(flat)
jung	(young)	dumm	(stupid)	froh	(happy)
kalt	(cold)	grob	(coarse)	klar	(clear)
warm	(warm)	hart	(hard)	rasch	(quick)
kurz	(short)	klug	(clever)	roh	(raw)
lang	(long)	scharf	(sharp)	schlank	(slender)
stark	(strong)			stolz	(proud)
schwach	(weak)			toll	(crazy)
				voll	(full)

   NOTE: The first column of adjectives with mandatory umlaut consists of pairs of opposites (**alt-jung,** etc.), which may help you remember them.

G. Irregular forms

1. The following adjectives and adverbs have irregular forms.

POSITIVE	COMPARATIVE	SUPERLATIVE	
groß	größer	größt–	(adds only –t in superlative)
gut	besser	best–	
hoch (hoh)*	höher	höchst–	(drops c from comparative)
nah(e)	näher	nächst–	(adds c in superlative)
viel	mehr	meist–†	

2. *Gern, lieber, am liebsten*

Gern (or **gerne**) is an adverb that adds the meaning of *like to* to a verb:

Ich reise.	(I travel.)
Ich reise gern.	(I *like to* travel.)
Er arbeitet zu Hause.	(He works at home.)
Er arbeitet gern zu Hause.	(He *likes to* work at home.)

Gern has irregular comparative and superlative forms.

Ich trinke gern Tee.	(I *like to* drink tea.)
Ich trinke lieber Kaffee.	(I'd *rather* drink coffee.)
Ich trinke am liebsten Wein.	(I *like to* drink wine *best of all.*)

II. COMMON FORMULAS THAT USE THE POSITIVE AND COMPARATIVE

1. *so . . . wie* with positive

The formula **so . . . wie** is used with the positive form of adverbs and predicate adjectives. Its two most common variants are:

nicht so schnell wie	(not as fast as)
genau so schnell wie	(just as fast as)

Er fährt nicht so schnell wie du.
Sie fährt genau so schnell wie er.

---

* **Hoch** is regular as a predicate adjective: **Die Preise sind *hoch.*** But when endings are added to **hoch,** the c drops from the stem: **Des sind *hohe* Preise.**

† When **meist–** takes adjective endings, it must be preceded by the definite article: *die* **meisten Studenten** = most students.

2. *als* with comparative

The conjunction **als** is used to compare two things, and consequently it is used with the comparative of adverbs and adjectives:

> Sie fährt schneller als du.
> Der Porsche ist schneller als der VW.

3. *immer* with comparative

Where English would say "faster and faster," or "more and more expensive," German uses the following formula:

> immer schneller (faster and faster)
> immer teurer (more and more expensive)
>
> Die Wagen werden immer schneller.
> Die Wagen werden immer teurer.

4. *je . . . desto . . .* with comparative

This formula is used to connect two comparatives:

> je mehr, desto besser   (the more the better)
>
> Je mehr er arbeitet,   (The more he works,
> desto müder wird er.   the more tired he gets.)

III. POSITIVE, COMPARATIVE, AND SUPERLATIVE FORMS WITH ADJECTIVE ENDINGS

A. Stem forms of attributive adjectives

Adjectives that immediately precede the nouns they modify are called *attributive adjectives*. The three basic forms of the adjective you have seen so far are all stem forms that take normal adjective endings when they directly precede a noun.

schnell + *endings*

> Das ist ein schneller Wagen.
> Er hat einen schnellen Wagen.
> Das sind schnelle Wagen.

schneller + *endings*

> Das ist ein schneller**er** Wagen.
> Er hat einen schneller**en** Wagen.
> Das sind schneller**e** Wagen.

schnellst– + *endings*

> Das ist der schnellst**e** Wagen.
> Er hat den schnellst**en** Wagen.
> Das sind die schnellst**en** Wagen.

NOTE: When **schnellst–** is used without endings as a predicate adjective, it occurs only in the matrix *am* **schnellsten**. When **schnellst–** is used as an attributive adjective with endings, the *am* _____ *en* matrix is not used.

PREDICATE ADJECTIVE	Sein Wagen ist *am* schnellst*en*.
ATTRIBUTIVE ADJECTIVE	Er hat den schnellsten Wagen.

Attributive adjectives take endings that vary according to gender and number. Look at the following examples in the nominative case:

> Dieser Anzug ist der billigste. (This suit is *the cheapest*.)
> Dieses Hemd ist das billigste.
> Diese Jacke ist die billigste.
> Diese Anzüge sind die billigsten.

NOTE: Dieser Anzug ist der billigste *and* Dieser Anzug ist am billigsten are equivalent forms. It is safer, however, to use the am _____ sten formula in the following drills.

DRILLS

Form Drills

Put the following adjectives and adverbs into the *comparative* and *superlative*.

Standard Forms (these also include positive forms ending in *–d, –t*, "s" sounds, *–e, –el* and *–euer*)

1. Sein Zimmer ist *klein*.
2. Ich finde dieses Buch *interessant*.

3. Dieser Porsche ist *schnell.*
4. Spanisch ist *leicht.*
5. Er fährt *langsam.*
6. Ihr Kleid ist *hübsch.*
7. Das Hilton ist *teuer.*
8. Hier ist es immer *voll.*
9. Seine Schwester ist *intelligent.*
10. Dieser Anzug ist *dunkel.*
11. Sie singt *leise.*
12. Hier ist das Wasser immer *klar.*

Forms with Umlauts (these drills also include words which do *not* take umlauts)

1. Im Januar ist es *kalt.*
2. Dieser Schnaps ist *stark.*
3. Marie war immer *schlank.*
4. Im Winter sind die Tage *kurz* und die Nächte *lang.*
5. Dieses Lokal ist *voll.*
6. Im Juli ist es *warm.*
7. Kurt ist *jung* aber er sieht *alt* aus.
8. Um Hamburg ist es *flach.*
9. Dieses Messer ist *scharf.*
10. Im Dezember sind die Nächte *klar.*

Irregular forms

1. Dieser Wein ist *gut.*
2. Er ißt *viel.*
3. Was trinken Sie *gern*?
4. Das Wohnzimmer ist *groß.*
5. Ihre Preise sind *hoch.*

Common Formulas

1. Karl ist _____ sein Bruder.
               (older than)

2. Es ist nicht _____ gestern.
              (as warm as)

3. Computer werden _____.
              (cheaper and cheaper)

4. Je _____, desto _____.
       (more)   (better)

5. Sie ist genau _____ ihre Mutter.
   (as pretty as)

6. Guter Wein wird _____ .
   (more and more expensive)

7. Je _____ er arbeitet, desto _____ wird er.
   (more)   (more tired)

8. Es ist _____ du glaubst.
   (more expensive than)

Predicate Adjectives and Adverbs

1. Es ist _____ gestern.
   (colder than)

2. Er fährt nicht _____ sein Bruder.
   (as fast as)

3. Wird es _____ ?
   (darker)

4. Die Preise werden _____ .
   (higher and higher)

5. Diese Cassetten sind _____ .
   (the cheapest)

6. Ich zahle _____ Miete _____ du.
   (more)   (than)

7. Sie wird _____ .
   (prettier and prettier)

8. Im Juni sind die Tage _____ und die Nächte _____ .
   (longest)   (shortest)

9. Es ist nicht _____ gestern.
   (as warm as)

10. Je _____ , desto _____ .
    (more)   (better)

11. Ich trinke _____ Cola.
    (like to)

12. Ich bleibe _____ hier.
    (would rather)

13. Ihre Preise sind _____ .
    (highest)

14. Es ist _____ du glaubst.
    (closer than)

15. Computer werden _____.

(cheaper and cheaper)

16. Dieser Wein ist _____ der andere.

(better than)

17. Sie trinkt _____ Wein.

(likes to [drink] best)

18. Es wird _____.

(warmer)

19. Er spielt nicht _____ du.

(as well as)

20. Guter Wein wird _____.

(more and more expensive)

21. Karl ist _____ sein Bruder.

(older than)

22. Je _____ er arbeitet, desto _____ wird er.

(more)   (more tired)

23. Im Januar ist es _____.

(coldest)

24. Er ißt nicht _____ ich.

(as much as)

25. Er wird _____.

(more and more tired)

26. Aber Mitzi, Karl ist doch zwanzig Jahre _____ du.

(older than)

Adjective Endings

1. Es ist _____ Haus in der Stadt.

(the largest)

2. _____ Mal bleibst du zu Hause.

(The next)

3. Er sucht _____ Wohnung.

(a larger)

4. Franz erzählt _____ Geschichten.

(the craziest)

5. Ich fahre mit _____ Zug.

(the next)

6. Haben Sie _____ Messer?

(a sharper)

7. _____ Leute kaufen _____ Wagen.
    (Most)   (a smaller)

8. Das findet man nur in _____ Restaurants.
                                (the best)

9. Es ist _____ Wagen in ganz Italien.
              (the fastest)

10. Ich brauche _____ Anzug.
                      (a darker)

11. Das ist _____ Schwester.
                (her younger)

12. Ich fahre zu _____ Tankstelle.
                      (the next)

Mixed Drills

1. Karl ist _____ sein Bruder.
                (older than)

2. Es ist nicht _____ gestern.
                    (as warm as)

3. Wird es _____?
                (darker)

4. Sie wird _____.
                (prettier and prettier)

5. Er sucht _____ Wohnung.
                (a larger)

6. Es ist _____ gestern.
              (colder than)

7. Ich trinke _____ Bier.
                  (like to [drink])

8. Diese Cassetten sind _____.
                            (cheapest)

9. Es ist _____ Haus in Hamburg.
              (the largest)

10. Ich fahre mit _____ Zug.
                      (the next)

11. Computer werden _____.
                        (cheaper and cheaper)

12. Ich zahle _____ Miete _____ du.
                  (more)   (than)

13. Je _____, desto _____.
          (more)   (better)

14. _____ Leute kaufen _____ Wagen.
       (Most)   (a smaller)

15. Er fährt nicht _____ sein Bruder.
                      (as fast as)

16. Im Januar ist es _____.
                        (coldest)

17. Es ist _____ du glaubst.
              (closer than)

18. Die Preise werden _____.
                         (higher and higher)

19. Haben Sie _____ Messer?
                 (a sharper)

20. Es ist _____ Wagen in ganz Italien.
              (the fastest)

21. Im Dezember sind die Tage _____ und die Nächte _____.
                                  (shortest)   (longest)

22. Ich bleibe _____ zu Hause.
                 (would rather [stay])

23. _____ Mal bleibst du zu Hause.
       (The next)

24. Dieser Wein ist _____ der andere.
                       (better than)

25. Er ißt nicht _____ ich.
                    (as much as)

26. Guter Wein wird _____.
                       (more and more expensive)

27. Ich brauche _____ Anzug.
                   (a darker)

28. Ihre Preise sind _____.
                        (the highest)

29. Je _____ er arbeitet, desto _____ wird er.
          (more)   (more tired)

30. Das findet man nur in _____ Restaurants.
                             (the best)

31. Er spielt nicht _____ du.
                       (as well as)

32. Es wird _____.
      (warmer)

33. Das ist _____ Schwester.
      (her younger)

34. Ich fahre zu _____ Tankstelle.
      (the next)

Express in German

1. It's colder than yesterday.
2. Is it getting darker?
3. He doesn't drive as fast as his brother.
4. He's looking for (**suchen**) a larger apartment.
5. I pay more rent than you.
6. She's getting prettier and prettier.
7. It's the largest house in Hamburg.
8. These cassettes are cheapest.
9. The more, the better.
10. I need a darker suit.
11. It's closer than you think.
12. It's getting warmer.
13. Most people buy a smaller car.
14. I'm driving to the next gas station.
15. I like to drink beer.
16. Computers are getting cheaper and cheaper.
17. Do you have a sharper knife?
18. He doesn't play as well as you.
19. I'd rather stay here.
20. You only find that in the best restaurants.
21. This wine is better than the other one.
22. The more he works the more tired he gets.
23. It's the fastest car in Italy.
24. In December the days are shortest and the nights longest.
25. That's her younger sister.
26. Karl is older than his brother.
27. The next time you're staying at home.

Prepositions

4

I. INTRODUCTION

The use of prepositions is a particularly rich and idiomatic aspect of language. One preposition can have many meanings and can be found in various syntactical surroundings. The English preposition *on,* for example, has extremes of meaning ranging from the literal to the figurative; it occurs in formal speech as well as slang; and it has settings and functions ranging from the prepositional phrase to verb prefixes and suffixes:

on the table	on the whole
on wheels	the tax on gasoline
on time	the march on Washington
on my honor	the come-on
on the spot	to put on
	turned on

German prepositions are just as rich and varied as their English counterparts.

A. The prepositional phrase

The meaning and function of a preposition can be best understood in the preposition's most stable setting, the *prepositional phrase*. Here is a simple example in English:

on the table

1. *On* is a preposition.

2. *The table* is the object of the preposition.

3. The whole prepositional phrase answers the question "where", i.e., it functions as an adverb of place.

Other prepositional phrases specify the "when" (time) or "how" (manner) of an action or situation.

B. German prepositional phrases

Look at these prepositional phrases:

auf dem Tisch	on the table
mit ihm	with him
für mich	for me
um die Ecke	around the corner
während der Ferien	during the vacation

These German examples show that the *object of a preposition* can be in various *cases*—any case, in fact, except the nominative:

mit *ihm*	(dative)
für *mich*	(accusative)
während *der Ferien*	(genitive)

The choice, however, is not free.

GENERAL RULES:

1. The case of the object of a preposition is determined by the preposition, which is said to "govern" or "take" it.

2. While most prepositions take only one case, certain others can take either of two cases. Here the choice is determined by the function of the whole prepositional phrase.

C. Contractions

Contractions often occur within prepositional phrases. In fact, certain contractions are so common that they are in effect mandatory:

MANDATORY CONTRACTIONS

an dem → am	in dem → im	zu dem→ zum
an das → ans	in das → ins	zu der → zur
	bei dem → beim	
	von dem → vom	

Some other contractions are common in colloquial German, but they are not mandatory:

auf das → aufs	hinter dem → hinterm	vor dem → vorm
durch das → durchs	über das → übers	vor das → vors
für das → fürs	unter das → unters	um das → ums
	unter dem → unterm	

Still other contractions are colloquial to the point of slurring: **auf'm, nach'm,** etc.

LEVEL ONE

I. PREPOSITIONS TAKING THE DATIVE

The following prepositions take only dative objects:

aus	gegenüber	seit
außer	mit	von
bei	nach	zu

A. AUS

Most common uses

1. *from* (with place name)

Herr Schmidt kommt aus Berlin.   (Mr. Schmidt comes *from* Berlin.)
Das Paket kam aus Deutschland.   (The package came *from* Germany.)

In such cases, **aus** indicates *origin*. Note that the first sentence means that Mr. Schmidt was either born in Berlin or that he has been living there for some time. Here the context plays an important role. If you grew up in California and were studying in New York, you would answer the New Yorker's question "Where do you come from?" with "From (**aus**) California." If you've been in New York long enough to feel at home there, you might answer the same question with "From (**aus**) New York, but originally from (**aus**) California."

2. *out of* (location)

Sie kommt gerade aus dem Haus.   (She's just coming *out of* the house.)

More specific uses

3. *out of, for* (motivation)

Er tat es aus Mitleid.   (He did it *out of* pity.)
Aus diesem Grund will er bleiben. (*For* this reason he wants to stay.)

In expressions like **aus Mitleid** (*out of pity*) neither German nor English uses the definite article.

4. *made* (*out*) *of*

Das ganze Haus ist aus Holz.   (The whole house is *made of* wood.)
Gute Mappen sind aus Leder.   (Good briefcases are *made of* leather.)

When **aus** is used in this sense, neither German nor English uses the definite article.

B. AUSSER

Most common uses

1. *except for, besides, but, aside from, other than*

Außer ihm kenne ich niemand in Hamburg.

(*Except for him* I don't know anyone in Hamburg.)
(*Besides him* I don't know anyone in Hamburg.)
(I don't know anyone in Hamburg *but him.*)

Note that *besides* means the same thing as *except for* in the above sentences.

2. *besides, in addition to*

Außer ihm kenne ich viele Leute in Hamburg.

(I know a lot of people in Hamburg *besides him*.)

Here *besides* means *in addition to* rather than *except for*.

More specific uses

3. *out of*

Er ist außer Atem (außer Gefahr). Der Automat ist außer Betrieb.

(He's *out of breath* [*out of danger*].)
(The [coin-operated] machine is *out of order*.)

When **außer** is used in the sense of *out of*, no article is used. In this, German is similar to English.

4. *beside* (*himself*, etc.)

Sie war außer sich.

(She was *beside herself*.)

When **außer** is used in this sense, reflexive pronouns are required. See page 190ff for reflexives.

C. BEI

Most common uses

1. *at, with* (referring to *someone's house* or *home*)

Er wohnt bei seinem Bruder.
Er wohnt bei seinen Eltern.

(He's living *at* his brother's place.)
(He's living *with* his parents.)

2. *near* (with locations)

Unser Haus liegt beim Bahnhof.
Budenheim liegt bei Mainz.

(Our house is *near* the station.)
(Budenheim is *near* Mainz.)

3. *at* (referring to a business or professional establishment)

Um drei bin ich beim Arzt.
Er ist jetzt beim Friseur.

(I'll be *at* the doctor's at three.)
(He's *at* the barber's now.)

Note that English uses a possessive (at the *doctor's* or at the *doctor's* office) where German just uses a dative object.

4. *at, for* (referring to place of work)

Er ist jetzt bei der Arbeit.	(He's *at* work now.)
Er arbeitet bei Mercedes-Benz.	(He works *for* Mercedes-Benz.)

More specific uses

5. *with* (on one's person)

Ich habe kein Geld bei mir.	(I don't have any money *with* me. [*on* me])

6. *by, while*

Störe ich beim Essen?	(Am I disturbing you *while* you're eating?)

7. *when* (normally referring to the weather)

Bei schlechtem Wetter bleiben wir zu Hause.	(*When* the weather's bad we stay home.)

8. *by*

Wie kannst du bei dem Licht lesen?	(How can you read *by* that light?)

D. GEGENÜBER

Most common use

1. *across from, opposite*

Er saß mir gegenüber.	(He sat *across from* me.)
Unserem Haus gegenüber ist eine Bäckerei.	(There's a bakery *across from* our house.)

Gegenüber normally follows its object.

E. MIT

Most common uses

1. *with*

Kommen Sie mit uns?   (Are you coming *with* us?)

2. *by* (with means of transportation)

Er ist mit dem Zug gekommen.   (He came *by* train.)

Where English uses only *by* to indicate the means of travel, German uses
mit and the definite article.

F. NACH

Most common uses

1. *to* (destination with place names)

Fahren Sie nach Hamburg?   (Are you going *to* Hamburg?)
(nach Deutschland, Europa?)   (*to* Germany, Europe?)

Nach is used with the names of towns, cities, states, countries, and continents
(i.e., names of towns and larger entities).

Note the following idiom:

Ich gehe nach Hause.   (I'm going *home*.)

2. *after* (in time expressions)

Es ist zehn nach fünf.   (It's ten *after* five.)
Nach der Arbeit geht er nach Hause.   (He goes home *after* work.)

NOTE: German uses the definite article in expressions like **nach der Arbeit**
or **nach dem Mittagessen**.

More specific use

3. *according to*

Seinem Brief nach geht es ihm gut.   (*According to* his letter he's fine.)

When **nach** means *according to,* it follows its object.

G. SEIT

Most common uses

1. *since* (a point in past time)

Wir wohnen seit dem ersten April in Freiburg.

(We've been living in Freiburg *since* the first of April.)

2. *for* (a period of time)

Sie wohnt seit einer Woche bei uns.

(She has been living at our place *for* a week.)

NOTE: **Seit** requires the present tense if it refers to an action that began in the past and is still going on. In such cases English uses the present perfect.

Sie wohnt seit einer Woche bei uns.

(She *has been living* at our place for a week.)

H. VON

Most common uses

1. *from*

Ich fahre von Stuttgart nach Köln.

(I'm driving *from* Stuttgart to Cologne.)

Heute habe ich einen Brief von Thomas bekommen.

(I got a letter *from* Thomas today.)

Contrast:
Heute habe ich einen Brief von Thomas bekommen. (with persons)
Heute habe ich einen Brief aus München bekommen. (with places)

Also Contrast:
Ich komme aus Stuttgart. (I come *from* Stuttgart, i.e., I live there.)
Ich fahre von Stuttgart nach Köln. (I'm driving *from* Stuttgart to Cologne.)

2. *from, off of*

Das Glas fiel vom Tisch.

(The glass fell *off of* [*from*] the table.)

3. *by*

Wir haben drei Novellen von Thomas Mann gelesen.	(We read three novellas *by* Thomas Mann.)

4. *of* (possessive)

Er ist ein Freund von mir (von Karl).	(He's a friend *of* mine [*of* Karl's].)

Note that a possessive (i.e., *mine, Karl's*) follows the English *of*-construction, whereas the German **von** is followed by a simple dative object.

I. ZU

Most common use

1. *to* (with places inside a town or city, with persons)

Er geht zum Bahnhof. (zur Post)	(He's going *to the* station. [*to the* post office])
Er geht zu seinem Freund. (zu ihm)	(He's going *to* his friend's [place]. [*to* his place])

NOTE: English uses a possessive (*to his friend's* or *to his place*) when a person's house or home is meant. German uses only a dative object.

Note the following idiomatic uses of **zu:**

Er ist zu Hause.	(He's [*at*] home.)
Wir gehen zu Fuß.	(We're *walking* [going *on foot*].)
zum Beispiel	(*for example*)
zum Schluß	(*finally, in conclusion*)

More specific uses

2. *at, for* (with holidays and occasions)

Wo warst du zu Weihnachten?	(Where were you *at* Christmas?)
Was hast du zu Weihnachten bekommen?	(What did you get *for* Christmas?)

Zu is used with all holidays and special occasions: **zu Weihnachten, zu Ostern, zu Pfingsten, zum Geburtstag.**

3. *at* (with prices)

Geben Sie mir zehn Briefmarken zu
einer Mark.

(Give me ten one-mark stamps. *lit.*:
at one mark each)

■ DRILLS

Fill-ins

Supply the missing prepositions and, where necessary, the missing articles.

1. Bitte, wie kommt man _____ Post?
   (to the)

2. _____ wem bist du ausgegangen?
   (With)

3. Dieser Zug fährt _____ München _____ Stuttgart.
   (from)   (to)

4. Sie kommt gerade _____ Haus.
   (out of the)

5. Ich warte schon _____ fünf Uhr hier.
   (since)

6. _____ ihm war niemand da.
   (Besides)

7. Ich war gestern _____ Hause.
   (at)

8. Das Hotel liegt _____ Bahnhof.
   (near the)

9. Sie wohnt noch _____ Eltern.
   (with her)

10. Ich bin Berliner. Ich komme _____ Berlin.
    (from)

11. Sind Sie _____ Zug gekommen?
    (by)

12. Ich habe einen Brief _____ Thomas bekommen.
    (from)

13. Er ist gerade _____ Arzt gegangen.
    (to the)

14. Er ist jetzt _____ Arzt.
    (at the)

15. Ich gehe jetzt _____ Hause.

16. Mein Glas ist _____ Tisch gefallen.
    (off the)

17. Sie ist jetzt _____ Arbeit.
    (at)

18. Kommst du nachher _____ mir?
    (to)

19. Wir wohnen _____ zwei Jahren hier.
    (for)

20. Er saß mir _____ .
    (across from)

21. Es ist zwanzig _____ acht (Uhr).
    (after)

22. Gestern habe ich ein Paket _____ Freiburg bekommen.
    (from)

23. Wir gehen _____ Fuß.
    (on)

More specific uses

1. Hast du zehn Mark _____ dir? (on you)
2. Der Automat ist _____ Betrieb. (out of order)
3. Gute Mappen sind _____ Leder. (made of leather)
4. Was hast du _____ Weihnachten bekommen? (for Christmas)
5. Seinem Brief _____ kommt er morgen an. (according to his letter)
6. _____ schlechtem Wetter bleiben wir zu Hause. (when the weather is bad)
7. Geben Sie mir zehn Briefmarken _____ einer Mark. (ten one mark stamps)
8. Das hast du nur _____ Mitleid getan. (out of pity)

Express in German

1. It's twenty after eight.
2. She's just coming out of the house.
3. I was at home yesterday.

4. Did you come by train?
5. I got a letter from Thomas.
6. W've been living here for two years.
7. How do I get to the post office?
8. This train goes (**fahren**) from Munich to Stuttgart.
9. He sat across from me.
10. She's at work now.
11. I got a package from Freiburg yesterday. (Begin with **Gestern** . . .)
12. He went to the doctor's.
13. I'm going home now.
14. Who did you go out with? (*lit.* "With whom")
15. Besides him no one was there.
16. I've been waiting here since five o'clock.
17. She's still living with her parents.
18. Are you coming to my place afterwards?
19. My glass fell off the table.
20. We're walking.
21. He's at the doctor's now.

More specific uses

1. What did you get for Christmas?
2. The machine is out of order.
3. Good briefcases are made of leather.
4. According to his letter he's arriving tomorrow.
5. Do you have ten marks on you?
6. Give me ten one mark stamps.
7. *When the weather is bad* we stay at home. (*Use a prepositional phrase.*)

LEVEL TWO

I. PREPOSITIONS TAKING THE ACCUSATIVE

The following prepositions take accusative objects:

bis	gegen
durch	ohne
für	um

A. BIS

Most common uses

1. *until* (in time expressions)

Ich bleibe bis nächste Woche hier.   (I'm staying here *until* next week.)

2. *as far as* (with places)

Ich fahre nur bis Salzburg.   (I'm only going *as far as* Salzburg.)

3. *to*

von Kopf bis Fuß   (from head *to* foot)
von oben bis unten   (from top *to* bottom)

4. *by* (with a definite time)

Es wird bis morgen fertig sein.   (It'll be ready *by* tomorrow.)

More specific uses

Bis is often found in conjunction with other prepositions. When it is, the *final preposition* of the pair determines the case. In the following examples, *in* and *an* take the accusative:

5. bis in = *into*

Wir arbeiteten bis (spät) in die Nacht.   (We worked [late] into the night.)

6. bis an = (*right*) *up to*

Das Wasser kam bis an die Tür.   (The water came [right] *up to* the door.)

B. DURCH

Most common use

1. *through*

Wir gingen durch den Park.   (We walked *through* the park.)

More specific use

2. *by, through*

Ich habe das durch Zufall gehört.	(I heard that *by* chance.)
Ich lernte ihn durch Freunde kennen.	(I met him *through* friends.)

C. FÜR

Most common use

1. *for*

Ist Post für mich da?	(Is there any mail *for* me?)
Für zwanzig Mark kriegst du ein gutes Essen.	(You can get a good meal *for* twenty marks.)

More specific use

2. *for, by*

Wort für Wort	(word *for* word)
Schritt für Schritt	(step *by* step)

D. GEGEN

Most common uses

1. *against*

Was haben Sie gegen ihn?	(What do you have *against* him?)

2. *into, (up) against*

Er ist gegen einen Baum gefahren.	(He ran *into* a tree.)

More specific use

3. *around, about, along toward* (up to a certain time or number but not exceeding it)

Es waren gegen hundert Leute da.	(There were *about* a hundred people there.)
Wir kommen gegen vier Uhr an.	(We're arriving *about* [*along toward*] four o'clock.)

In these examples **gegen** means *about* or *approximately,* but in a restricted sense: the number or time referred to cannot be exceeded (up to four o'clock, but not after; up to a hundred people, but no more).

E. OHNE

Most common use

1. *without*

Er ist ohne seinen Mantel weggegangen.	(He left *without* his coat.)
Geh nicht ohne mich.	(Don't go *without* me.)

F. UM

Most common uses

1. *around*

Er kommt gerade um die Ecke.	(He's just coming *around* the corner.)
Sie saßen alle um den Tisch.	(They were all sitting *around* the table.)

2. *at* (in time expressions)

Er ist um elf Uhr gekommen.	(He came *at* eleven o'clock.)

■ DRILLS

Fill-ins

Supply the missing prepositions and, where necessary, the missing articles.

1. Er hat das Buch _____ mich bestellt.
   (for)

2. Sie kommt gerade _____ Ecke.
   (around the)

3. Geh nicht _____ deine Mappe.
   (without)

4. Ich habe nichts _____ ihn.
   (against)

5. Es wird _____ morgen fertig sein.
                  (by)

6. Wir sind _____ Stadt gefahren.
               (through the)

7. Georg hat viel Geld _____ seinen neuen Mantel ausgegeben.
                            (for)

8. Er hat sie _____ Kopf _____ Fuß angesehen.
                  (from)   (to)

9. Er ist _____ acht Uhr gekommen.
              (at)

10. Dieser Zug fährt nur _____ München.
                            (as far as)

11. Er ist _____ Baum gefahren.
              (into a)

12. Sie ist _____ ihren Mantel weggegangen.
               (without)

13. Wer nicht _____ uns ist, ist _____ uns.
                  (for)   (against)

14. Wir bleiben _____ nächsten Montag.
                   (until)

More specific uses

1. Sie kommt _____ sechs Uhr an. (about six o'clock)
2. Ich habe ihn _____ Freunde kennengelernt. (through friends)
3. Übersetzen Sie nicht Wort _____ Wort! (word for word)
4. Wir arbeiteten _____ spät _____ Nacht. (late into the night)

Express in German

1. Don't go without your briefcase.
2. This train only goes (**fahren**) as far as Munich.
3. He ordered the book for me.
4. We drove through the city.
5. I don't have anything against him.
6. She left without her coat.
7. George spent a lot of money for his new coat.
8. She's just coming around the corner.
9. It'll be ready by next week.
10. He ran into a tree.

11. She came at eight o'clock.
12. We're staying until next Monday.

More specific uses

1. I met him through friends.
2. She came about six o'clock.
3. Don't translate word for word.
4. We worked late into the night.

LEVEL THREE

I. TWO-WAY PREPOSITIONS

Look at the difference between the prepositional phrases in the following sentences:

LOCATION	Paul is *in the city* today.
DESTINATION	Paul is driving *into the city* today.

In the first sentence the prepositional phrase *in the city* gives Paul's location—*where* he is. In the second sentence the phrase *into the city* gives Paul's destination—*where* he's going (*to*). The preposition *into* is used when there is motion in a definite direction or toward a certain destination. When there is no motion in a definite direction, the preposition *in* is used. (You wouldn't say: "He's living *into* the city.")

German uses two-way prepositions to make the same distinction. But instead of choosing between two prepositions (as English does with *in* and *into*), German chooses between the dative and accusative case.

II. SUMMARY: DATIVE OR ACCUSATIVE?

A. DATIVE: location (no motion toward a destination)
[wo = where]

When there is *no motion toward a destination,* two-way prepositions take dative objects, and the prepositional phrase answers the question wo?

(*where?*)

> Wo ist er? Er ist **in der Stadt.**
> (*Where* is he? He's *in the city*.)

B. ACCUSATIVE: motion toward a destination
   (wohin = *where to*)

When there is *motion toward a destination,* two-way prepositions take accusative objects and the prepositional phrase answers the question **wohin?** (*where to?*)

> **Wohin** geht er? Er geht **in die Stadt.**
> (Where's he going? He's going *into the city*.)

It is important to note that it is not just *motion* but rather *motion toward a specific destination* that determines whether you choose the dative or accusative:

> Er ist den ganzen Tag **in der Stadt** herumgelaufen.
> (He's been running around *in the city* all day.)

> Er ist **in die Stadt** gegangen.
> (He went *into the city*.)

Both of the above examples involve motion. In the first sentence, the person is already in the city, so the city is not his destination, but rather his location, and consequently **in** takes the dative. The second sentence tells you where he's going (to): in die Stadt (*into the city*). A definite destination is given, and consequently **in** takes the accusative.

III. LIST OF TWO-WAY PREPOSITIONS

an	über
auf	unter
hinter	in
vor	neben
	zwischen

A. AUF

1. *on* (*on top of*)

Auf is used with horizontal surfaces: floors, chairs, tabletops. It is *not* used with vertical surfaces such as walls or windows.

wo + dative: Es lag auf dem Tisch.
                     (It was lying on the table.)

wohin + accusative: Ich warf es auf den Tisch.
                       (I threw it on [to] the table.)

2. *in* (with languages)

auf deutsch
auf englisch
auf französisch , etc.

Compare the following two sentences:

Er sagte es auf deutsch .
(He said it *in* German.)

Übersetzen Sie aus dem Englischen ins Deutsche .
(Translate from English *into* German.)

In the first sentence **deutsch** is an adverb and therefore not capitalized. The second sentence uses **deutsch** and **englisch** as adjectival nouns (see p. 320ff). For this reason, they are capitalized and they take normal adjective endings.

Note the following idiomatic uses of **auf:**

auf dem Land sein   (to be in the country)
aufs Land gehen   (to go to the country)

auf einer Reise sein   (to be on a trip)
auf eine Reise gehen   (to go on a trip)

B. AN

1. *on, onto*

In contrast to **auf, an** is normally used with *vertical surfaces,* e.g., a wall or a blackboard.

| wo + dative: | Das Bild hing an der Wand. |
| | (The picture was hanging on the wall.) |

| wohin + accusative: | Ich hängte es an die Wand. |
| | (I hung it on the wall.) |

2. dative: *at* (*at the edge of*)

	LOCATION	an der Grenze	at the border
		am Rand	at the edge
		am Strand	at the beach
		am Fenster	at the window

3. accusative: *to* (*up to the edge of*)

	DESTINATION	an die Grenze	to the border
		an den Rand	to the edge
		an den Strand	to the beach
		ans Fenster	to the window

NOTE: **An** usually means *up to, but no farther than* a given point:

Wir fahren an die Grenze.
(We're driving [up] to the border, but not across it.)

Note the following idiomatic uses of **an:**

an der Universität	at the university
an der Ecke	on the corner
an die Arbeit gehen	to go to work

C. HINTER

1. *behind, in back of*

| wo + dative: | Er arbeitet hinter dem Haus. |
| | (He was working behind the house.) |

| wohin + accusative: | Er ist gerade hinter das Haus ge-gangen. |
| | (He just went behind the house.) |

D. IN

1. *in, into, to*

wo + dative:	Er ist in der Küche.
	(He's in the kitchen.)
wohin + accusative:	Er geht in die Küche.
	(He's going into the kitchen.)

Note the following idiomatic uses of **in:**

ins Theater (Konzert) gehen	to go to the theater (concert)
in der Schule sein	to be in (at) school
in die Schule gehen	to go to school
im 3. Stock	on the 4th (!) floor*
in der Schweiz,	in Switzerland, the
der Bundesrepublik	Federal Republic (of Germany)
in die Schweiz,	to Switzerland, the
die Bundesrepublik	Federal Republic
aus dem Englischen ins Deutsche[†]	from German into English
Ich wohne in der Hauptstraße.	(I live on Main Street.)

but:

Ich wohne Hauptstraße 187.   (I live at 187 Main Street.)

NOTE: German does not use a preposition when the street number is given.

NOTE: in **der** Schweiz, etc.
in **die** Schweiz, etc.

Die Schweiz, die Bundesrepublik and all other feminine names of countries require the use of the definite article.

---

* **im dritten Stock:** In German, the first (ground) floor is called **das Erdgeschoß,** the second floor **der erste Stock,** the third floor **der zweite Stock,** and so forth. For this reason, the number of the floor is always one less in German than it is in English.

[†] Sie übersetzte es aus dem Englischen **ins Deutsche.** Lit.: She translated it from the English into the German. German uses adjectival nouns in such expressions; for a full explanation, see Adjectival Nouns, p. 320ff.

E. NEBEN

1. *next to, alongside of, beside*

wo + dative: Es steht neben dem Bett.
(It is standing next to the bed.)

wohin + accusative: Stell es neben das Bett.
(Put it next to the bed.)

F. ÜBER

1. *over, above*

wo + dative: Das Bild hing über meinem Schreibtisch.
(The picture hung over my desk.)

wohin + accusative: Ich hängte das Bild über meinen Schreibtisch.
(I hung the picture over my desk.)

2. *across (over), on the other side*

wohin + accusative: Sie gehen hier über die Straße.
(You go across the street here.)

NOTE: In this sentence the idea of destination consists in going *from* one side of the street *to* the other.

3. *more than, over* = **über** + accusative

Es kostet über fünfzig Mark. (It costs more than fifty marks.)
Er ist über siebzig Jahre alt. (He's over seventy.)

G. UNTER

1. *under*

wo + dative: Der Koffer ist unter dem Bett.
(The suitcase is under the bed.)

wohin + accusative: Stell den Koffer unter das Bett.
(Put the suitcase under the bed.)

2. *less than, under* = **unter** + accusative

Diese Anzüge kosten alle unter fünf
hundert Mark.

(All of these suits cost less than five
hundred marks.)

Note the following idiomatic uses of **unter:**

Das ist unter meiner Würde.	(That's *beneath* my dignity.)
unter uns gesagt	(just *between* you and me)
unter dem Einfluß von	(*under* the influence of)
unter Freunden	(*among* friends)

H. VOR

1. *in front of* (*before*)

wo + dative: Der Wagen steht vor der Tür.
                 (The car's standing in front of the door.)

wohin + accusative: Fahr den Wagen vor die Tür.
                 (Drive the car [up] in front of the door.)

Note the following idioms:

vor allem	above *all*
vor Angst	out of fear
vor Freude	for joy

I. ZWISCHEN

1. *between*

wo + dative: Ihr Wagen steht zwischen den zwei
                 anderen da.
                 (Your car is standing between those
                 two over there.)

wohin + accusative: Stellen Sie Ihren Wagen zwischen
                 die zwei anderen da.
                 (Park your car between those two
                 over there.)

DRILLS

Fill-ins

Supply the missing prepositions, and, where necessary, the article or possessive adjective.

1. Mein Wagen steht _____ Haus.
   (in front of the)

2. Er warf seinen Mantel _____ Bett.
   (onto the)

3. Es stand heute _____ Zeitung.
   (in the)

4. Ich hängte das Bild _____ Schreibtisch.
   (over the)

5. Er sagte es _____ deutsch.
   (in)

6. Komm sofort _____ Haus!
   (into the)

7. Deine Brille ist _____ Zeitung.
   (under the)

8. Der Nachttisch steht _____ Bett.
   (next to the)

9. Stell es _____ Tür.
   (in front of the)

10. Die Garage ist gleich _____ Haus.
    (behind the)

11. Stell die Lampe _____ Sofa und _____ Schreibtisch.
    (between the)   (the)

12. Schreiben Sie nicht _____ Bücher.
    (in the)

13. Meine Serviette ist _____ Tisch gefallen.
    (under the)

14. Das Bild hing _____ Sofa.
    (over the)

15. Fahr deinen Wagen _____ zwei anderen da.
    (alongside of the)

16. Basel liegt _____ Grenze _____ Deutschland und
                        (on the)   (between)

    _____ Schweiz.

17. Er schläft mit dem Bart _____ Decke.
                                  (under the)

18. Es kostet _____ vierhundert Mark.
                    (over)

19. Legen Sie es _____ Tisch!
                      (on the)

20. Fahren Sie den Wagen _____ Haus!
                              (in front of the)

21. Sie stand _____ Fenster.
                    (at the)

22. Er ging _____ Straße.
                (across the)

23. Es ist _____ Kühlschrank gefallen.
                (behind the)

24. Er ging _____ Straßenlaterne auf und ab.
                  (under the)

25. Deine Schuhe sind _____ Bett.
                          (under the)

26. Leg deinen Mantel _____.
                          (over mine*)

27. Er hat es _____ Tafel geschrieben.
                    (on the)

28. Deine Mappe liegt _____ Sofa.
                          (on the)

Idiomatic uses

1. Morgen fahre ich _____ Land.
                        (to the)

2. Sie studiert jetzt _____ Universität.
                          (at the)

3. Wir gehen _____ Kino.
                  (to the)

---

* Use the possessive adjective *mein* plus the appropriate adjective ending.

4. _____vergiß deine Reiseschecks nicht.
   (Above all)

5. Ich fahre nächste Woche _____ Schweiz.
   (to)

6. Sie steht _____ Ecke.
   (on the)

7. Er wohnt jetzt _____ Land.
   (in the)

8. Sie wohnen _____ dritten Stock.
   (on the)

9. Gehen wir jetzt _____ Arbeit.
   (to)

10. Er wohnt _____ Hauptstraße.
    (on)

11. _____ gesagt hat er unrecht.
    (Between you and me)

12. Übersetzen Sie es _____ Englischen _____ Deutsche.
    (from)   (into)

13. Wir gehen bald _____ Reise.
    (on a)

Synthetic Exercises

Form complete sentences in the tenses indicated. Both dative and accusative prepositional objects are involved.

1. Garage / sein / gleich / hinter / Haus (*present*)
2. Meine Serviette / fallen / unter / Tisch (*present perfect*)
3. Es / stehen / heute / in / Zeitung (*past*)
4. Sie / stehen / an / Fenster (*past*)
5. Er / werfen / Mantel / auf / Bett (*past*)
6. Mein Wagen / stehen / vor / Haus (*present*)
7. Er / schreiben / es / an / Tafel (*present perfect*)
8. Es / fallen / hinter / Kühlschrank (*present perfect*)
9. Komm sofort / in / Haus / ! (*imperative*)
10. Nachttisch / stehen / neben / Bett (*present*)
11. Stell es / vor / Tür / (*imperative*)
12. Ich / hängen / Bild / über / Schreibtisch (*past*)
13. Er / gehen / unter / Straßenlaterne / auf und ab (*past*)

14. Legen Sie / Ihr / Mantel / über / mein / (*imperative*)
15. Stellen Sie / Lampe / zwischen / Sofa / und / Schreibtisch / (*imperative*)
16. Er / gehen / über / Straße (*past*)
17. Basel / liegen / an / Grenze / zwischen / Deutschland / und / Schweiz (*present*)
18. Deine Mappe / liegen / auf / Sofa (*present*)

Idiomatic uses

1. Sie / studieren / jetzt / an / Universität (*present*)
2. Ich / fahren / nächste Woche / in / Schweiz (*present*)
3. Gehen wir / jetzt / an / Arbeit / ! (*imperative*)
4. Er / wohnen / in / Hauptstraße (*present*)
5. Ich / fahren / morgen / auf / Land (*present*)
6. Sie / wohnen / in / zweit- / Stock (*present*)
7. Übersetzen Sie / Sätze / aus / Englisch / in / Deutsch / ! (*imperative*)
8. Sie / stehen / an / Ecke (*present*)
9. Wir / gehen / bald / auf / Reise (*present*)

Express in German

1. The garage is right behind the house.
2. He threw his coat on the bed.
3. It was (**stehen**) in the newspaper today.
4. Drive the car in front of the house.
5. Put (**legen**) it on the table.
6. He wrote it on the board.
7. Your shoes are under the bed.
8. He said it in German.
9. I hung the picture over the desk.
10. Come into the house immediately!
11. Don't write in the books!
12. She was standing at the window.
13. It costs over four hundred marks.
14. It fell behind the refrigerator.
15. My car is (**stehen**) in front of the house.
16. The night table is next to the bed.
17. Put it in front of the door.
18. My napkin fell under the table.

19. Your briefcase is on the sofa.
20. Basel is **(liegen)** on the border between Germany and Switzerland.
21. Put **(legen)** your coat over mine.
22. He went across the street.
23. He walked back and forth under the streetlight.
24. Put the lamp between the sofa and the desk.

Idiomatic uses

1. I'm driving to the country tomorrow.
2. They live on the fourth floor. (!)
3. He lives on Main Street.
4. She's standing on the corner.
5. He's living in the country now.
6. We're going to the movies.
7. Let's go to work now.
8. I'm driving to Switzerland next week.
9. Translate it from English into German.
10. She's studying at the university now.
11. We're going on a trip soon.

LEVEL FOUR

I. PREPOSITIONS REQUIRING THE GENITIVE

The following prepositions require genitive objects:

(an)statt	trotz
während	wegen

A. (AN)STATT

1. *instead of*

Anstatt is more formal than **statt**.

> Statt eines Anzugs kaufte ich eine Jacke und Hose.
> (*Instead of* a suit I bought a sportscoat and slacks.)

NOTE: The genitive case is *not used* when the noun object of **statt** is not preceded by an article or adjective.

> Statt Bier trinken wir Wein.
> (Instead of beer we'll drink wine.)

Idiom: **Stattdessen** = instead of that

B. TROTZ

1. *in spite of*

> Trotz seiner Erkältung kommt er mit.
> (*In spite of* his cold he's coming along.)

Idiom: **Trotzdem** = in spite of that, nonetheless

C. WÄHREND

1. *during*

> Während des Tages bin ich nie zu Hause.
> (*During* the day I'm never home.)

D. WEGEN

1. *because of, due to, on account of*

Wegen der hohen Preise fahren wir diesen Sommer nicht nach Paris.
(*Because of* the high prices we're not going to Paris this summer.)

Idiom: **Weswegen** = *why, on what account, what for*

> Weswegen machen Sie das?
> (*What* are you doing that *for?*)

Idioms: **meinetwegen, deinetwegen, seinetwegen, ihretwegen, unsertwegen, euretwegen, ihretwegen, Ihretwegen**

Meinetwegen, etc. = *for my sake, on my account, because of me.*

> Ich hoffe, Sie tun das nicht nur meinetwegen.
> (I hope you're not doing that just *on my account.*)

Meinetwegen, etc. = *as far as I'm concerned, for all I care.*

Meinetwegen kannst du machen, was du willst.
(*As far as I'm concerned* you can do whatever you want.)

■ DRILLS

Fill-ins

Supply the missing elements.

1. _____ Kaffee trinke ich Tee.
   (Instead of)

2. _____ Semesters sehen wir Charlotte sehr selten.
   (During the)

3. _____ Farbe finde ich den Wagen schön.
   (In spite of the)

4. _____ neuen Anzugs kaufe ich mir eine Jacke und Hose.
   (Instead of a)

5. _____ Arbeit muß er viel reisen.
   (Because of his)

6. _____ Einkommens ist er immer pleite.
   (In spite of his)

7. _____ Sommers bleiben wir zu Hause.
   (During the)

8. _____ Nebels sind wir sehr langsam gefahren.
   (Due to the)

Idiomatic uses

1. _____ können Sie jetzt nach Hause gehen.
   (For all I care)

2. _____ haben wir es gemacht.
   (In spite of that)

3. _____ fuhr er nach Lübeck.
   (Instead of that)

4. Er tat es _____.
   (because of me)

Express in German

1. Because of his work he has to travel a lot.
2. In spite of his income he's always broke.
3. During the summer we stay at home.
4. Instead of coffee I'm going to drink tea.
5. In spite of the color I find the car pretty.
6. Instead of a new suit I'm going to buy a jacket and slacks.
7. Due to the fog we drove very slowly.
8. During the semester I don't see Charlotte very often.

Idiomatic uses

1. We did it in spite of that.
2. Instead of that he drove to Lübeck.
3. For all I care you can go home.
4. He did it because of me. (*Use* **tun.**)

■ MIXED DRILLS (all levels)

Fill-ins

1. Geh nicht _____ deine Mappe.
   (without)

2. Dieser Zug fährt _____ München _____ Stuttgart.
   (from)   (to)

3. Er warf seinen Mantel _____ Bett.
   (on the)

4. Sie kommt gerade _____ Haus.
   (out of the)

5. Es stand heute _____ Zeitung.
   (in the)

6. Ich habe nichts _____ ihn.
   (against)

7. Es fiel _____ Kühlschrank.
   (behind the)

8. Mein Glas fiel _____ Tisch.
   (off the)

9. Deine Schuhe sind _____ Bett.
                      (under the)

10. Sie kommt gerade _____ Ecke.
                     (around the)

11. Wir wohnen _____ zwei Jahren hier.
                (for)

12. Fahren Sie den Wagen _____ Haus.
                       (in front of the)

13. Er saß mir _____.
                (across from)

14. _____ Sommers bleiben wir zu Hause.
       (During the)

15. Komm sofort _____ Haus!
              (into the)

16. _____ ihm war niemand da.
       (Besides)

17. _____ Farbe finde ich den Wagen schön.
     (In spite of the)

18. Es wird _____ morgen fertig sein.
             (by)

19. Meine Serviette fiel _____ Tisch.
                  (under the)

20. Sie wohnt noch _____ Eltern.
              (with her)

21. Der Nachttisch steht _____ Bett.
               (next to the)

22. _____ Arbeit muß er viel reisen.
    (Because of his)

23. Sie stand _____ Fenster.
          (at the)

24. Wir sind _____ Stadt gefahren.
         (through the)

25. Wie komme ich _____ Post?
            (to the)

26. _____ Kaffee trinke ich Tee.
    (Instead of)

27. Legen Sie es _____ Tisch.
          (on the)

28. Sie kommen _____ Freiburg.
(from)

29. Wir bleiben _____ nächsten Montag.
(until)

30. Deine Mappe liegt _____ Sofa.
(on the)

31. _____ Einkommens ist er immer pleite.
(In spite of his)

32. Sie ist jetzt _____ Arbeit.
(at)

33. Er kam _____ acht Uhr.
(at)

34. Sind Sie _____ Zug gekommen?
(by)

35. _____ Nebels sind wir sehr langsam gefahren.
(Due to the)

36. Leg deinen Mantel _____.
(over mine)

More specific or idiomatic uses

1. Hast du zehn Mark _____ dir? (on you)
2. Morgen fahre ich _____ Land. (to the country)
3. Ich habe ihn _____ Freunde kennengelernt. (through friends)
4. Der Automat ist _____ Betrieb. (out of order)
5. Ich fahre nächste Woche _____ Schweiz. (to Switzerland)
6. _____ Brief _____ kommt er morgen an. (According to his letter)
7. _____ können Sie nach Hause gehen. (For all I care)
8. Sie wohnen _____ dritten Stock. (on the)
9. Gehen wir jetzt _____ Arbeit. (to work)
10. Sie kam _____ sechs Uhr. (about six o'clock)
11. Gute Mappen sind _____ Leder. (made of leather)
12. Wir arbeiteten _____ spät _____ Nacht. (late into the night)
13. _____ fuhr er nach Lübeck. (Instead of that)
14. Wir gehen bald _____ Reise. (on a trip)
15. Geben Sie mir zehn Briefmarken _____ Mark. (ten one mark stamps)
16. Übersetzen Sie es _____ Englischen _____ Deutsche. (from English into German)

Express in German

1. How do I get to the post office?
2. She's just coming around the corner.
3. It was in the newspaper today.
4. Put it on the table.
5. They come from Freiburg.
6. Don't go without your briefcase.
7. Because of his work he has to travel a lot.
8. Come into the house immediately!
9. Did you come by train?
10. Drive the car in front of the house.
11. She came at eight o'clock.
12. In spite of his income he's always broke.
13. Your briefcase is on the sofa.
14. He sat across from me.
15. It fell behind the refrigerator.
16. We've been living here for two years.
17. Your shoes are under the bed.
18. This train goes from Munich to Stuttgart.
19. During the summer we stay at home.
20. I don't have anything against him.
21. My napkin fell under the table.
22. She's just coming out of the house.
23. It'll be ready by tomorrow.
24. Instead of coffee I'm going to drink tea.
25. He threw his coat on the bed.
26. Besides him no one was there.
27. We drove through the city.
28. She was standing at the window.
29. Due to the fog we drove very slowly.
30. She's still living with her parents.
31. We're staying until next Monday.
32. My glass fell off the table.
33. Put your coat over mine.
34. In spite of the color I find the car pretty.
35. She's at work now.

More specific or idiomatic uses

1. Do you have ten marks on you?
2. I'm driving to the country tomorrow.

3. I met him through friends.
4. They live on the fourth floor. (!)
5. The machine is out of order.
6. She came about six o'clock.
7. I'm driving to Switzerland next week.
8. Instead of that he drove to Lübeck.
9. Good briefcases are made of leather.
10. According to his letter he's arriving tomorrow.
11. Let's go to work now.
12. We worked late into the night.
13. We're going on a trip soon.
14. For all I care you can go home.
15. Translate it from English into German.
16. Give me ten one mark stamps.

Time Expressions
5

I. HOURS AND MINUTES

A. Asking the time

The two common ways of asking the time of day are:

> Wie spät ist es? and Wieviel Uhr ist es?
> (What time is it?)

NOTE: In the expression **wieviel Uhr, wieviel** does not take an adjective ending.

B. UM = at

Where English uses the preposition *at* (e.g., *at* eight o'clock), German uses the preposition **um** (**um** acht Uhr):

> Er kommt um acht Uhr.
> (He's coming *at* eight o'clock.)

Um is used to indicate *exact* time. To indicate approximate time **gegen** is used:

> Er kommt gegen acht Uhr.
> (He's coming *along toward* [*about*] eight o'clock.)

C. Full, half, and quarter hours and minutes

1. Full hours

> Es ist acht (Uhr). (It's eight [o'clock].)

NOTE 1: **Um** is not used in telling a person the time of day, i.e. in answering the question **Wie spät ist es?** This corresponds to English usage: English does not use the preposition *at* in such cases.

NOTE 2: The word **Uhr** may be omitted, just as the word *o'clock* may be. When it is omitted from the German equivalent of *one o'clock,* however, the word **eins** must be used:

> Es ist ein Uhr.   but   Es ist eins.

2. Half hours

In English the *half* hour always refers back to the *last* full hour: it's half *past seven.* In German, however, it refers to the next full hour: it's half (of the way to) eight.

> 7:30   Es ist halb acht.
> (It's *half past seven.*)

3. Quarter hours

The most common way of telling time is to use the prepositions **nach** (*after* the hour) and **vor** (*before* the hour):

> 8:15   Es ist viertel nach acht.
> (It's quarter *after* eight.)
>
> 7:45   Es ist viertel vor acht.
> (It's quarter *to* eight.)

German has an alternate way of reporting quarter hours that is essentially the same as the way half hours are told. This construction does not use prepositions. All the quarter hours refer to the *next* full hour, rather than to the *last* one:

7:15	Es ist viertel acht. (a *quarter* of the way to *eight*)
(7:30	Es ist halb acht. [*half* of the way *to eight*])
7:45	Es ist dreiviertel acht. (*three quarters* of the way *to eight*)

4. Minutes

Expressions referring to minutes require the preposition **nach** or **vor:**

3:10	Es ist zehn (Minuten) nach drei.
3:25	Es ist fünfundzwanzig (Minuten) nach drei.
3:35	Es ist fünfundzwanzig (Minuten) vor vier.

NOTE 1: **Nach** and **vor** are used like their English equivalents *after* (*past*) and *before* (*to*): **nach** is used up to the half hour and refers to the last full hour (3:29 = neunundzwanzig nach drei) and **vor** is used after the half hour and refers to the *next* full hour (3:31 = neunundzwanzig vor vier).

NOTE 2: Like the word *minutes,* the word **Minuten** is often omitted.

NOTE 3: Occasionally, the half hour may be used as a reference rather than the full hour. This is the case especially when the approximate time is already known:

Es ist fünf nach (vor) halb.
(It's five minutes after [before] the half hour.)

5. Timetable time

Railroads, bus stations, airports, theaters, etc. use a 24-hour system:

Der Zug kommt um **20.15** (zwangzig Uhr fünfzehn) in Mainz an.
(The train arrives in Mainz at *8:15 p.m.*)

NOTE: In such cases, quarters and halves are not used. They are replaced by the numbers 15, 30, and 45:

20:15	zwanzig Uhr fünfzehn
15:30	fünfzehn Uhr dreißig
8:45	acht Uhr fünfundvierzig

II. DAYS AND PARTS OF DAYS

The parts of the day are all *masculine* with the exception of **die Nacht** and **die Mitternacht.**

der Morgen	morning	die Nacht	night
der Vormittag	forenoon	die Mitternacht	midnight
der Mittag	noon		
der Nachmittag	afternoon		
der Abend	evening		

All expressions referring to whole days are *masculine.* These include:

1. the word *day:* **der Tag**

2. the days of the week:

der Sonntag	der Donnerstag
der Montag	der Freitag
der Dienstag	der Samstag (Sonnabend)
der Mittwoch	

3. dates: der fünfundzwanzigste Mai

A. AM

All time expressions referring to days and parts of days may be used with **am**—with the *exception* of **Nacht** and **Mitternacht.**

The resulting expression may indicate:

1. *a one-time occurrence*

Er kommt am Donnerstag (am dreiundzwanzigsten Mai, am Abend).
(He's coming *on* Thursday [*on* the twenty-third of May, *in* the evening].)

2. *a regularly repeated occurrence*

Die Rechnungen kommen immer am Montag (am ersten Januar, am Morgen.
(The bills always come *on* Monday [*on* the first of January, *in* the morning].)

EXCEPTIONS: **in** der Nacht
um Mitternacht

NOTE: The word is **am** (not **an**) and is a contraction of **an dem.**

As in English, the preposition may be omitted *before days of the week:*

> Er kommt Mittwoch. (He's coming Wednesday.)

B. Adverbs of time

The days of the week and the parts of the day can be used as adverbs. The adverb is formed by adding an –s ending to the noun. As is always the case in German, adverbs are *not capitalized.*

In contrast to the **am**-expressions (am Montag, etc.), these adverbs can only be used to indicate *repeated occurrences:*

> Er arbeitet nachmittags (nachts, samstags).
> (He works afternoons [nights, Saturdays].)

EXCEPTION: During the day = **tagsüber.**

NOTE: There is no purely adverbial form of dates. The formula is:

> Er arbeitet immer am ersten Januar.
> (He always works *on the first* of January.)

III. WEEKS, MONTHS, SEASONS, AND YEARS

The *months* and the *seasons* are all *masculine:*

MONTHS

der Januar	der Mai	der September
der Februar	der Juni	der Oktober
der März	der Juli	der November
der April	der August	der Dezember

SEASONS

der Frühling	spring	der Herbst	autumn, fall
der Sommer	summer	der Winter	winter

The word for *week* is feminine: **die Woche, –n.**
The word for *year* is neuter: **das Jahr, –e.**

A. IM and IN DER

1. Months and seasons (im)

Im (the contraction of **in dem**) is used with the names of the months and seasons:

> Er ist **im** März hier gewesen.
> (He was here *in* March.)

> Sie kommt **im** Herbst.
> (She's coming *in* the fall.)

2. Weeks (in der, in)

a. **In der zweiten Woche** = in the second week.

Like English, German does not normally use the phrase *in the week* without some sort of modification, e.g., in the *second* week of our trip.

b. **In einer Woche, in zwei Wochen** = in a week, in two weeks, etc.

These expressions are also always in the dative case.

NOTE: The preposition **während** takes the genitive case.

> **während der Woche**   during the week

3. Years (im)

> Er ist **im Jahr(e) 1985** nach Frankfurt gezogen.
> Er ist **1985** nach Frankfurt gezogen.
> (He moved to Frankfurt *in 1985*.)

In naming a specific year, German either uses (*a*), the full phrase **im Jahr(e)*** *plus the year* or (*b*), it uses the year alone, *without a preposition*. You can't refer to years the way we do in English: ~~in 1985~~.

Both **im Jahr(e) 1985** and **1985** are correct, but the shorter form is far more common in everyday speech.

---

* The **e** in **im Jahr***e* is an old dative singular ending that is still retained in a number of common idioms, e.g., **zu Haus***e* and **nach Haus***e*.

IV. DEFINITE AND INDEFINITE TIME

A. Accusative case for definite time

The accusative case is used to indicate definite time when no preposition is involved:

> Letzten Sonntag blieb ich den ganzen Tag* zu Hause.
> (*Last Sunday* I stayed home *all day.*)

> Sie fährt nächste Woche nach Deutschland.
> (She's going to Germany *next week.*)

> Wir gehen jeden Winter skilaufen.
> (We go skiing *every winter.*)

> Er hat uns voriges Jahr besucht.
> (He visited us *last year.*)

NOTE: When German uses **ganz** in time expressions, the phrase always begins with the definite article:

> *Die* ganze Woche = all week.
> *Den* ganzen Tag = all day.

Note also that **letzt−** (last), **nächst−** (next), **vorig−** (last), and **jed−** (every) are very common in expressions of definite time.

B. Combinations of GESTERN, HEUTE, MORGEN, and parts of days

English may combine the words *yesterday* and *tomorrow* with words referring to parts of the day (e.g., *morning, afternoon, evening*) in order to form more exact time expressions:

> yesterday afternoon
> tomorrow evening

German functions in a similar manner:

> gestern nachmittag
> morgen abend

---

* **den** ganzen Tag. When German uses **ganz** (all) with singular nouns the expression must be preceded by a definite article (**den** ganzen Tag = all day).

Unlike English, however, German uses this same method to form time expressions referring to *today*. Instead of saying *this* morning, *this* evening, German says **heute** morgen, **heute** abend.

To form this kind of time expression, one may, with one exception, choose one word from column A and one from column B.

A	B
gestern	morgen
heute	vormittag
morgen	mittag
	nachmittag
	abend

The one exception is the German expression for *tomorrow morning:* **morgen früh,** (not morgen morgen).

NOTE: When the parts of the day (e.g., **morgen, vormittag**) are used in conjunction with **gestern, heute,** or **morgen,** they are adverbs of time rather than nouns and are therefore *not capitalized.*

C. Genitive case for indefinite time

Eines Tages ist er einfach weggegangen.
(*One day* he just went away.)

Expressions of this kind begin with the word **ein.**

V. OTHER COMMON TIME EXPRESSIONS

A. Other time expressions requiring prepositions

As we have seen, a time expression without a preposition uses:

the accusative case for definite time
the genitive case for indefinite time

When a preposition is involved, the rules are as follows.

1. Dative prepositions and accusative prepositions

Obviously, when a preposition requires dative objects only or accusative objects only, the appropriate case *must be used.* For example:

Er wohnt seit einer Woche hier.
(He's been living here *for a week*.)

Seit always takes a dative object; therefore the dative must be used in time expressions with **seit.**

NOTE: **Seit** einer Woche = *for* a week.

Seit is used with the *present tense* if the time expression refers to something that *began in the past and is still going on*. Where German uses the present tense to stress that the action (or condition) is still going on at the present time, English normally uses the present perfect: He *has been* living here for a week.

2. Two-way prepositions

When a two-way preposition is used in time expressions, the case is determined as follows:

a. Point in time (when? / **wann?**) = dative

If the prepositional phrase answers the question "When?" (at what *point in time?*), the two-way preposition takes the dative.

Sie sind vor einer Woche wegegangen.   (They left *a week ago*.)
Sie kommen in einer Woche zurück.   (They're coming back *in a week*.)

When did they leave?   Answer: vor einer Woche (dative).
When are they coming back?   Answer: in einer Woche (dative).

b. Period of time (how long? / **wie lange?**) = accusative

If the prepositional phrase answers the question "How long?" (for what period of time), the two-way preposition takes the accusative:

Er ist über eine Woche da geblieben.   (He stayed there *over a week*.)
Ich fahre auf ein Jahr* nach   (I'm going to Germany *for a year*.)
Deutschland.

---

* *Auf* **ein Jahr** and *für* **ein Jahr.** Conversational German tends increasingly to use **für** rather than **auf.**

How long did he stay there?   Answer: über eine Woche (accusative).
How long am I going for?   Answer: auf ein Jahr (accusative).

Auf must be used with verbs of motion (e.g., **fahren**). With other verbs, such as **sein** and **bleiben,** the accusative of definite time is used:

Ich blieb eine Woche in Frankfurt.
(I stayed in Frankfurt [*for*] *a week.*)

c. Seit *and* auf: *a comparison*

seit: *for* a period of past time
auf: *for* a period of future time

Both **seit** and **auf** can mean *for* in time expressions, and they both suggest *periods of time.* Furthermore, they are both normally used with the present tense in German. The difference between them is this:

Seit einem Jahr   refers to a year already past.
Auf ein Jahr   refers to a year yet to come.

Ich wohne seit einem Jahr in Deutschland. (The year is behind me.)
Ich fahre auf ein Jahr nach Deutschland.   (The year is ahead of me.)

B. Dates

Look at the following ways of asking for the date and giving it:

QUESTION	ANSWER
Der wievielte* ist heute?	Heute ist der siebte (7.) Juni.
Den wievielten haben wir heute?	Heute haben wir den siebten (7.) Juni.
(What's the date today?)	(Today is the seventh [7th] of June.)

NOTE: Where English says *the seventh of June,* German says simply **der siebte Juni.** The English preposition *of* has no counterpart in the German expression.

---

* Literally, **der wievielte** = *the how-many-eth.*

C. TAGELANG = for days

The German equivalents of *for days, for weeks, for months, for years,* etc., are formed by adding -lang to the *plural form of the noun.* Since they are adverbs, they are *uncapitalized.*

tagelang	monatelang
wochenlang	jahrelang

D. Expressions using -mal or MAL

1. **Einmal** = *once, one time* (**-mal**).

once, one time	einmal
twice, two times	zweimal
ten times	zehnmal
a hundred times	hundertmal

Expressions indicating the number of times (how many times?) are formed by adding **-mal** to the cardinal number.

NOTE 1: The only exception is **ein**mal. (The cardinal number is **eins.**)

NOTE 2: In expressions such as *a* hundred times, *a* thousand times, German does not have an equivalent to the English *a* (**hundertmal, tausendmal**).

NOTE 3: German never uses the word ~~Zeit~~ in such a context.

2. **Das erste Mal** = *the first time* (**Mal**).

das dritte (achte, nächste Mal)   the third (eighth, next) time

Here English and German behave similarly. In this case **Mal** is a noun and is therefore capitalized.

Again one must remember that German never uses ~~Zeit~~ in this context.

3. **Zum** ersten Mal = *for the* first time (**Mal**).

zum dritten (letzten) Mal   *for the* third (last) time

Contrast:

Das letzte Mal hast du es gemacht.	(You did it *the last time.*)
Ich sage dir das zum letzten Mal.	(I'm telling you that *for the* last time.)

■ DRILLS

Hours and Minutes

Fill in the blanks. Do *not* use "railroad" time.

1. Er kommt _____. (at eight o'clock)
   _____. (at quarter after seven)
   _____. (at quarter to three)
   _____. (at five-thirty)
   _____. (at ten to nine)
   _____. (at quarter to one)
   _____. (at five after eight)
   _____. (at twenty to five)
   _____. (at six-thirty)
   _____. (at twelve o'clock)

2. Es ist _____. (twenty after two)
   _____. (quarter to six)
   _____. (twelve-thirty)
   _____. (ten after four)
   _____. (twenty-five to ten)
   _____. (three-thirty)
   _____. (five o'clock)
   _____. (eleven-thirty)
   _____. (quarter after seven)
   _____. (quarter to one)

Days and Parts of Days

1. Er kommt _____ (on Friday, on Sunday).
2. Er arbeitet _____ (Saturdays, Wednesdays, nights).
3. _____ (Evenings) bleibt er zu Hause.
4. Ich sehe ihn _____ (on the twenty-fifth).
5. Er kommt heute _____ (in the afternoon, at midnight).
6. _____ (During the day) ist es sehr schön.
7. _____ (Sundays) regnet es immer.
8. Er kommt _____ (in the evening).
9. Ich fahre _____ (on Tuesday, on Monday) ab.
10. _____ (At night) ist es viel ruhiger.

Weeks, Months, Seasons, and Years

1. Er kommt _____ (in May, in December, in August).
2. _____ (In 1982) war ich in Innsbruck.
3. Wir fahren _____ (in March, in February, in April) nach Mainz.
4. _____ (During the week) muß er arbeiten.
5. _____ (In the fall, in the spring) ist es sehr schön hier.
6. Ich bin _____ (in 1970) geboren.

Definite and Indefinite Time

1. Wir gehen _____ (this evening) ins Kino.
2. Haben Sie ihn _____ (yesterday afternoon) besucht?
3. _____ (Tomorrow morning) muß ich arbeiten.
4. _____ (Next year) bin ich in Berlin.
5. _____ (One morning) war er einfach nicht mehr da.
6. Besuchen Sie uns _____ (next week)?
7. Er kommt _____ (tomorrow evening).
8. Er blieb _____ (all day) zu Hause.
9. _____ (One day) ist er weggegangen.
10. So geht es _____ (every spring).

Other Common Time Expressions

1. Er ist _____ (a month ago) weggegangen.
2. Ich bin _____ (over a year) da geblieben.
3. Wir sind nur _____ (once) in Frankreich gewesen.
4. Ich wohne _____ (for a month) hier.
5. Er hat _____ (for years) hier gewohnt.
6. Ich fahre _____ (for a month) nach Wien.
7. Sie ist _____ (a week ago) gekommen.
8. _____ (The next time) bleibe ich zu Hause.
9. _____ (In a week, in two years) ist er wieder da.
10. Sie ist _____ (four times) da gewesen.
11. Heute haben wir _____ (the eighth of January).
12. Ich lese diese Novelle _____ (for the first time).

Mixed Drills

1. Er kommt _____ (at ten to nine).
2. Ich fahre _____ (on Monday) ab.

3. Sie ist _____ (four times) da gewesen.
4. Er hat _____ (for years) hier gewohnt.
5. Wir haben ihn _____ (yesterday evening) besucht.
6. Sie ist _____ (a month ago) weggegangen.
7. _____ (The next time) bleibst du zu Hause.
8. Es ist genau _____ (twenty-five to ten).
9. Wir gehen _____ (this evening) ins Kino.
10. Sie arbeitet _____ (Saturdays).
11. Heute haben wir _____ (the eighth of January.)
12. Wir fahren _____ (in February) nach Mainz.
13. _____ (During the day) ist es sehr heiß.
14. Besuchen Sie uns _____ (next week)?
15. Ilse kommt _____ (at five-thirty).
16. Ich lese dieses Buch _____ (for the first time).
17. Mark ist _____ (in 1970) geboren.
18. Ich bin _____ (at quarter after one) zurück.
19. _____ (In the fall) ist es sehr schön hier.
20. Sie wohnen _____ (for a month) hier.
21. Ich arbeite _____ (tomorrow morning).
22. _____ (Sundays) regnet es immer.
23. Es ist _____ (ten after four).
24. Ich bin _____ (over a year) da geblieben.
25. Er blieb _____ (all day) zu Hause.
26. Sie fährt _____ (for a month) nach Wien.
27. Ich bin nur _____ (once) da gewesen.
28. Wir sehen ihn _____ (on the twenty-fifth.)
29. _____ (Evenings) bleiben sie immer zu Hause.
30. Er arbeitet _____ (nights).
31. _____ (One morning) ging sie einfach weg.
32. _____ (In 1982) war ich in Innsbruck.

Express in German

1. I've only been there once.
2. We're going (**fahren**) to Mainz in February.
3. He's lived here for years.
4. It's ten after four.
5. Are you going to visit us next week?
6. I'm leaving on Monday.
7. She's been living here for a month.

8. He works nights.
9. We visited him yesterday evening.
10. I stayed there over a year.
11. It's exactly twenty-five to ten.
12. She left a month ago.
13. In 1982 I was in Innsbruck.
14. Ilse's coming at five-thirty.
15. The next time you're staying home.
16. I'll be back at quarter after one.
17. It always rains Sundays.
18. We're going to the movies this evening.
19. She's been there four times.
20. He's coming at ten to nine.
21. Today is the eighth of January.
22. I'm reading it for the first time.
23. Mark was born in 1970.
24. She works Saturdays.
25. During the day it's very hot.
26. In the fall it's very pretty here.
27. One morning she simply went away.
28. I'm working tomorrow morning.
29. We're going to see him on the twenty-fifth.
30. She's going to Vienna for a month.
31. He stayed home all day.

Modal
Auxiliaries

6

LEVEL ONE

I. INTRODUCTION

Look at the following sentences:

> He's going home.
> He's doing it.

These are simple declarative statements of fact. Often, however, one wants
to add something to simple statements of this kind:

> He *must* go home.
> He *can* do it.

As you can see, you can do this by using additional verbs like *must* or *can*.
German has a set of such verbs and they are called *modal auxiliaries,* or
modals, for short. They are treated as a group because they all affect sen-

tence structure the same way. The following table shows you the German modals and their English counterparts:

ability	Er kann es machen.	He can (is able to) do it.
necessity	Er muß es machen.	He must (has to) do it.
permission	Er darf es machen.	He may do it.
desire	Er will es machen.	He wants to do it.
obligation	Er soll es machen.	He's supposed to do it.

II. STRUCTURE OF GERMAN SENTENCES WITH MODAL AUXILIARIES

The following sentence is a simple declarative statement of fact; it *does not* use a modal:

Ich gehe nach Hause.

When the modal **muß** is added to the sentence, the following changes take place:

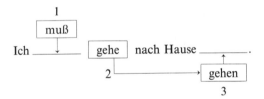

Ich muß nach Hause gehen.

1. **Muß** (the conjugated form of the modal) must occupy the second (verb) position in the sentence.

2. **Gehe,** which was in second position before, moves to the end of the sentence.

3. Since a modal expression cannot have *two* conjugated verbs, **gehe** appears at the end of the sentence as *an infinitive:*

Ich muß nach Hause gehen.

III. OMISSION OF *ZU* IN MODAL EXPRESSIONS

I must go home.   Ich muß nach Hause gehen.
I have *to* go home.

I can do it.   Ich kann es machen.
I'm able *to* do it.

Some English equivalents of the German modals require the word *to:* I have *to* go home, I'm able *to* do it. Others do not: I must go home, I can do it.

German, however, *never* uses zu before infinitives *in modal expressions.*

IV. CONJUGATION OF MODAL AUXILIARIES

KÖNNEN

	PRESENT TENSE		PAST TENSE	
	ich kann	wir können	ich konnte	wir konnten
	du kannst	ihr könnt	du konntest	ihr konntet
	er kann	sie können	er konnte	sie konnten
STEMS	**kann–**	**könn–**	**konn–**	

A. Present tense stems

1. *Present tense stems*

With one exception, German modals have two stems in the present tense:

one for the infinitive and plural forms (e.g., könn–)

one for the singular forms (e.g., kann–)

2. *Present tense endings*

a. The 1st and 3rd person singular take *no endings;* they use *only the* stem.

1ST PERSON SINGULAR: ich kann
3RD PERSON SINGULAR: er kann

b. The other four forms take the regular present tense endings.

B. Past tense stem and endings

The past tense of German modals is formed by adding *weak past tense endings* to the *past tense stem of the modal:*

ich	—te	wir	—ten
du	—test	ihr	—tet
er	—te	sie	—ten

V. FORMS AND MEANINGS OF GERMAN MODALS

A. KÖNNEN

	PRESENT TENSE		PAST TENSE	
	ich kann	wir können	ich konnte	wir konnten
	du kannst	ihr könnt	du konntest	ihr konntet
	er kann	sie können	er konnte	sie konnten
STEMS	kann–	könn–	konn–	

1. can, to be able to (ability)

Er kann es machen   (He *can* do it.)
Er konnte es machen.   (He *was able to* [*could*] do it.)

2. can, may (possibility)

Das kann sein.   (That *may* be.)

3. to know (ability)

Er kann Deutsch.   (He *knows* German. [He can read,
                                 write, and speak it.])

NOTE: German has three words that correspond to English *know:*

wissen: to know a fact

Ich **weiß**, wo das ist.
(I *know* where that is.)

kennen: to know a person or to be familiar with a place or a subject.

Ich **kenne** ihn (München) sehr gut.
(I *know* him (Munich) very well.)

können: to know in the sense of having a facility in something.

Er **kann** Algebra.
(He *knows* [can do] Algebra.)

B. MÜSSEN

	PRESENT TENSE		PAST TENSE	
	ich muß	wir müssen	ich mußte	wir mußten
	du mußt	ihr müßt	du mußtest	ihr mußtet
	er muß	sie müssen	er mußte	sie mußten
STEMS	**muß–**	**müss–**	**muß–**	

1. must, to have to (necessity)

Ich **muß** morgen früh aufstehen.
Ich **mußte** gestern arbeiten.

(I *have to* get up early tomorrow.)
(I *had to* work yesterday.)

C. DÜRFEN

	PRESENT TENSE		PAST TENSE	
	ich darf	wir dürfen	ich durfte	wir durften
	du darfst	ihr dürft	du durftest	ihr durftet
	er darf	sie dürfen	er durfte	sie durften
STEMS	**darf–**	**dürf–**	**durf–**	

1. may, to be permitted to, to be allowed to (permission)

Darf ich heute abend ins Kino gehen?

(*May* I go to the movies tonight?)

Gestern durfte ich nicht ausgehen.   (I *wasn't allowed to* go out yesterday.)

NOTE: In informal speech you often hear **können** (**Kann** ich heute abend ins Kino gehen?) instead of **dürfen.** This corresponds to the colloquial English "*Can* I go?" instead of the more formal "*May* I go?"

D. MÖGEN

	PRESENT TENSE		PAST TENSE	
	ich mag	wir mögen	ich mochte	wir mochten
	du magst	ihr mögt	du mochtest	ihr mochtet
	er mag	sie mögen	er mochte	sie mochten
STEMS	**mag–**	**mög–**	**mocht–**	

(The simple past tense forms of **mögen** are not very common in spoken German.)

1. *to like* (*liking, fondness*)

Ich mag ihn nicht.   (I *don't like* him.)
Ich mochte das Essen nicht.   (I *did*n't *like* the meal.)

2. *may* (*possibility*)

Das mag wohl sein.   (That *may* well be.)

E. WOLLEN

	PRESENT TENSE		PAST TENSE	
	ich will	wir wollen	ich wollte	wir wollten
	du willst	ihr wollt	du wolltest	ihr wolltet
	er will	sie wollen	er wollte	sie wollten
STEMS	**will–**	**woll–**	**woll–**	

1. to want to (desire, volition)

Er **will** diesen Sommer nach Deutschland fahren.
(He *wants to* go to Germany this summer.)

Das **wollte** ich dir sagen.
(I *wanted to* tell you that.)

2. to claim to, consider oneself (assertion, opinion)

Gerhard **will** ein großer Tennisspieler sein.
(Gerhard *claims to* be (thinks he is) a great tennis player.)

F. SOLLEN

	PRESENT TENSE		PAST TENSE	
	ich soll	wir sollen	ich sollte	wir sollten
	du sollst	ihr sollt	du solltest	ihr solltet
	er soll	sie sollen	er sollte	sie sollten
STEMS	**soll–**	**soll–**	**soll–**	

1. to be supposed to (obligation)

Er **soll** um fünf Uhr kommen.
(He *is supposed to* come at five o'clock.)

Er **sollte** das gestern machen.
(He *was supposed to* do that yesterday.)

2. to be said to, to be supposed to (supposition)

Dieser Film **soll** sehr gut sein.
(This film *is supposed to* be very good.)

3. shall

Wo **soll** ich es hinstellen?
(Where *shall* I put it?)

G. Forms of German modals (summary)

1. Present tense stems of modals

Five of the German modals have *two stems:* one stem for the infinitive and plural forms, and a different stem for the singular.

INFINITIVE	PLURAL STEM	SINGULAR STEM
müssen	müss–	muß–
können	könn–	kann–
dürfen	dürf–	darf–
mögen	mög–	mag–
wollen	woll–	will–

The one remaining modal has only *one* present tense stem:

INFINITIVE	PLURAL STEM	SINGULAR STEM
sollen	soll–	soll–

2. Present tense forms

The present tense endings of the modals are unusual: the 1st and 3rd person singular *take no endings,* i.e., they use only the stem:

ich kann	——	wir könn	en
du kann	st	ihr könn	t
er kann	——	sie könn	en

3. Past tense stems of modals

The past tense forms of the modals have only *one stem:*

INFINITIVE	PAST TENSE STEM
müssen	muß–
können	konn–
dürfen	durf–
mögen	moch–
wollen	woll–
sollen	soll–

4. Past tense forms

ich konn	te	wir konn	ten
du konn	test	ihr konn	tet
er konn	te	sie konn	ten

VI. OMISSION OF INFINITIVES IN MODAL EXPRESSIONS

He *must* go home.   Er muß nach Hause gehen.
                      Er muß nach Hause.

He *can* do it.   Er kann es machen.
                      Er kann es.

In German the infinitive may be omitted from modal expressions when:

1. a goal or destination is stated or implied in the sentence:

    Ich muß nach Hause gehen.   Ich muß nach Hause.

2. the idea of *to do* (**machen, tun**) is present.

    Er kann das machen.   Er kann das.

3. the context makes the infinitive repetitious:

    Muß er heute zu Hause bleiben?   Ja, er muß.
    (Does he have to *stay* home today?   Yes, he has to.)

NOTE: Example 3 is similar to English usage; examples 1 and 2 are not.

■ DRILLS

Fill-ins: Present Tense

Supply the correct present tense form of the modal auxiliary.

1. Wir _____ später kommen.
        (können)

2. Er _____ das morgen machen.
         (müssen)

3. Was _____ du machen?
          (wollen)

4. _____ wir mitkommen?
      (Dürfen)

5. _____ du mir helfen?
      (Können)

6. Wir _____ um zehn Uhr zu Hause sein.
            (sollen)

7. Ich _____ diese Suppe nicht.
            (mögen)

8. Wir _____ ihn gleich finden.
             (müssen)

9. _____ er Deutsch?
      (Können)

10. Er _____ ein guter Freund von dir sein.
            (wollen)

11. _____ ich Ihnen helfen?
       (Dürfen)

12. _____ Sie mir ein gutes Restaurant empfehlen?
        (Können)

13. Dieser Film _____ sehr gut sein.
                   (sollen)

14. Ich _____ immer früh aufstehen.
             (müssen)

15. Sie (they) _____ hier bleiben.
                   (wollen)

16. _____ ich heute abend ins Kino gehen?
        (Dürfen)

17. Wir _____ ihn nicht.
             (mögen)

Fill-ins: Past Tense

Supply the correct past tense form of the modal auxiliary.

1. Wir _____ die Rechnung kaum bezahlen.
          (können)

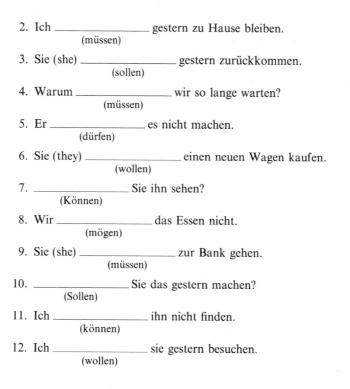

2. Ich _____ gestern zu Hause bleiben.
          (müssen)

3. Sie (she) _____ gestern zurückkommen.
            (sollen)

4. Warum _____ wir so lange warten?
           (müssen)

5. Er _____ es nicht machen.
        (dürfen)

6. Sie (they) _____ einen neuen Wagen kaufen.
           (wollen)

7. _____ Sie ihn sehen?
     (Können)

8. Wir _____ das Essen nicht.
        (mögen)

9. Sie (she) _____ zur Bank gehen.
           (müssen)

10. _____ Sie das gestern machen?
     (Sollen)

11. Ich _____ ihn nicht finden.
       (können)

12. Ich _____ sie gestern besuchen.
       (wollen)

Form and Structure Drills

Insert the modal auxiliaries into the following sentences. The tense required is indicated by the tense of the verb in the original sentence. For example, when the verb is in the past tense, the modal must also be in the past tense.

> Examples: Ich gehe jetzt zur Bank. (müssen)
>   Ich *muß* jetzt zur Bank *gehen.*
>
>   Er blieb zu Hause. (wollen)
>   Er *wollte* zu Hause *bleiben.*

1. Ich stehe immer früh auf. (müssen)
2. Wir kommen später. (können)
3. Ich besuchte ihn gestern. (wollen)

4. Kommen sie mit? (dürfen)
5. Er ist ein guter Freund von dir. (wollen)
6. Ich blieb gestern zu Hause. (müssen)
7. Dieser Film ist sehr gut. (sollen)
8. Wir bezahlten die Rechnung nicht. (können)
9. Was machst du? (wollen)
10. Wir finden ihn gleich. (müssen)
11. Sie kam gestern zurück. (sollen)
12. Hilfst du mir? (können)
13. Er machte es nicht. (dürfen)
14. Sie ging zur Bank. (müssen)
15. Sie bleiben hier. (wollen)
16. Ich fand ihn nicht. (können)
17. Wir sind um zehn Uhr zu Hause. (sollen)
18. Er macht das morgen. (müssen)
19. Sie kauft einen neuen Wagen. (wollen)
20. Gehst du heute abend ins Kino? (dürfen)
21. Sie machten es gestern. (sollen)
22. Warum warteten wir so lange? (müssen)

Synthetic Exercises

Form complete sentences in both the present tense and the simple past tense
(unless otherwise indicated).

Example: Er / müssen / gehen / nach Hause

Er *muß* nach Hause gehen.
Er *mußte* nach Hause gehen.

1. Ich / können / finden / ihn nicht
2. Sie (she) / müssen / gehen / zur Bank
3. Er / dürfen / machen / es nicht
4. Wir / können / kommen / später
5. Er / wollen / sein / ein guter Freund von dir (*present tense only*)
6. Ich / müssen / aufstehen / immer früh
7. Ich / mögen / diese Suppe nicht (*present tense only*)
8. Wir / sollen / sein / um zehn Uhr zu Hause
9. Können / er / Deutsch / ?
10. Sie (they) / wollen / kaufen / einen neuen Wagen

Fill-ins: Present and Past Tenses

Using the English cues, supply the correct German modal auxiliary.

Example: Ich _____ nach Hause gehen.
                              (had to)

Ich _____ mußte _____ nach Hause gehen.

1. Wir _____ später kommen.
            (can)

2. Sie (she) _____ zur Bank gehen.
                      (had to)

3. Was _____ du machen?
            (do you want to)

4. _____ wir mitkommen?
        (May)

5. Wir _____ die Rechnung kaum bezahlen.
            (could)

6. Ich _____ immer früh aufstehen.
            (have to)

7. Dieser Film _____ sehr gut sein.
                    (is supposed to)

8. Er _____ ein guter Freund von dir sein.
            (claims to)

9. _____ du mir helfen?
        (Can)

10. Warum _____ so lange warten?
              (did we have to)

11. Er _____ es nicht machen.
          (was allowed to)

12. Sie (they) _____ einen neuen Wagen kaufen.
                    (wanted to)

13. Wir _____ um zehn Uhr zu Hause sein.
            (are supposed to)

14. Wir _____ später kommen.
            (can)

15. Ich _____ diese Suppe nicht.
            (like)

16. Sie (she) _____ gestern zurückkommen.
          (was supposed to)

17. _____ ich heute abend ins Kino gehen?
        (May)

18. Wir _____ ihn gleich finden.
            (have to)

19. Sie (they) _____ hier bleiben.
                (want to)

20. _____ er Deutsch?
    (Does he know)

Express in German

1. I *could*n't find him.
2. They *want to* stay here.
3. *May* we come along?
4. She *had to* go to the bank.
5. *Can* you help me?
6. We *are supposed to* be home at ten o'clock.
7. I always *have to* get up early.
8. She *was supposed to* come back yesterday.
9. *Does* he *know* German?
10. What *do* you *want to* do?
11. I *don*'t *like* this soup.
12. He *was*n't *allowed* to do it.
13. We *have to* find him right away.
14. He *claims to* be a good friend of yours.
15. We *could* hardly pay the bill.
16. This film *is supposed to* be very good.
17. *May* I go to the movies this evening?
18. They *wanted to* buy a new car.
19. Why *did* we *have to* wait so long?
20. We *can* come later.

LEVEL TWO

I. COMPOUND TENSES OF MODAL AUXILIARIES

As our starting point we will take

                    Er muß nach Hause gehen

and form its compound future and perfect tenses.

A. Future with auxiliary WERDEN

In German, the future tense is composed of **werden** *plus an infinitive.*
This rule also applies to the future tense of modal auxiliaries:

PRESENT TENSE	Er muß nach Hause gehen.
FUTURE TENSE	Er wird nach Hause gehen müssen.

The only difference between the two sentences is that the modal has changed
tenses.

The present tense form:　**muß**
has been replaced by:　**wird . . . müssen.**

B. Present perfect

The modals all use **haben** as their auxiliary in forming the present perfect.
There are, however, two ways to form the present perfect of modal
expressions:

1. **Haben** + *past participle*

The past participle of **müssen** is **gemußt.** If the dependent infinitive is
omitted from the modal expression, the present perfect is formed in the
usual way:

PRESENT TENSE	Er muß nach Hause.
PRESENT PERFECT	Er hat nach Hause gemußt.

2. **Haben** + *double infinitive*

Now look at a modal expression that contains a dependent infinitive:

PRESENT TENSE	Er muß nach Hause gehen.
PRESENT PERFECT	Er hat nach Hause gehen müssen.

When there is a *dependent infinitive* in a modal expression, the present perfect is formed with the *infinitive of the modal* (e.g., **müssen**), rather than the
past participle (e.g., **gemußt**). The infinitive form of the modal comes right
after the dependent infinitive, hence the name "double infinitive."

You might say that the past participle

gemußt

"changes into" an infinitive when it appears after a dependent infinitive:

gehen <u>müssen</u>

NOTE: This is true for all modal constructions in perfect tenses:

WITHOUT DEPENDENT INFINITIVE	WITH DEPENDENT INFINITIVE
Ich habe . . . gekonnt	Ich habe . . . gehen können
Ich habe . . . gedurft	Ich habe . . . gehen dürfen
Ich habe . . . gewollt	Ich habe . . . gehen wollen
Ich habe . . . gesollt	Ich habe . . . gehen sollen
Ich habe . . . gemocht	Ich habe . . . gehen mögen

NOTE: All modal auxiliaries require **haben** (rather than **sein**) to form their perfect tenses.

C. Past perfect

This tense can be treated like the present perfect; the only difference is that **hatte** replaces **hat:**

WITH DEPENDENT INFINITIVE	Ich hatte nach Hause gehen <u>müssen</u>.
WITHOUT DEPENDENT INFINITIVE	Ich hatte es gemußt.

D. Word order in dependent clauses

Look at the following example:

> Ich wußte nicht, **daß** er nach Hause gegangen ist.

The conjugated verb form is normally in *final position* in subordinate clauses. However, when a double-infinitive construction is involved, the conjugated verb form precedes the two infinitives:

> Ich wußte nicht, daß er <u>hat</u> mitkommen wollen.

E. Summary

1. Principal parts of the modal auxiliaries

INFINITIVE	PAST TENSE	PAST PARTICIPLE	3RD PERSON SINGULAR PRESENT
müssen	mußte	gemußt	muß
können	konnte	gekonnt	kann
dürfen	durfte	gedurft	darf
mögen	mochte	gemocht	mag
wollen	wollte	gewollt	will
sollen	sollte	gesollt	soll

2. Tenses of modal auxiliaries

WITHOUT DEPENDENT INFINITIVE		WITH DEPENDENT INFINITIVE
Ich muß es.	have to (go)	Ich muß nach Hause gehen.
Ich mußte es.	had to (go)	Ich mußte nach Hause gehen.
Ich werde es müssen.	will have to (go)	Ich werde nach Hause gehen müssen.
Ich habe es gemußt.	have had to (go)	Ich habe nach Hause gehen müssen.
Ich hatte es gemußt.	had had to (go)	Ich hatte nach Hause gehen müssen.

a. Tense change

The only elements that change in the sentences above are the forms of the modal (muß, mußte, werde . . . müssen, etc.). All modals form their perfect tenses with **haben** (NOT with **sein**).

> *Hence:*   Ich habe es gemußt.
> Ich habe gehen müssen.

b. Double infinitives (perfect tenses)

PRESENT PERFECT   Ich habe es gemußt.   Ich habe nach Hause gehen müssen.
PAST PERFECT   Ich hatte es gemußt.   Ich hatte nach Hause gehen müssen.

When no dependent infinitive is involved, the perfect tense of a modal sentence requires a past participle (Ich habe es **gemußt**).

When a dependent infinitive is used to complete the meaning of the sentence, *the infinitive form of the modal is used instead of a past participle* (Ich habe nach Hause gehen **müssen**).

NOTE: In such cases the *infinitive of the modal* is always the *last word* in its clause and is always immediately preceded by the dependent infinitive (e.g., gehen **müssen**).

 DRILLS

Future Tense with *Werden*

Put the following sentences into the future tense by using the auxiliary *werden*.

        Example: Sie **müssen** nach Hause gehen.
                       Sie **werden** nach Hause gehen **müssen.**

1. Können Sie ihn besuchen?
2. Ich muß früh aufstehen.
3. Sie wollen hier bleiben.
4. Er muß wohl lange warten.
5. Wir können die Rechnung kaum bezahlen.
6. Er darf es wohl nicht machen.
7. Wir können wohl später kommen.
8. Sie will zur Bank gehen.
9. Ich muß das morgen machen.

Past and Present Perfect Tenses

Put the following sentences into the past tense and the present perfect tense. (Both sentences requiring a double infinitive construction and those requiring a past participle of the modal auxiliary are included in this exercise.)

        Examples: Sie **müssen** nach Hause gehen.

                      Sie **mußten** nach Hause gehen.
                      Sie **haben** nach Hause gehen **müssen.**

                      Das **kann** er.

                      Das **konnte** er.
                      Das **hat** er **gekonnt.**

1. Wir können nicht kommen.
2. Ich muß heute zu Hause bleiben.
3. Sie wollen einen neuen Wagen kaufen.

4. Kann er Deutsch?
5. Sie will es einfach nicht tun.
6. Ich muß immer früh aufstehen.
7. Wir wollen Tennis spielen.
8. Können Sie ihn besuchen?
9. Sie müssen viel lesen.
10. Ich will in die Stadt.
11. Wir können die Rechnung kaum bezahlen.
12. Er darf es nicht machen.
13. Ich mag die Suppe nicht.
14. Was willst du machen?
15. Ich muß nach Hause.
16. Dürfen Sie das machen? Ja, wir dürfen es.
17. Er muß lange warten.
18. Wir müssen das heute machen.
19. Sie will zur Bank gehen.
20. Ich kann es nicht machen.

Synthetic Exercises: Future Tense

Use the following words to form sentences in the future tense.

1. Ich / müssen / machen / das morgen
2. Wir / können / kommen / nicht
3. Er / müssen / warten / wohl lange
4. Sie / wollen / bleiben / hier
5. Können / Sie / besuchen / ihn / ?
6. Er / dürfen / machen / es nicht

Synthetic Exercises: Past Tense and Present Perfect Tense

Use the following words to form sentences in the past and present perfect tenses.

1. Sie / wollen / machen / es einfach nicht
2. Ich / müssen / aufstehen / früh
3. Sie / wollen / kaufen / einen neuen Wagen
4. Wir / können / machen / es nicht
5. Ich / müssen / nach Hause
6. Wir / wollen / spielen / Tennis
7. Ich / mögen / die Suppe nicht
8. Sie / müssen / lesen / viel

9. Wir / können / bezahlen / die Rechnung kaum
10. Ich / wollen / in die Stadt
11. Ich / müssen / bleiben / heute zu Hause
12. Können / er / Deutsch / ?
13. Sie / wollen / gehen / zur Bank

Express in German

1. We *wanted to* play tennis. (*past* and *perfect*)
2. I *had to* get up early. (*past* and *perfect*)
3. We *won't be able* to come. (*future*)
4. They *wanted to* buy a new car. (*past* and *perfect*)
5. I *had* (to go) home. (*past* and *perfect*)
6. We *could* hardly pay the bill. (*past* and *perfect*)
7. They*'ll want to* stay here. (*future*)
8. They *had to* read a lot. (*past* and *perfect*)
9. I *wanted* (to go) downtown. (*past* and *perfect*)
10. He *won't be allowed* to do it. (*future*)
11. I *didn't* like the soup. (*past* and *perfect*)
12. She simply *didn't want to* do it. (*past* and *perfect*)
13. I*'ll have to* do that tomorrow. (*future*)
14. *Did* he *know* German? (*past* and *perfect*)
15. He*'ll have to* wait a long time. (*future*)
16. She *wanted to* go to the bank. (*past* and *perfect*)
17. I *had to* stay at home today. (*past* and *perfect*)
18. *Will* you *be able to* visit him? (*future*)

LEVEL THREE

I. HELFEN, LASSEN, AND THE SENSES

Structurally, **helfen, lassen,** and the verbs indicating the senses behave like modal auxiliaries:

I hear him coming.	Ich höre ihn kommen.
I heard him coming (come).	Ich hörte ihn kommen.
I'll hear him coming (come).	Ich werde ihn kommen hören.
I (have) heard him coming (come).	Ich habe ihn kommen hören.
I had heard him coming (come).	Ich hatte ihn kommen hören.

Like the modals, these verbs require a *double-infinitive construction* to form their perfect tenses *when there is a dependent infinitive* (e.g., **kommen**) *involved:*

Ich habe ihn kommen hören.
but: Ich habe es gehört.

After verbs of this type, English very often uses a present participle (e.g., coming). It should be noted that German always uses a dependent *infinitive* (e.g., **kommen**)—never a present participle:

Ich höre ihn kommen.
(I hear him *coming*.)

A. The senses

In theory, *all* of the verbs used to indicate the senses behave as **hören** does in the examples above. In practice, however, **sehen** and **hören** are the sense verbs most frequently used.

Ich sehe ihn kommen.	I see him coming.
Sie hörte einen Wagen vorbeifahren.	She heard a car drive by.

B. HELFEN

Er half mir die Bücher zurückbringen.	(He helped me take the books back.)

In the sentence above, both verbs have objects: **mir** is the dative object of **helfen,** and **die Bücher** is the accusative object of **zurückbringen.**

C. LASSEN

Lassen has two basic meanings:

1. *to let or to allow (permission)*

Er ließ mich seinen Wagen nehmen.	(He let me take his car.)
Ich ließ ihn gehen.	(I let him go.)

Note that the objects of **lassen** are in the accusative case (**mich, ihn**).

2. to have (something done); to have or make (someone do something)

Er ließ den Wagen reparieren.   (He had the car repaired.)

When English uses *have* in this sense, it completes the expression with a past participle (to have the car *repaired,* to have a suit *cleaned*). But no matter which sense it is used in, lassen *always takes a dependent infinitive:*

> Er ließ den Wagen reparieren.
> Ich ließ ihn gehen.

NOTE: The second use of **lassen** (to have something done) indicates that the subject of the sentence is not actually performing the action described but is having someone else perform it. English often does not make this distinction clearly. Instead of:

We're having a house built.

you can say: We're building a house.

To a German, this last sentence would mean that you are building the house with your own hands. If someone else is doing the work, a German says:

> Wir lassen uns* ein Haus bauen.

 DRILLS

Fill-ins: Present or Past Tense

Fill in the blanks, using the English verb as your cue.

1. Ich _____ ihn kommen.
          (see)

2. Er _____ den Wagen vorbeifahren.
          (heard)

3. Sie (she) _____ mir die Bücher zurückbringen.
               (helped)

---

* **Uns** is a dative of reference that means "for ourselves."

4. Wir _____ uns ein Haus bauen.
   (had)

5. _____ du ihn klingeln?
   (Do you hear)

6. Ich _____ ihm das Problem lösen.
   (am helping)

7. Er _____ den Wagen reparieren.
   (is having)

8. Ich _____ sie in den Zug einsteigen.
   (saw)

9. Sie (they) _____ mich Ihren Wagen nehmen.
   (let)

10. Pfadfinder _____ alten Damen Pakete tragen.
    (help)

Present Perfect Tense

Put the following sentences into the present perfect.

1. Er ließ den Wagen reparieren.
2. Ich hörte ihn die Tür zumachen.
3. Sie half mir das Problem lösen.
4. Ich sah den Wagen vorbeifahren.
5. Er ließ mich den Brief lesen.
6. Wir hörten ihn weggehen.
7. Sie halfen mir die Pakete tragen.
8. Ich sah ihn kommen.
9. Ich ließ mir die Haare schneiden.
10. Sie hörten den Wagen wegfahren.
11. Er ließ ihn gehen.

Future Tense with *Werden*

Put the following sentences into the future tense, using the auxiliary *werden*.

1. Ich lasse es mir schicken.
2. Wir hören sie klopfen.
3. Ich sehe ihn hereinkommen.
4. Hörst du ihn klingeln?
5. Wir lassen uns ein Haus bauen.

Synthetic Exercises

Form complete sentences in the present, past and perfect tenses.

1. Ich / sehen / ihn / kommen
2. Wir / lassen / uns / Haus / bauen
3. Er / helfen / mir / Problem / lösen
4. Ich / hören / Wagen / wegfahren
5. Er / lassen / mich / Wagen / nehmen
6. Sie / helfen / mir / Bücher / zurückbringen
7. Ich / sehen / ihn / in / Büro / gehen

Express in German

1. I see him coming.
2. He let me read the letter. (*past* and *perfect*)
3. We heard her leave. (*past* and *perfect*)
4. He helped me solve the problem. (*past* and *perfect*)
5. I'm going to have it sent. (*future*)
6. They saw the car drive by. (*past* and *perfect*)
7. Boy Scouts help old ladies carry packages.
8. He had the car repaired. (*past* and *perfect*)
9. We'll hear him knock. (*future*)
10. I let him go. (*past* and *perfect*)
11. I'll see him come. (*future*)
12. He helped me take the books back. (*past* and *perfect*)
13. She's letting us take her car.
14. We heard him close the door. (*past* and *perfect*)
15. I saw him go into his office. (*past* and *perfect*)
16. We're having a house built.
17. I had my hair cut. (*past* and *perfect*)
18. Will you hear her ring? (*future*)

Passive Voice

7

LEVEL ONE

I. COMPARISON WITH ACTIVE VOICE

SUBJECT	VERB	OBJECT
A lot of students	read	this novel.

The subject is performing the action here (a lot of students *read*), and the object (this novel) is being acted upon.

This same sentence can be put into the *passive voice:*

ACTIVE	PASSIVE
A lot of students *read* this novel.	This novel *is* (*being*) *read* by a lot of students.

The subject of the passive sentence is *not* itself acting; on the contrary, it *is being acted upon,* i.e., it is *passive.* The person(s) performing the action is found in a prepositional phrase following the verb (*by* a lot of students) and is called the "agent."

It is the verb form, however, that really shows whether the sentence is active or passive:

ACTIVE	X *reads* (*is reading*).	Here X is *acting*.
PASSIVE	X *is read* (*is being read*).	Here X is being *acted upon*.

II. FORMATION OF PASSIVE SENTENCES

The German passive sentence follows essentially the same pattern. It can be formed from its active counterpart in three steps:

1. The *accusative object* of the active sentence becomes the *nominative subject* of the passive sentence:

ACTIVE	PASSIVE
Viele Studenten lesen diesen Roman.	Dieser Roman . . .
(A lot of students read *this novel*.)	(*This novel* . . .)

2. The active verb form is replaced by:

> *a conjugated form of* **werden** + *a past participle*

ACTIVE	PASSIVE
Viele Studenten lesen diesen Roman.	Dieser Roman wird . . . gelesen.

NOTE: **Werden** must agree with the subject of the *passive* sentence. In these examples, the subject of the active sentence is plural whereas the subject of the passive sentence is singular.

ACTIVE		PASSIVE	
Viele Studenten lesen . . .		Dieser Roman wird . . . gelesen.	
(plural)	(plural)	(singular)	(singular)

3. The subject of the active sentence is replaced by:

> **von** + *a dative object*

ACTIVE	PASSIVE
Viele Studenten lesen diesen Roman	Dieser Roman wird von vielen Studenten gelesen.

This construction corresponds to the *by*-construction in English:

von vielen Studenten
(by a lot of students)

In a passive sentence this dative object (e.g., **Studenten**) is called the agent; that is, it is used to indicate the person or thing performing the action.

NOTE 1: *the **durch**-construction*

Jedes Jahr werden viele Häuser durch Feuer zerstört.
(Every year a lot of houses are destroyed *by* fire.)

Durch + *an accusative object* is used to express agency when the agent is an impersonal force such as fire, wind, rain, etc. The **durch**-construction is usually called for when *by* is used in the sense of *as the result of* or *by means of*.

durch Feuer zerstört	destroyed by (as the result of) fire
durch Penicillin geheilt	cured by (means of) penicillin
durch kein Argument überzeugt	not convinced by (means of) any argument

but:

von vielen Studenten gelesen   read by a lot of students

Read by means of students or *as the result of students* doesn't make sense.

NOTE 2: *omission of the agent*

Whenever the presence of an agent makes a passive sentence sound wooden and unnatural, the agent is simply omitted. This is almost always the case when the agent is a pronoun.

Changing active sentences into passive ones is a useful first approach to the passive voice. But passive sentences have a style and logic of their own: they are not mechanical, point-for-point transformations of active sentences. This becomes clear when one tries to put sentences such as the following into the passive voice:

Mary loves John.
I had a good supper last night.

The results are awkward in every sense of the word:

> John is loved by Mary.
> A good supper was had last night by me.

The passive must be drilled primarily within the context of the passive itself. For this reason, we shall take the sentence

> Dieser Roman wird von vielen Studenten gelesen

as our model and form its past, future, and perfect tenses.

III. TENSES OF THE PASSIVE VOICE

A. Present tense

As you have seen, the present tense of the German passive is made up of a present tense form of *werden* + a past participle:

werden   *past participle*
Dieser Roman wird von vielen Studenten gelesen.
(This novel *is read* by a lot of students.)

NOTE 1: Where German uses a form of *werden* with the past participle, English uses a form of the verb "to be," e.g., "is," or "is being."

NOTE 2: In German passive constructions, the past participle (e.g., **gelesen**) appears at the *end of the sentence*.

B. Past tense

PRESENT   Dieser Roman wird von vielen Studenten gelesen.
PAST   . . . . wurde . . . . gelesen.

Here the present tense form of **werden:**   **wird**
is replaced by the past tense form: **wurde.**

C. Future with auxiliary

PRESENT   Dieser Roman wird von vielen Studenten gelesen.
FUTURE   . . . . wird . . . . gelesen werden.

The present tense form of **werden:**   **wird**
is replaced by the future tense form: **wird . . . werden.**

D. Present perfect

PRESENT   Dieser Roman wird von vielen Studenten gelesen.
PRESENT PERFECT . . . . ist . . . . gelesen worden.

The principle is again basically the same:
the present tense form: **wird**
is replaced by a present perfect form: **ist . . . worden.**

NOTE: **ist . . . worden**
The normal past participle of **werden** is **geworden.** However, the passive
uses a contracted form in which the usual **ge–** prefix is missing:

ist gelesen worden.

E. Past perfect

PRESENT PERFECT   ist . . . gelesen worden.
PAST PERFECT   war . . . gelesen worden.

Dieser Roman war von vielen Studenten gelesen worden.

IV. ENGLISH AND GERMAN PASSIVE FORMS: SUMMARY AND COMPARISON

Compare the German verb forms with the English ones in the following
sentences:

This novel *is* (*being*) read by most students.
. . . . *was* (*being*) . . . .
. . . . *will be* read . . . .
. . . . *has been* read . . . .
. . . . *had been* read . . . .

Dieses Buch wird von den meisten Studenten gelesen.
. . . . wurde . . . . gelesen.
. . . . wird . . . . gelesen werden.
. . . . ist . . . . gelesen worden.
. . . . war . . . . gelesen worden.

is (*being*) read	**wird** ... gelesen
was (*being*) read	**wurde** ... gelesen
will be read	**wird** ... gelesen **werden**
has been read	**ist** ... gelesen **worden**
had been read	**war** ... gelesen **worden**

You will notice:

1. *Read* and **gelesen** occur in every tense. The past participle is the *unchanging* part of passive constructions in both languages.

2. Whereas English uses a form of *to be* and the past participle to form the passive, German uses a form of:

werden + PAST PARTICIPLE

PRESENT	wird ... gelesen
PAST	wurde ... gelesen
FUTURE	wird ... gelesen werden
PRESENT PERFECT	ist ... gelesen worden
PAST PERFECT	war ... gelesen worden

All changes of tense in the passive affect only the form of **werden** (in German) and the form of *to be* (in English).

3. **ist ... worden**

Werden uses **sein** as its auxiliary. The passive uses a contracted form of **geworden** in which the usual **ge–** prefix is missing: **ist** gelesen **worden**
war gelesen **worden**

 DRILLS

Active-Passive

Put the following active sentences into the passive.

1. Fast alle Studenten lesen dieses Buch.
2. Der Chef erledigt solche Sachen.
3. Viele Ärzte empfehlen das.
4. Ein Freund bringt mich nach Hause.
5. Isaac Stern spielt Beethovens Violinkonzert.
6. Mein Mann holt mich ab.

Tense Formation (Past and Present Perfect)

Put the following sentences into the simple past tense and the present perfect tense.

1. Mein Wagen wird heute repariert.
2. Wir werden von Freunden abgeholt.
3. Sie wird von einem Freund nach Hause gebracht.
4. Der Fernseher wird heute geliefert.
5. Er wird immer von der Presse kritisiert.
6. Werden die Briefe abgeschickt?
7. Das wird geändert.
8. Alles wird gut vorbereitet.
9. Sie wird ans Telefon gerufen.
10. Die Bar wird von der Polizei geschlossen.
11. Er wird heute operiert.
12. Ihr Haus wird heute verkauft.
13. Wird er eingeladen?
14. Das Abendessen wird später serviert.
15. Werden die Bücher zurückgebracht?
16. Das wird von vielen Ärzten empfohlen.
17. Unser Wagen wird gestohlen.
18. Zwei Zimmer werden für uns reserviert.
19. Beethovens Violinkonzert wird von Isaac Stern gespielt.
20. Die Rechnungen werden gleich bezahlt.

Tense Formation (Future Tense)

Put the following present tense sentences into the future tense.

1. Das wird geändert.
2. Er wird heute operiert.
3. Wir werden von Freunden abgeholt.
4. Wird er eingeladen?
5. Das wird gleich erledigt.

Tense Formation (Mixed Tenses)

Put the following present tense sentences into the tenses indicated in parentheses.

1. Sein Wagen wird heute repariert. (*past*)
2. Sie wird von einem Freund nach Hause gebracht. (*present perfect*)

3. Das wird geändert. (*future*)
4. Er wird immer von der Presse kritisiert. (*past*)
5. Alles wird gut vorbereitet. (*past perfect*)
6. Werden die Briefe abgeschickt? (*present perfect*)
7. Er wird heute operiert. (*present perfect*)
8. Sie wird ans Telefon gerufen. (*past*)
9. Zwei Zimmer werden für uns reserviert. (*present perfect*)
10. Die Bar wird von der Polizei geschlossen. (*past*)
11. Wird er eingeladen? (*future*)
12. Die Rechnungen werden bezahlt. (*past perfect*)
13. Ihr Haus wird heute verkauft. (*past*)
14. Wir werden von Freunden abgeholt. (*future*)
15. Werden die Bücher zurückgebracht? (*present perfect*)

The Variable Factor: The Form of *Werden*

Supply the form of *werden* suggested by the English words in parentheses.

1. (are)   Die Läden _____ um halb sieben geschlossen.
2. (was)   Sie _____ ans Telefon gerufen.
3. (have been) _____ die Briefe abgeschickt _____?
4. (is)   Tennis _____ überall gespielt.
5. (will be)   Das _____ geändert _____.
6. (was)   Ihr Haus _____ gestern verkauft.
7. (has been)   Die Bar _____ von der Polizei geschlossen _____.
8. (is being)   Das Abendessen _____ später serviert.
9. (had been)   Alles _____ gut vorbereitet _____.
10. (will be)   Wir _____ wohl abgeholt _____.
11. (was)   Sie _____ von einem Freund nach Hause gebracht.
12. (has been)   Es _____ noch nicht gefunden _____.
13. (is)   Dieses Buch _____ von vielen Studenten gelesen.
14. (was)   Das Hotel _____ durch Feuer zerstört.
15. (has been)   Unser Wagen _____ gestohlen _____.
16. (will be)   Er _____ eingeladen _____.
17. (is)   Am Sonntag _____ keine Post gebracht.
18. (was)   Er _____ immer von der Presse kritisiert.
19. (have been) Zwei Zimmer _____ für uns reserviert _____.
20. (are)   _____ Briefmarken hier verkauft?
21. (was)   Sie _____ nie wieder gesehen.
22. (will be)   Das _____ gleich erledigt _____.
23. (has been)   Er _____ noch nicht identifiziert _____.

24. (is being)   Der Fernseher _____ heute geliefert.
25. (had been)   Die Rechnungen _____ schon bezahlt _____.
26. (was)   Sein Wagen _____ heute repariert.
27. (have been) _____ die Bücher zurückgebracht _____?
28. (was)   Er _____ von einem Lastwagen überfahren.
29. (will be)   Er _____ heute operiert _____.
30. (is)   Das _____ von vielen Ärzten empfohlen.

Synthetic Exercises

Form complete passive sentences in the tenses indicated.

1. Tennis / gespielt / überall (*present*)
2. Es / gefunden / noch nicht (*present perfect*)
3. Sie / gerufen / an / Telefon (*past*)
4. Wir / abgeholt / wohl (*future*)
5. An / Sonntag / keine Post / gebracht (*present*)
6. Hotel / zerstört / durch Feuer (*past*)
7. Alles / vorbereitet / gut (*past perfect*)
8. Läden / geschlossen / um halb sieben (*present*)
9. Er / identifiziert / noch nicht (*present perfect*)
10. Das / erledigt / gleich (*future*)
11. Fernseher / geliefert / heute (*present*)
12. Ihr Haus / verkauft / gestern (*past*)
13. Sie / gesehen / nie wieder (*past*)
14. Zwei Zimmer / reserviert / für uns (*present perfect*)
15. Abendessen / serviert / später (*present*)
16. Rechnungen / bezahlt / schon (*past perfect*)
17. Er / eingeladen / morgen (*future*)
18. Bar / geschlossen / von / Polizei (*present perfect*)
19. Briefmarken / verkauft / hier (*present*)
20. Das / empfohlen / von / viel- / Ärzte (*present*)
21. Er / überfahren / von / Lastwagen (*past*)

Express in German

1. Tennis is played everywhere.
2. She was called to the phone.
3. It hasn't been found yet.
4. The TV is being delivered today.
5. His car was repaired today.

6. Have the books been brought back?
7. That will be taken care of right away.
8. Dinner is being served later.
9. Everything had been well prepared.
10. She was taken home by a friend. (Use **bringen.**)
11. Our car has been stolen.
12. The stores are closed at six-thirty.
13. The hotel was destroyed by fire.
14. We'll probably be picked up.
15. No mail is delivered on Sunday. (Use **bringen.**)
16. The bar has been closed by the police.
17. He was always criticized by the press.
18. The bills had already been paid.
19. He'll be invited tomorrow.
20. Are stamps sold here?
21. Have the letters been sent off?
22. She was never seen again.
23. Two rooms have been reserved for us.
24. Their house was sold yesterday.
25. This book is read by a lot of students.
26. He was run over by a truck.
27. He hasn't been identified yet.
28. He'll be operated (on) today.
29. That's recommended by a lot of doctors.

LEVEL TWO

I. PASSIVE: SPECIAL PROBLEMS

A. The false or apparent passive

1. Passive (*Action performed on the subject*)

Look at the following example of a true passive sentence:

> Der Wagen **wird** repariert.   (The car *is being* repaired.)

Something is happening to the subject: the car *is being* repaired. The passive voice focuses attention on an action or a process.

2. False passive (*Condition*)

Now look at an example of the *false passive:*

> Der Wagen ist repariert.   (The car *is* repaired.)

Nothing is happening to the subject: the car is repaired and you can get in and drive it. In other words, the *false passive* focuses on the *result* of an action, that is, on a *condition*.

To recapitulate:

1. **Der Wagen *wird* repariert** means that the car is in the process of being repaired.

2. **Der Wagen *ist* repariert** means that it is already repaired (a *state* or *condition* rather than an action.)

The difference in meaning is clear. If someone says, "Der Wagen **wird** repariert," he means that the car is in the shop and that he can't drive it. If he says, "Der Wagen **ist** repariert," he means that it's fixed and he can drive it again.

Grammatically, the false passive is the same as:

sein + *an adjective*

The past participle functions exactly like an adjective:

> Der Wagen ist **rot.**
> Der Wagen ist **repariert.**

This makes forming the past tense quite simple:

> Der Wagen **war** rot.
> Der Wagen **war** repariert.

NOTE: The distinction between passive (action) and false passive (condition) also holds for the past tense.

ACTION   Der Laden **wurde** um sechs Uhr geschlossen.
                (The store was closed at six o'clock.)

CONDITION   Der Laden war den ganzen Tag geschlossen.
                 (The store was closed all day.)

B. Passive with absentee subjects

Passive sentences may have a definite subject or an indefinite subject—or even no apparent subject at all.

Most passive sentences do have a definite subject:

ACTIVE	PASSIVE
Man repariert den Wagen.	Der Wagen wird repariert.

As you have already seen, the *accusative* object of an active sentence (e.g., **den Wagen**) appears as the *nominative* subject of the corresponding passive sentence (e.g., **der Wagen**).

But look at the following sentence:

> Man arbeitet nicht am Sonntag.

In this active sentence there is no *accusative* object! Its passive counterpart would be:

> X wird am Sonntag nicht gearbeitet.

Since a verb (e.g., **wird**) cannot be in the first position of a sentence without turning the sentence into a question, **es** is used as an *indefinite subject:*

> Es wird am Sonntag nicht gearbeitet.

NOTE: **Werden** agrees with the indefinite subject **es** (es **wird**).

But if another element of the passive sentence (e.g., a time expression) can sensibly be put in the first position, this may be done, and the indefinite subject **es** is then omitted:

> Am Sonntag wird nicht gearbeitet.

As you can see, the result is a sentence without an apparent subject. In this case the subject is an *implied* **es,** and for that reason the verb remains in the *3rd person singular:* wird.

Further examples:

ACTIVE	PASSIVE
Man tanzt heute abend.	Es wird heute abend getanzt.
	Heute abend wird getanzt.
Man raucht nicht hier.	Hier wird nicht geraucht.

As before, the passive sentences begin either with:

1. **es** (an indefinite subject), or,

2. another element of the sentence that can sensibly occupy the first position (most often a time expression).

NOTE: These German sentences have no literal English translations:

GERMAN PASSIVE	ENGLISH EQUIVALENT
Heute abend wird getanzt.	There's a dance this evening.
	There'll be dancing this evening.
Hier wird nicht geraucht.	There's no smoking here.
	No smoking.

As the above examples show, this special use of the passive is a highly idiomatic area of the language. For the most part you'll do best to learn such expressions as frozen idioms.

■ DRILLS

False or Apparent Passive

Form "false passive" sentences in the tenses indicated.

1. Dies- / Tisch / sein / schon reserviert (*present* and *past*)
2. Restaurant / sein / geschlossen (*present* and *past*)

3. Zeitungen / sein / ausverkauft (*present* and *past*)
4. Laden / sein / ganz- / Tag / geschlossen (*past*)
5. Rechnung / sein / schon bezahlt (*present*)
6. Alles / sein / verloren (*present* and *past*)
7. Unser Haus / sein / schon verkauft (*present*)
8. Alles / sein / gut vorbereitet (*present* and *past*)
9. Das / sein / schon erledigt (*present*)
10. Er / sein / geschieden (*present* and *past*)
11. Dies- / Plätze / sein / belegt (*present*)
12. Fernseher / sein / repariert (*present* and *past*)

Express in German

Use false passive sentences only.

1. That's already taken care of.
2. The TV is repaired.
3. The newspapers were sold out.
4. The bill is already paid.
5. She's divorced.
6. The restaurant was closed.
7. The house is sold.
8. This table is reserved.
9. Everything was well prepared.
10. These seats are taken.
11. The store was closed all day.
12. All is lost.

Express in German

This exercise contains both passive and false passive sentences.

1. The T.V. is being repaired.
2. These seats are taken.
3. The newspapers were sold out.
4. That's being taken care of.
5. The store was closed all day.
6. Our house is being sold.
7. A table is being reserved for us.

8. Everything was well prepared.
9. The bill is already paid.

Passive with Indefinite Subjects

Active–passive

Put the following sentences into the passive voice. (Do *not* express the agent, e.g., *von ihm / by him.*)

1. Hier raucht man nicht.
2. Man arbeitet nicht am Sonntag.
3. Der Zug hält nicht vor Frankfurt.
4. Sie machen abends nicht auf.
5. Wir tanzen heute abend.
6. Sie liefern nicht am Samstag.
7. Wir servieren ab elf Uhr.
8. Wir haften nicht für Gepäck.

Tense Formation

Put the following sentences into the simple past tense.

1. Abends wird nicht aufgemacht.
2. Ab elf Uhr wird serviert.
3. Am Samstag wird nicht geliefert.
4. Für Gepäck wird nicht gehaftet.
5. Vor Frankfurt wird nicht gehalten.

Synthetic Exercises

Form passive sentences in the tense or tenses indicated.

1. Heute abend / getanzt (*present*)
2. Ab elf Uhr / serviert (*present* and *past*)
3. Hier / geraucht / nicht (*present*)
4. Am Samstag / geliefert / nicht (*present* and *past*)
5. Für Gepäck / gehaftet / nicht (*present* and *past*)
6. Abends / aufgemacht / nicht (*present* and *past*)
7. Am Sonntag / gearbeitet / nicht (*present*)
8. Vor Frankfurt / gehalten / nicht (*present* and *past*)

Express in German (Use Passive Sentences Only)

Begin the sentences with the words in parentheses.

1. There's no smoking here. (*Hier . . .*)
2. There were no stops before Frankfurt. (*Vor Frankfurt . . .*)
3. There are no deliveries on Saturday. (*Am Samstag . . .*)
4. There's a dance tonight. (*Heute abend . . .*)
5. Not responsible for luggage. (*Für Gepäck . . .*)
6. There's no work on Sundays. (*Am Sonntag . . .*)

LEVEL THREE

I. THE PASSIVE WITH MODAL AUXILIARIES

A. English and German passive forms

Look at an example, in German and in English, of a simple passive sentence:

Das Haus wird verkauft.   The house *is being sold.*

The passive is often used with modal auxiliaries. Here's an example:

Das Haus muß verkauft werden.   The house *has to be sold.*

The following table shows you passive expressions with modals in all of the simple and compound tenses:

The house	*has to*	be sold.	Das Haus	muß	verkauft werden.
	had to	be sold.		mußte	verkauft werden.
	will have to	be sold.		wird	verkauft werden müssen.
	has had to	be sold.		hat	verkauft werden müssen.
	had had to	be sold.		hatte	verkauft werden müssen.

This construction is made up of two elements:

A Conjugated Form of the Modal + A Passive Infinitive

muß   verkauft werden

1. The passive infinitive

As you already know, a passive expression is composed of:

werden + *a past participle.*

The passive infinitive is made up of the same elements. It's just that **werden** is in the infinitive form and *follows* the past participle:

verkauft werden

The passive infinitive remains unchanged in all tenses.

2. Tense change

The only elements that change in the above sentences are the forms of **müssen:** *shifts in tense affect only the modal part of the expression.* Since **verkauft werden** is a passive infinitive, the double infinitive expression is used in the perfect tenses of modals with the passive voice:

Passive infinitive Infinitive of modal
Das Haus hat verkauft werden müssen.

Double infinitive constructions are discussed in detail on pp. 158–60.

3. Omission of zu *with infinitives in modal expressions*

It must be sold.   Es muß verkauft werden.
It has *to* be sold.

It should be sold.   Es sollte verkauft werden.
It ought *to* be sold.

German never uses **zu** in modal expressions. (See also p. 146, "Omission of **zu** in Modal Expressions.")

B. The rationale behind the German forms

Note that in each case only a simple change takes place.

1. Present tense

The previous sections have dealt with passive constructions without modals:

Das Haus wird verkauft.

When a modal is added, the following changes take place:

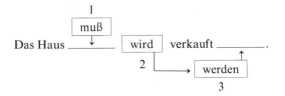

Das Haus muß verkauft werden.

1. **Muß** (a conjugated form of a modal) is needed in the second (or verb) position of the sentence.

2. **Wird,** which was in this position before, is forced out and to the end of the sentence.

3. Because a modal expression cannot have *two* conjugated verb forms, **wird** becomes **werden** (the infinitive form).

2. Past tense

PRESENT PASSIVE   Das Haus **muß** verkauft werden.
PAST PASSIVE   . . . . **mußte** . . . .

Here we merely substitute the past tense of the modal (mußte) for its present tense (muß).

3. Future with auxiliary

PRESENT PASSIVE   Das Haus **muß** verkauft werden.
FUTURE PASSIVE   . . . . **wird** . . . . **müssen.**

Only the modals change tenses in the passive voice; therefore, we may say that the present form: **muß**
is replaced by: **wird . . . müssen.**

4. Present perfect

Here the principle is essentially the same. The change may be viewed as a simple replacement:

> Das Haus muß verkauft werden.
>
> . . . . hat . . . . müssen.

NOTE: *double infinitive construction*

The perfect of **muß** is **hat . . . gemußt.** Here, however, **gemußt** "changes to" **müssen** because of the passive infinitive **verkauft werden.** (See also p. 157, "Compound Tenses of Modal Auxiliaries.")

> Das Haus hat *verkauft werden* müssen.

5. Past perfect

This tense can be treated like the present perfect. The only difference is that **hatte** replaces **hat:**

> Das Haus hatte verkauft werden müssen.

■ DRILLS

Form Drill

Form new sentences in the present tense by adding the suggested modals to the following passive sentences.

> Example: Das Haus *wird* verkauft. (müssen)
> Das Haus *muß* verkauft *werden.*

1. Der Kühlschrank wird repariert. (müssen)
2. Das Sofa wird heute gebracht. (sollen)
3. Das Haus wird renoviert. (müssen)
4. Der Wagen wird nicht verkauft. (können)
5. Die Briefe werden heute abgeschickt. (sollen)
6. Das wird bei der Bank gemacht. (müssen)
7. Hähnchen wird mit den Fingern gegessen. (dürfen)

Tense Drill

Put the following sentences into the past and present perfect tenses.

Example: Der Brief *muß* gleich geschrieben werden.
. . . . *mußte* . . . .
. . . . *hat* . . . . *müssen.*

1. Das muß gleich erledigt werden.
2. Er muß heute operiert werden.
3. Das Fenster kann nicht aufgemacht werden.
4. Das Haus muß renoviert werden.
5. Das kann nicht gemacht werden.
6. Das muß geändert werden.

The Constant Factor: The Passive Infinitive

Complete the following sentences by supplying the passive infinitive.

Example: Das Haus muß _____.
                              (be sold)
            Das Haus muß *verkauft werden.*

1. Das muß bei der Bank _____.
                                    (be done)

2. Der Kühlschrank mußte _____.
                                    (be repaired)

3. Das Sofa soll heute _____.
                                  (be brought)

4. Das Fenster hat nicht _____ können.
                                    (be opened)

5. Er mußte heute _____.
                          (be operated (on))

6. Der Wagen kann nicht _____.
                                    (be sold)

7. Das Haus hat _____ müssen.
                        (be renovated)

8. Die Briefe sollen heute _____.
                                      (be sent off)

9. Das muß gleich _____.
                          (be taken care of)

10. Das konnte nicht _____ .
      (be done)

11. Das hat _____ müssen.
      (be changed)

The Variable Factor: The Form of the Modal

Complete the following sentences in the tense indicated.

Example: Das Haus _____ verkauft werden _____ . (*perfect*)
                      (had to)
            Das Haus *hat* verkauft werden *müssen*.

1. Die Briefe _____ heute abgeschickt werden. (*present*)
      (are supposed to)

2. Er _____ heute operiert werden. (*past*)
      (had to)

3. Hähnchen _____ mit den Fingern gegessen werden. (*present*)
      (may)

4. Das _____ gleich erledigt werden _____ . (*perfect*)
      (had to)

5. Der Kühlschrank _____ repariert werden. (*past*)
              (had to)

6. Das Haus _____ renoviert werden _____ . (*future*)
      (will have to)

7. Das _____ bei der Bank gemacht werden. (*present*)
      (has to)

8. Das Fenster _____ nicht aufgemacht werden _____ . (*perfect*)
              (could)

9. Der Wagen _____ nicht verkauft werden. (*past*)
              (could)

10. Das Sofa _____ heute gebracht werden. (*present*)
      (is supposed to)

11. Das _____ geändert werden _____ . (*future*)
      (will have to)

12. Das _____ nicht gemacht werden _____ . (*perfect*)
      (could)

Express in German

1. The refrigerator had to be repaired. (*past*)
2. The sofa is supposed to be brought today.
3. That couldn't be done. (*perfect*)
4. That has to be done at the bank.
5. He had to be operated (on). (*past*)
6. The house will have to be renovated. (*future*)
7. The letters are supposed to be sent off today.
8. That had to be taken care of right away. (*perfect*)
9. The car couldn't be sold. (*past*)
10. That will have to be changed. (*future*)
11. The window couldn't be opened. (*perfect*)
12. Fried chicken may be eaten with your (*lit.* "the") fingers.

Reflexive Pronouns and Verbs

8

A. Introduction

A verb is said to be *reflexive* when its subject and its object are the same person (or thing):

I cut myself.

I and *myself* obviously refer to the same person. *Myself*, the direct object of the verb *cut*, is called a *reflexive pronoun*. Whenever the object of a verb is identical with the subject, a reflexive pronoun is used. When an object and a subject are *not* identical, the object will be a noun or a *personal* pronoun.

REFLEXIVE	I cut *myself*.
NON-REFLEXIVE	I cut *the bread*. I cut *it*.

B. Reflexive pronouns

English uses the suffixes *-self* or *-selves* (e.g., my*self*, him*self*, our*selves*, them*selves*) to form reflexive pronouns.

German doesn't use suffixes; it has a set of reflexive pronouns that are identical to the usual personal pronouns in all but the 3rd person singular and plural, where the reflexive pronoun is **sich.**

	SINGULAR		PLURAL	
	Accusative	*Dative*	*Accusative*	*Dative*
1st PERSON	mich	mir	uns	uns
2nd PERSON	dich	dir	euch	euch
3rd PERSON	**sich**	**sich**	**sich**	**sich**

NOTE: The polite form of the reflexive pronoun is not capitalized:

Setzen Sie *sich.*
(Have a seat.)

C. Usage

A reflexive pronoun must be used when an object (*any object*) is identical with the subject of a sentence, which means that a reflexive pronoun can be:

1. *the direct object*

REFLEXIVE	NON-REFLEXIVE
Er hat **sich** geschnitten.	Er hat **es** (**das Brot**) geschnitten.
(He cut himself.)	(He cut it [the bread].)

2. *the indirect object*

REFLEXIVE	NON-REFLEXIVE
Er kaufte **sich** eine Krawatte.	Er kauft **ihm** (**seinem Bruder**) eine Krawatte.
(He bought himself a tie.)	(He bought him [his brother] a tie.)
Er bestellte **sich** ein Bier.	Er bestellte **ihr** (**seiner Freundin**) ein Bier.
(He ordered himself a beer.)	(He ordered her [his girlfriend] a beer.)

3. *the object of a preposition*

Er hat kein Geld bei **sich.**
(He doesn't have any money on him.)

D. German verbs with reflexive direct objects

A number of verbs can be used either reflexively or non-reflexively:

REFLEXIVE	NON-REFLEXIVE
Er machte sich fertig.	Er machte es fertig.
(He got (himself) ready.)	(He got it ready.)

NOTE 1: English often omits a reflexive pronoun where German cannot. The following examples contrast English and German usage:

He's getting ready.	Er macht sich fertig.
He's shaving.	Er rasiert sich.
He's washing.	Er wäscht sich.

NOTE 2: Look at the following sentences:

REFLEXIVE	NON-REFLEXIVE
Er zog sich an.	Er zog seinen Mantel an.
(He *got dressed.*)	(He *put on* his coat.)

As you can see, there can be considerable differences in meaning and translation, depending on whether a verb is used reflexively or non-reflexively:

an · ziehen	*to put on* (an article of clothing)
sich an · ziehen	*to get dressed*

1. Verbs that can be reflexive or non-reflexive

	NON-REFLEXIVE	REFLEXIVE
an · ziehen	Er zog seinen Mantel an. (He put on his coat.)	Er zog sich an. (He got dressed.)
aus · ziehen	Er zog seinen Mantel aus. (He took off his coat.)	Er zog sich aus. (He got undressed.)
bedienen	Bedienen Sie den Kunden da drüben. (Serve the customer over there.)	Bedienen Sie sich. (Serve (help) yourself.)
erinnern	Er erinnerte mich daran. (He reminded me of it.)	Er erinnerte sich daran. (He remembered it.)

fertig · machen	Er machte es fertig. (He got it ready.)	Er machte sich fertig. (He got ready.)
hin · legen	Er legte das Buch hin. (He laid the book down.)	Er legte sich hin. (He lay down.)
interessieren	Das interessiert ihn. (That interests him.)	Er interessiert sich dafür. (He's interested in it.)
rasieren	Er rasiert einen Kunden. (He's shaving a customer.)	Er rasiert sich. (He's shaving.)
schneiden	Er hat das Brot geschnitten. (He cut the bread.)	Er hat sich geschnitten. (He cut himself.)
setzen	Er setzte es aufs Sofa. (He set it on the sofa.)	Er setzte sich aufs Sofa. (He sat down on the sofa.)
waschen	Er wäscht den Wagen. (He's washing the car.)	Er wäscht sich. (He's washing.)
wundern	Das hat ihn gewundert. (That surprised him.)	Er hat sich gewundert. (He was surprised.)

2. Verbs that are only reflexive

The following verbs are always used with reflexive pronouns:

sich amüsieren	Haben Sie sich gut amüsiert? (Did you have a good time?)
sich beeilen	Er mußte sich beeilen. (He had to hurry.)
sich entschließen	Hat er sich schon entschlossen? (Has he already decided?)
sich erkälten	Ich habe mich erkältet. (I've caught a cold.)
sich freuen auf + acc.	Er freut sich auf die Ferien. (He's looking forward to the vacation.)
sich freuen über + acc.	Er freut sich darüber. (He's happy about it.)

sich genieren	Genieren Sie sich nicht!
	(Don't be embarrassed.)
sich gewöhnen an + *acc.*	Ich kann mich nicht daran gewöhnen.
	(I can't get used to it.)
sich irren	Sie irren sich.
	(You're mistaken.)
sich schämen über + *acc.*	Schämen Sie sich nicht?
	(Aren't you ashamed?)

E. Verbs with reflexive indirect objects

Reflexive indirect objects fall into three basic groups:

1. Normal indirect objects

> Er kaufte sich (ihm, seinem Bruder) eine Krawatte.

In this sentence the reflexive pronoun may be replaced by a noun or a personal pronoun. A sentence of this kind is complete even if the dative expression is omitted:

> Er kaufte eine Krawatte.

The addition of an indirect object tells us who the tie is being bought for:

> for *himself* (for *his brother,* etc.)

but it doesn't affect the basic meaning of the verb in any way.

2. Reflexives with parts of the body

Compare the following German sentences with their English equivalents:

Er hat sich den Arm gebrochen.	(He broke *his* arm.)
Ich wasche mir die Hände.	(I'm washing *my* hands.)
Er will sich die Zähne putzen.	(He wants to brush *his* teeth.)

In such expressions, English uses a possessive pronoun (*my, his*) when referring to parts of the body. German, on the other hand, uses a definite article preceded by a dative reflexive pronoun (e.g., **mir die** Hände).

3. Purely reflexive indirect objects

In each of the following pairs of examples, the first verb is used non-reflexively and the second verb is a purely reflexive idiom. Compare their meanings:

merken	Ich habe nichts gemerkt.
(to notice)	(I didn't notice anything.)
sich etwas merken	Ich werde es mir merken.
(to keep [something] in mind, make a mental note of)	(I'll keep it in mind.)
an · sehen	Ich sah es lange an.
(to look at)	(I looked at it for a long time.)
sich etwas an · sehen	Ich habe mir das Haus angesehen.
(to take a look at something)	(I took a look at the house.)
vor · stellen	Bitte, stellen Sie mich vor.
(to introduce)	Introduce me, please.
sich etwas vor · stellen	Das kann ich mir vorstellen.
(to imagine something)	(I can imagine that.)

In all of these cases the addition of the indirect object has a profound effect on the meaning of the verb. The pronouns in these idiomatic expressions must always be reflexive: they may *not* be replaced by nouns or personal pronouns.

 DRILLS

Replacement Drills

Restate the following sentences using the suggested subjects. Remember to make the necessary changes in both the *verb* and the *reflexive pronoun*.

1. Wir müssen uns beeilen. (er, ich)
2. Ich interessiere mich für Musik. (er, wir)
3. Er setzte sich an den Tisch. (ich, sie [they])
4. Hast du dich erkältet? (sie [she])

 5. Sie irren sich. (du, ihr)
 6. Ich will mir einen Fernseher kaufen. (er, wir)
 7. Er wird sich wundern. (du, Sie)
 8. Er hat sich den Arm gebrochen. (ich)
 9. Erinnerst du dich an den Film? (ihr, Sie)
10. Das kann ich mir vorstellen, (du, Sie)
11. Haben Sie sich noch nicht angezogen? (du, er)
12. Wir freuen uns auf die Ferien. (ich, sie [she])
13. Sie bestellte sich ein Steak. (ich, er)
14. Hast du dich geschnitten? (er, Sie)
15. Habt ihr euch nicht geniert? (du, Sie)
16. Ich will mir das Haus ansehen. (sie [she], wir)
17. Er zog sich aus und ging ins Bett. (ich, sie [they])
18. Haben Sie sich schon entschlossen? (du, er)
19. Ich will mir die Hände waschen. (er, wir)
20. Ich will mich für eine Weile hinlegen. (er, sie [they])
21. Sie können sich nicht daran gewöhnen. (ich, er)
22. Das mußt du dir merken. (ich, er)
23. Schämt er sich nicht? (du, Sie)
24. Ich freue mich sehr darüber. (er, wir)

Fill-ins

Supply the correct *reflexive* pronouns.

 1. Er hat _____ erkältet.
 2. Ich freue _____ auf die Ferien.
 3. Hast du _____ noch nicht angezogen?
 4. Setzen Sie _____.
 5. Darf ich _____ vorstellen?
 6. Erinnerst du _____ an den Film?
 7. Ich bestelle _____ ein Steak.
 8. Er zog _____ aus und ging ins Bett.
 9. Hast du _____ entschlossen?
10. Ich will _____ das Haus ansehen.
11. Bedienen Sie _____.
12. Hast du _____ nicht geniert?
13. Er will _____ die Hände waschen.
14. Du wirst _____ wundern.
15. Ich kann _____ nicht daran gewöhnen.

16. Hast du ＿＿＿＿＿＿＿ gut amüsiert?
17. Er hat ＿＿＿＿＿＿＿ den Arm gebrochen.
18. Ich will ＿＿＿＿＿＿＿ für eine Weile hinlegen.
19. Hast du ＿＿＿＿＿＿＿ noch nicht rasiert?
20. Das kann ich ＿＿＿＿＿＿＿ vorstellen.
21. Sie freut ＿＿＿＿＿＿＿ sehr darüber.
22. Ich muß ＿＿＿＿＿＿＿ jetzt fertigmachen.
23. Das muß ich ＿＿＿＿＿＿＿ merken.
24. Schämst du ＿＿＿＿＿＿＿ nicht?
25. Er will ＿＿＿＿＿＿＿ waschen.
26. Ich muß ＿＿＿＿＿＿＿ die Zähne putzen.
27. Er will ＿＿＿＿＿＿＿ einen Fernseher kaufen.

Synthetic Exercises

These exercises include both reflexive and some non-reflexive sentences.
Use the present tense except where otherwise indicated.

> Examples: Er / setzen / auf / Sofa
> Er setzt sich auf das Sofa.
>
> Er / setzen / Glas / auf / Tisch (*past*)
> Er setzte das Glas auf den Tisch.

1. Er / müssen / beeilen
2. Sie / interessieren / für Musik
3. Ich / freuen / auf / Ferien
4. Genieren / du / nicht / ? (*present perfect*)
5. Ich / müssen / waschen / Hände
6. Er / erkälten (*present perfect*)
7. Er / müssen / waschen / Wagen
8. Amüsieren / du / gut / ? (*present perfect*)
9. Setzen / Sie (*imperative*)
10. Ich / müssen / putzen / Zähne
11. Erinnern / du / an / Film / ?
12. Ich / müssen / fertigmachen / jetzt
13. Er / hinlegen / Buch (*past*)
14. Sie / irren / !
15. Ich / können / gewöhnen / nicht daran
16. Entschließen / Sie / schon / ? (*present perfect*)
17. Er / erinnern / mich / daran (*past tense*)

Express in German

1. He has to hurry.
2. I have to get ready now.
3. You're wrong.
4. He caught cold.
5. I want to wash my hands.
6. She's interested in music.
7. I have to wash the car.
8. Did you cut yourself?
9. I want to lie down for a while.
10. He bought himself a TV.
11. Sit down.
12. I want to take a look at the house.
13. Haven't you shaved yet?
14. May I introduce myself?
15. He got undressed and went to bed.
16. You'll be surprised.
17. He laid the book down.
18. I'm looking forward to the vacation.
19. Weren't you embarrassed?
20. I have to brush my teeth.
21. Did you have a good time?
22. Haven't you gotten dressed yet?
23. I ordered myself a steak.
24. Help (serve) yourself!
25. Hans broke his arm.
26. I can imagine that.
27. Aren't you ashamed?
28. Do you remember the movie?
29. He reminded me of it.
30. I'll have to keep that in mind.
31. Have you decided yet?
32. She's very happy about it.
33. I can't get used to it.

Conjunctions

9

LEVEL ONE

I. INTRODUCTION

Conjunctions—as the name implies—join units of language together: words to words, phrases to phrases, clauses to clauses.

WORDS	*Hans **and** I* are going swimming.
PHRASES	Are you going *by train **or** by plane*?
CLAUSES	*I'm not going **because** I have too much to do.*

In both English and German, you have to select the right conjunction to define the right relationship. This is a *lexical* problem, a matter of vocabulary. But when it comes to joining *clauses* to *clauses* or *sentences* to *sentences,* German presents a *structural* problem. Look at these two German sentences:

Ich gehe nicht ins Kino. Ich habe den Film schon gesehen.
(I'm not going to the movies.) (I've already seen the movie.)

Note what happens when these sentences are connected with two different conjunctions, **denn** and **weil,** both of which mean *because:*

Ich gehe nicht ins Kino, denn ich habe den Film schon gesehen.
Ich gehe nicht ins Kino, weil ich   den Film schon gesehen habe.

These two *compound sentences* mean the same thing, but **denn** has not affected the word order of the clause it introduces, whereas **weil** has.

GENERAL RULES

A. Coordinating conjunctions

Some German conjunctions *do not* affect the word order of the clauses they introduce:

> Ich gehe nicht.   Ich habe zuviel zu tun.
> Ich gehe nicht, denn ich habe zuviel zu tun.
> (I'm not going *because* I have too much to do.)

Denn is a *coordinating* conjunction; it does not affect word order:

> . . . , denn ich habe zuviel zu tun.

As far as word order is concerned, coordinating conjunctions are not counted as sentence elements, that is, the verb stays in its normal (second) position in the clause:

0	1	2	3
CONJUNCTION	SUBJECT	VERB	OTHER
. . . , **denn**	ich	**habe**	zuviel zu tun

Clauses joined by coordinating conjunctions are called *coordinate clauses.*

B. Subordinating conjunctions

Other conjunctions *do* affect the word order of the clauses they introduce:

> Ich gehe nicht.   Ich habe zuviel zu tun.
> Ich gehe nicht, weil   ich   zuviel zu tun habe.
> (I'm not going *because* I have too much to do.)

When a clause is introduced by a *subordinating* conjunction, the conjugated verb comes at the end of its clause:

> . . . , weil ich zuviel zu tun habe.

Clauses introduced by subordinating conjunctions are called *subordinate clauses.*

C. Punctuation

Commas are used between *joined clauses.* This holds for both coordinate and subordinate clauses.

II. COORDINATING CONJUNCTIONS

The coordinating conjunctions—**denn, und, oder, aber,** and **sondern**—*do not* affect word order.

1. **denn** *because, since, for* (causal)

> Ich komme heute nicht, denn ich muß arbeiten.
> (I'm not coming today *because* I have to work.)

2. **oder** *or*

> Soll ich einkaufen gehen, oder gehst du?
> (Shall I go shopping *or* are you going?)

NOTE: . . . , oder gehst du?

The coordinating conjunction doesn't affect the word order of a question. **Oder** is "inert" and **gehst** is the first element in the clause.

3. **und** *and*

> Ich machte die Tür auf, und da stand er.
> (I opened the door *and* there he stood.)

4. **aber** *but, however*

> Ich suchte ihn, aber ich konnte ihn nicht finden.
> (I looked for him *but* I couldn't find him.)

5. **sondern** *but, rather, on the contrary*

Ich komme nicht zu dir, sondern du kommst zu mir.
(I'm not coming to your place *but* (*rather*) you're coming to mine.)

NOTE: **Sondern** (not **aber**) is used after a negative first clause when the words *rather* or *on the contrary* can sensibly be used in the equivalent English sentence. (The word *but* in the sentence "I looked for him *but* I couldn't find him" can't logically be replaced by *rather* or *on the contrary*.)

III. OMISSION OF REDUNDANT ELEMENTS: ELLIPSIS

Er war aufgestanden und (er war) ins Wohnzimmer gegangen.
(He had gotten up and [he had] gone into the living room.)

Wir tun es jetzt oder (wir tun es) gar nicht.
(We'll do it now or [we'll] not [do it] at all.)

Wir sind nicht weitergefahren sondern (wir) haben in Zürich übernachtet.
(We didn't drive farther but (we) spent the night in Zurich.)

In German, as in English, elements common to both clauses of a compound sentence are often eliminated from the second clause. This is often the case in clauses introduced by **oder, und,** and **sondern.** But ellipsis is not found after **denn** and the *subordinating conjunctions,* and it is rare after **aber.** In this, too, German is similar to English:

Er ist zu Hause geblieben, denn er hatte zuviel zu tun.
(He stayed home because *he* had too much to do.)

The second **er** / *he* cannot be omitted.

NOTE 1: Common elements can be omitted only when both clauses use normal declarative word order (subject first, verb second). Look at the following sentence:

Er kaufte etwas, und dann ging er nach Hause.
(He bought something and then he went home.)

The second clause doesn't use normal declarative word order; the subject **er** is in *third* position rather than in first position. For this reason, the word **er** cannot be omitted from the second clause.

NOTE 2: Punctuation is affected by ellipsis. Omission of sentence elements makes the second clause incomplete and it is not preceded by a comma.

DRILLS

Drills

Sentence combinations using conjunctions.

Combine the following sentences with the German conjunctions corresponding to the English in parentheses.

1. Ich bin nicht sicher. Ich glaube, er ist in seinem Büro. (but)
2. Sie machte das Licht aus. Sie ging ins Bett. (and)
3. Soll ich ein Taxi anrufen? Willst du zu Fuß gehen? (or)
4. Wir sind nicht weitergefahren. Wir haben in München übernachtet. (but)
5. Er stand um zwei Uhr auf. Er konnte nicht schlafen. (because)
6. Soll ich ihn abholen? Wollen Sie es machen? (or)
7. Es ist ein hübscher Mantel. Ich finde ihn zu teuer. (but)
8. Ich gehe zur Apotheke. Dann gehe ich nach Hause. (and)
9. Er konnte es nicht machen. Er war gar nicht hier. (because)
10. Ich gehe nicht zu Nicki. Ich gehe zu Erika. (but)

LEVEL TWO

I. SUBORDINATING CONJUNCTIONS

The subordinating conjunctions *do* affect word order.

A. Word order in the subordinate clause

In clauses introduced by subordinating conjunctions, the conjugated verb is forced to the end of the clause.

MAIN CLAUSE   SUBORDINATE CLAUSE
Es ist gar nicht teuer, obwohl es ein gutes Restaurant ist.
(It isn't at all expensive, although it's a good restaurant.)

B. Word order in the main clause

A sentence can also begin with a subordinate clause. In this case the *main clause begins with a conjugated verb.*

SUBORDINATE CLAUSE   MAIN CLAUSE

Obwohl es ein gutes Restaurant ist, ist es gar nicht teuer.
(Although it's a good restaurant, it isn't at all expensive.)

NOTE: This is in keeping with the *normal word order* of the German declarative sentence that requires the conjugated verb to be the second element of the sentence. A subordinate clause functions as a single (although extended) sentence element as far as word order is concerned. Thus a conjugated verb coming right after a subordinate clause is, in fact, occupying the second (verb) position.

1	2
Obwohl es ein gutes Restaurant ist,	ist es gar nicht teuer.
Trotzdem	ist es gar nicht teuer.

C. Separable prefix verbs in subordinate clauses

Separable prefix verbs in subordinate clauses present a slight problem. First look at a separable prefix verb in a simple sentence:

Sie kommt morgen zurück.

Now look at the same sentence used as a subordinate clause:

Sie sagt, daß sie morgen zurückkommt.

When the conjugated part of the verb goes to the end of the clause, it joins up with its prefix again and is written as one word: zurückkommt.

II. CONJUNCTIONS PRESENTING SPECIAL PROBLEMS

A. When

1. **als** (a subordinating conjunction used in expressions of *past time*)

2. **wenn** (a subordinating conjunction used with *future time* and also to mean *if* and *whenever*)

3. **wann** (a question word that can also function as a subordinating conjunction)

1. **Als** (*when*) may refer to a point in past time:

> *When* I found him . . .
> Als ich ihn fand . . .

or to an extended, uninterrupted period of past time:

> *When* I lived in Munich . . .
> Als ich in München wohnte . . .

NOTE: **Als** is also used in narrating past events using the present tense—a literary technique. With this exception, **als** may be used only with the *past* or *past perfect* tenses. It is rarely used with the present perfect tense.

2. **Wenn** corresponds to the English *when* in the sense of *whenever* (recurrence):

> *When*(*ever*) he comes . . . (he stays with us).
> Wenn er kommt . . .

It is also used to imply the *future:*

> *When* he comes . . . (he will stay with us).
> Wenn er kommt . . .

or to express the English word *if:*

> *If* he comes . . . (he will stay with us).
> Wenn er kommt . . .

NOTE: As you can see, the clause **Wenn er kommt . . .** is dependent upon its broader context to indicate whether it refers to the *future* or means *if* or *whenever.*

3. **Wann** is a question word:

> Wann kommt er?
> *When* is he coming?

Wann can also introduce a subordinate clause:

> Ich weiß, wann er kommt.
> (I know *when* he's coming.)

Ich fragte ihn, **wann** er kommt.
(I asked him *when* he's coming.)

NOTE: In such cases, **wann** functions as a subordinating conjunction. For this reason, the conjugated verb is at the end of the subordinate clause. (This is the case when *any question word* introduces a subordinate clause.)

DRILLS

Fill-ins

Fill in the German word suggested by the English cue *and the context of the sentence.*

1. Ich lernte ihn kennen, _____ ich an der Universität war.
                              (when)

2. _____ sie nach Berlin fahren, bleiben sie in einem guten Hotel.
   (When)

3. _____ werden Sie Zeit haben?
         (When)

4. Ich gebe es ihm, _____ ich ihn sehe.
                        (when)

5. Er war sehr müde, _____ er ankam.
                        (when)

6. Wir kauften es, _____ wir in München waren.
                      (when)

7. Wissen Sie, _____ er zurückgekommen ist?
                  (when)

8. _____ er das Büro verläßt, macht er die Fenster zu.
   (Whenever)

Express in German

1. He was very tired when he arrived.
2. When will you have time?
3. I'll give it to him when I see him.
4. Whenever he leaves the office, he closes the windows.
5. I met him when I was at the university.

6. Do you know when he came back?
7. When they go to Berlin, they always stay in a good hotel.
8. We bought it when we were in Munich.

B. If / if (whether)

1. **Wenn** means *if* in the sense of *in the event that.*

> **Wenn** er kommt, gebe ich es ihm.
> (*If* (*in the event that*) he comes, I'll give it to him.)

2. **Ob** means *if* in the sense of *whether.*

> Ich weiß nicht, **ob** er heute kommt.
> (I don't know *if* (*whether*) he's coming today.)

■ DRILLS

Fill-ins

Fill in the German word suggested by the English cue *and the context of the sentence.*

1. Wissen Sie, _____ er es gefunden hat?
   (if)

2. Ist es dir recht, _____ wir später kommen?
   (if)

3. Ich weiß nicht, _____ sie zu Hause ist.
   (if)

4. _____ er Sie nach meiner Adresse fragt, geben Sie sie ihm.
   (if)

5. Weißt du, _____ sie heute abend kommen kann?
   (if)

Express in German

1. I don't know if she's home.
2. If he asks you for my address, give it to him.
3. Do you know if she can come this evening?

4. Is it all right with you if we come later?
5. Do you know if he's found it?

C. *After / afterwards*

1. **Nachdem** is a subordinating conjunction (it introduces a subordinate clause):

> Ich komme zu dir, nachdem ich gegessen habe.
> (I'll come to your place *after* I have eaten.)

Nachdem may be used only with the present perfect and past perfect tenses.

2. **Nach** is a preposition (it introduces prepositional phrases):

> Ich komme nach dem Essen zu dir.
> (I'll come to your place *after dinner*.)

3. **Nachher** is an adverb of time (like **heute, morgen,** etc.):

> Ich komme nachher zu dir.
> (I'll come to your place *afterwards*.)

■ DRILLS

Fill-ins

Fill in the German word suggested by the English cue *and the context of the sentence.*

1. _____ dieser Sendung gehe ich ins Bett.
    (After)

2. _____ gehe ich nach Hause.
    (After that)

3. Ich rufe dich an, _____ ich mit ihm gesprochen habe.
    (after)

4. Warum kommst du nicht _____ der Party zu mir?
    (after)

5. Kommen Sie zurück, _____ Sie es erledigt haben.
    (after)

6. Wir können _____ essen.
    (afterwards)

Express in German

1. Why don't you come to my place after the party?
2. Come back after you have taken care of it.
3. We can eat afterwards.
4. I'll call you up after I've spoken with him.
5. After this program I'm going to bed.
6. After that I'm going home.

D. Before / before (that)

1. **Bevor** is a subordinating conjunction:

> **Bevor** er **wegging,** gab er mir den Schlüssel.
> (*Before* he left he gave me the key.)

2. **Vor** is a preposition. It can mean *before*:

> Er geht immer **vor elf Uhr** ins Bett.
> (He always goes to bed *before eleven o'clock*.)

or *ago:*

> Das war **vor zwei Jahren.**
> (That was *two years ago*.)

3. **Vorher** is an adverb of time:

> Das hast du mir schon **vorher** gesagt.
> (You've told me that *before*.)

DRILLS

Fill-ins

Fill in the German word suggested by the English cue *and the context of the sentence.*

1. Hören Sie auf, _____ es zu spät ist.
       (before)

2. Kannst du es _____ Donnerstag machen?
       (before)

3. Ich habe es nie _____ gesehen.
                   (before)

4. Machen Sie das Licht aus, _____ Sie nach Hause gehen.
                                     (before)

5. Sie geht nie _____ sechs Uhr nach Hause.
              (before)

Express in German

1. Can you do it before Thursday?
2. Turn off the light before you go home.
3. She never goes home before six o'clock.
4. Stop before it's too late.
5. I've never seen it before.
6. Come before dinner.
   Before I've eaten?
   Yes, sure, before.

E. Since, since then, because

1. **Seitdem** (*since*) refers to a *period of time:*

   Seitdem er weniger **arbeitet**, sieht er viel besser aus.
   (*Since* he *has been working* less he looks much better.)

   Seitdem sie **zurückgekommen ist**, wohnt sie in der Hauptstraße.
   (*Since* she *came back* she's been living on Main Street.)

Choice of tenses with **seitdem:**

When *since* refers to a continuing action, German uses:

seitdem + present tense

    Seitdem er weniger **arbeitet,** . . .
    Since he *has been working* less, . . .

By contrast, English uses the present perfect in such cases.

When *since* refers to a one-time past action, German uses:

seitdem + present perfect

    Seitdem sie **zurückgekommen ist,** . . .
    Since she *came back,* . . .

German must use the present perfect in such cases, whereas English tends to use the simple past.

2. **Seitdem** is also an adverb of time that means *since then:*

CONTINUING ACTION (PRES.) Seitdem sieht er besser aus.
(*Since then* he's been looking better.)

ONE-TIME ACTION (PRES. PERF.) Seitdem habe ich ihn nur einmal gesehen.
(*Since then* I've only seen him once.)

3. **Seit** is a preposition used in time expressions:

Sie wohnt seit zwei Wochen in der Hauptstraße.
(She's been living on Main Street *for two weeks*.)

Note that **seit** is used with the present tense when it refers to an action that began in the past and is still going on. English uses the present perfect in such situations.

4. **Weil** (*because, since*) indicates a strong causal connection:

Ich konnte nicht einkaufen gehen, weil ich kein Geld hatte.
(I couldn't go shopping *because* I didn't have any money.)

5. **Da** (*since, because*) indicates a less strong causal connection—or no strict causal connection at all.

NOTE: The choice of **weil** or **da** depends on how strong a causal connection you wish to convey:

weil If you consider your reasons for an action to be *absolutely compelling* you use **weil** (not **da**):

Ich arbeite, weil ich Geld verdienen muß.
(I work *because* I have to earn money.)

weil / da If you consider your reasons *good and adequate* (but not absolutely compelling), you can use either **weil** or **da:**

Ich ging heute schwimmen, weil es so schön war.
(I went swimming today *because* it was so nice.)

Da es heute so schön war, ging ich schwimmen.
(*Since* it was so nice today, I went swimming.)

da If the reason is—in your eyes at least—*not at all compelling or forcing,* you use **da** (not **weil**):

Da ich noch zehn Minuten hatte, trank ich noch eine Tasse Kaffee.
(*Since* I still had ten minutes, I drank another cup of coffee.)

Da ich sowieso* nach München fahre, werde ich Tante Elvira besuchen.
(*Since* I'm going to Munich *anyway*, I'll visit Aunt Elvira.)

 DRILLS

Fill-ins

Fill in the German word suggested by the English cue *and the context of the sentence.*

1. Hast du ihn gesehen, _____ er zurückgekommen ist?
   (since)

2. Ich lese dieses Buch nur, _____ ich muß.
   (because)

3. _____ ich zur Bibliothek gehe, bringe ich deine Bücher zurück.
   (Since)

4. Albrecht wohnt _____ August nicht hier.
   (since)

5. _____ ich heute nachmittag Zeit habe, werde ich meine
   (Since)
   Freundin besuchen.

6. Wir haben ihn nicht gesehen, _____ er in Salzburg wohnt.
   (since)

7. Sie ging nach Hause, _____ sie müde war.
   (because)

8. _____ habe ich ihn nicht gesehen.
   (Since then)

---

* **Sowieso** (*anyway*) often accompanies **da** in such cases. In the last example, the visit to Aunt Elvira and the going to Munich are obviously not connected in any compelling causal way. As a matter of fact, Aunt Elvira would be insulted if she heard the word **sowieso**.

Express in German

1. Since I'm going to the library, I'll take your books back.
2. We haven't seen him since he's been living in Salzburg.
3. Albrecht hasn't lived here since August.
4. She went home because she was tired.
5. Since I have time this afternoon, I'm going to visit my girlfriend.
6. Have you seen him since he came back?
7. Since then we haven't seen them.
8. I'm only reading this book because I have to.

F. *As long as, as soon as, as often as* (*every time*)

1. **Solange** means *as long as* and refers to a period of time:

> Wir bleiben, solange du willst.
> (We'll stay *as long as* you want.)

2. **Sobald** means *as soon as* and refers to a point in time:

> Wir gehen, sobald du fertig bist.
> (We'll go *as soon as* you're ready.)

3. **Sooft** means *as often as*, *every time* (*that*) and refers to a series of occurrences:

> Sooft ich daran denke, werde ich böse.
> (*Every time* I think of it I get mad.)

■ DRILLS

Fill-ins

Fill in the German word suggested by the English cue.

1. Machen Sie es, _____ Sie können.
   (as soon as)

2. Bleiben Sie, _____ Sie wollen.
   (as long as)

3. _____ wir ihn sehen, sieht er müde aus.
   (Every time)

4. Nächsten Sommer arbeite ich, _____ ich kann.
   (as long as)

5. Rufen Sie mich an, _____ er ankommt.
   (as soon as)

6. _____ ich daran denke, muß ich lachen.
   (Every time)

Express in German

1. Next summer I'm going to work as long as I can.
2. Call me up as soon as he arrives.
3. Every time I think of it I have to laugh.
4. Do it as soon as you can.
5. Every time we see him, he looks tired.
6. Stay as long as you want.

G. Other subordinating conjunctions

The following subordinating conjunctions, unlike the preceding ones, present few problems to English speakers because they correspond almost exactly to their English counterparts.

1. **Daß** means *that*:

> Er zeigte uns, **daß** er es **konnte.**
> (He showed us *that* he could do it.)

2. **Bis** means *until* and is both a subordinating conjunction and a preposition:

> Warten Sie, **bis ich zurückkomme.**
> (Wait *until* I get back.)

> Warten Sie **bis ein Uhr.**
> (Wait *until one o'clock.*)

3. **Damit** (so daß) means *so that:*

> Ich sage es dir nochmal, damit du es nicht vergißt.
> (I'll tell you again *so that* you won't forget it.)

4. **Obwohl** (obgleich) means *although, even though:*

> Obwohl es ein gutes Restaurant ist, ist es nicht sehr teuer.
> (*Although* it's a good restaurant, it's not very expensive.)

5. **Während** is both a subordinating conjunction meaning *while:*

> Während Sie in Berlin waren, kam ein Paket für Sie an.
> (*While* you were in Berlin, a package arrived for you.)

and a preposition meaning *during:*

> Während des Tages bin ich nie zu Hause.
> (*During the day* I'm never home.)

6. **Indem** means *by* (do)*ing* (something). Compare the English and German equivalents carefully:

> Ich spare viel Geld, indem ich in der Mensa* esse.
> (I save a lot of money *by eating* in the *mensa*.)

■ DRILLS

Sentence Combinations Using Conjunctions

Combine the following sentences using the suggested conjunctions. Note that both *coordinating* and *subordinating* conjunctions are involved. Be sure to use correct word order.

1. Hören Sie auf. (before) Es ist zu spät.
2. Sie wird es machen. (when) Sie kommt zurück.
3. Er zeigte uns. (that) Er konnte es tun.
4. Ich rufe dich an. (after) Ich habe mit ihm gesprochen.
5. (Since) Ich fuhr sowieso durch Heidelberg. Ich besuchte Onkel Max.

---

* **Die Mensa** is the state-subsidized dining hall at a German university. Eating there is optional—and potentially hazardous.

6. Kannst du nicht warten? (until) Wir sind zu Hause.
7. (If) Er fragt Sie nach meiner Adresse. Geben Sie sie ihm.
8. Ich bin nicht sicher. (but) Ich glaube, er ist in seinem Büro.
9. Wir kauften es. (when) Wir waren in München.
10. Weißt du? (if) Sie kann heute abend kommen.
11. Rufen Sie mich an. (as soon as) Er kommt an.
12. Ich konnte nicht einkaufen gehen. (because) Ich hatte kein Geld.
13. Sie machte das Licht aus. (and) Sie ging ins Bett.
14. Es kam. (while) Sie waren weg.
15. (Every time) Ich sehe ihn. Er sieht müde aus.
16. Er sieht besser aus. (since) Er arbeitet weniger.
17. Wir sparen viel Geld. (by . . . ing) Wir essen zu Hause.
18. (Whenever) Er verläßt das Büro. Er macht die Fenster zu.
19. Soll ich ihn abholen? (or) Willst du es machen?
20. Sag mir die Flugnummer. (so that) Ich kann dich abholen.
21. Wissen Sie? (if) Er hat es gefunden.
22. Wir kennen sie nicht sehr gut. (although) Sie wohnen gleich nebenan.
23. Ich hatte gehört. (that) Er war krank.
24. Machen Sie das Licht aus. (before) Sie gehen nach Hause.
25. (When) Sie fahren nach Berlin. Sie bleiben immer in einem guten Hotel.
26. Kommen Sie zurück. (after) Sie haben es erledigt.
27. (Since) Ich gehe zur Bibliothek. Ich bringe deine Bücher zurück.
28. Wir sind nicht weitergefahren. (but) Wir haben in Zürich übernachtet.
29. Ich bleibe hier. (until) Du kommst zurück.
30. Hast du ihn gesehen? (since) Er ist zurückgekommen.
31. Ich lernte ihn kennen. (when) Ich war an der Universität.
32. Sie ging nach Hause. (because) Sie war müde.
33. Bleiben Sie hier. (as long as) Sie wollen.
34. (Although) Er ist siebzig Jahre alt. Er geht jeden Tag ins Büro.
35. Wissen Sie? (when) Er kommt zurück.
36. Es ist ein hübscher Mantel. (but) Ich finde ihn zu teuer.
37. Ich trank eine Tasse Kaffee. (while) Ich wartete auf dich.
38. Ist es dir recht? (if) Wir kommen später.
39. Ich sage es dir. (so that) Du bist vorbereitet.
40. Er konnte es nicht machen. (because) Er war gar nicht hier.
41. Ich lerne viel. (by . . . ing) Ich arbeite für ihn.

Synthetic Exercises

Use *all* of the following elements to make complete compound sentences.
Be careful to reorder the elements should this be necessary.

Example: Ich sage es dir nochmal, // *damit* / du / vergessen / es / nicht
Ich sage es dir nochmal, damit du es nicht vergißt.

1. Weißt du, *ob* / sie / können / kommen / heute abend / ?
2. Ich lernte ihn kennen // *als* / ich / sein / an / Universität
3. Er zeigte uns // *daß* / er / können / tun / es
4. Kannst du nicht warten // *bis* / wir / sein / zu Hause / ?
5. Es ist ein hübscher Mantel // *aber* / ich / finden / ihn / zu teuer
6. Wir kennen sie nicht sehr gut // *obwohl* / sie / wohnen / gleich nebenan
7. Ich trank eine Tasse Kaffee // *während* / ich / warten / auf dich
8. *Wenn* / er / verlassen / Büro // macht er die Fenster zu
9. Machen Sie das Licht aus // *bevor* / Sie / gehen / nach Hause
10. Er sieht viel besser aus // *seitdem* / er / arbeiten / weniger
11. *Da* / ich / gehen / zu / Bibliothek // bringe ich deine Bücher zurück
12. Wir sind nicht weitergefahren // *sondern* / übernachten / in München
13. Ich rufe dich an // *nachdem* / ich / sprechen / mit ihm
14. Ist es dir recht // *wenn* / wir / kommen / später / ?
15. *Obwohl* / er / sein / siebzig Jahre alt // geht er jeden Tag ins Büro
16. Sag mir die Adresse // *damit* / ich / können / abholen / dich
17. Er konnte es nicht machen // *denn* / er / sein / gar nicht hier
18. Hast du ihn gesehen // *seitdem* / er / zurückkommen / ?
19. *Sooft* / wir / sehen / ihn // sieht er müde aus
20. Ich lerne viel // *indem* / ich / arbeiten / für ihn

Express in German

Most of these sentences contain conjunctions. A few of them, however, contain adverbs or prepositions that can be confused with conjunctions.

1. We bought it when we were in Munich.
2. Do you know if he has found it?
3. Stay here as long as you want.
4. She went home because she was tired.
5. I'll stay here until you come back.
6. It's a pretty coat but I think (**finden**) it's too expensive.
7. Turn off the light before you go home.
8. When they go to Berlin, they always stay in a good hotel.
9. He looks much better since he's been working less.
10. I'll call you up after I've spoken with him.
11. Shall I pick him up or do you want to do it?

12. We save a lot of money by eating at home.
13. It came while you were gone (**weg**).
14. Since I was driving through Heidelberg anyway, I visited Uncle Max.
15. She never goes home before six o'clock.
16. Have you seen him since he returned?
17. I met him when I was at the university.
18. Is it all right with you if we come later?
19. Why don't you come to my place after the party?
20. Every time we see him, he looks tired.
21. I'm not sure, but I think he's in his office.
22. Tell me the flight number so that I can pick you up.
23. She'll do it when she comes back.
24. Stop it before it's too late.
25. Since then I haven't seen him.
26. He showed us that he could do it.
27. Come back after you have taken care of it.
28. I'm learning a lot by working for him.
29. Can't you wait until we're home?
30. We didn't drive further but spent the night in Zürich.
31. I drank a cup of coffee while I was waiting for you.
32. Dieter hasn't lived here since August.
33. We don't know them very well even though they live right next door.
34. Do you know when he's coming back?
35. Since I'm going to the library, I'll take your books back.
36. We can eat afterwards.
37. Call me as soon as he arrives.
38. I'm telling you so that you'll be prepared.
39. She turned out the light and went to bed.
40. Whenever he leaves the office, he closes the windows.
41. I couldn't go shopping because I didn't have any money.
42. Do you know if she can come this evening?
43. We're only staying here until tomorrow.
44. If he asks you for my address, give it to him.
45. I'd heard that he was sick.
46. He couldn't do it because he wasn't even (**gar nicht**) here.
47. I've never seen it before.

Subjunctive II
10

LEVEL ONE

I. USE OF THE SUBJUNCTIVE IN CONDITIONAL SENTENCES: INTRODUCTION

A. The subjunctive mood

Mood comes from the word *modus* (mode) and it means *a way*—in this case, a way of talking about things. English and German have two basic moods: *indicative* and *subjunctive*.

The *indicative* is used to make *statements of fact:*

> He *needs* the book. He *will buy* it.

The indicative may also be used in conditional sentences (If . . . , then . . .):

> If he *needs* the book, he *will buy* it.

In the example above, it *may be a fact* that he needs the book. (We have implied neither that he does need it nor that he does not need it; we are merely making a statement that *agrees with the possible fact* of his needing the book.)

RULE: The indicative is used to make statements that agree with:

1. facts as they *are* (He needs the book.)

2. facts as they *may be* (If he needs the book . . .)

The *subjunctive,* on the other hand, is used to make *statements that are contrary to fact:*

> If he *needed* the book, he *would buy* it.

The implication is, however, that the person in question *does not need* the book and that he *is not going to buy it.*

Similarly:

> If I knew his address, I would write him.

The implied fact is that I do not know his address and that I will not write him.

And again:

> If I had enough money, I would stay longer.

The fact is that I do not have enough money and therefore cannot stay longer.

The examples above are all present tense situations:

> If I had the money (right *now*), I'd stay longer.
> If he needed the book (right *now*), he'd buy it.

The subjunctive also has past tense forms:

> If I *had had* the money (back *then*), I would *have stayed* longer.
> If he *had needed* the book (back *then*), he would *have bought* it.

B. The English subjunctive in conditional sentences

1. Present tense

The *present tense* forms of the English *subjunctive* are ordinarily identical with the *past tense* forms of the *indicative:*

PAST INDICATIVE   He *needed* it.
PRESENT SUBJUNCTIVE   If he *needed* it . . .

There is, however, a basic difference in time, and therefore in meaning, between the past tense of the indicative and the present tense of the subjunctive:

PAST INDICATIVE   He *had* enough money (yesterday).
                           (*past time* using a *past tense form*)
PRESENT SUBJUNCTIVE   If he *had* enough money (now) . . .
                           (*present time* using a *past tense form*)

The present tense of the subjunctive can be easily recognized in English: *past tense forms* are used in a *present tense situation.*

NOTE: There are only a few present subjunctive forms that are different from the past indicative forms:

          PAST INDICATIVE   He *was* here.
but: PRESENT SUBJUNCTIVE   If he *were* here . . .

2. *Past tense*

The *past tense* forms of the English subjunctive are the same as the *past perfect* forms of the *indicative:*

PAST PERFECT INDICATIVE   He *had had* the money.
PAST SUBJUNCTIVE   If he *had had* the money . . .

PAST PERFECT INDICATIVE   He *had needed* it.
PAST SUBJUNCTIVE   If he *had needed* it . . .

SUMMARY

The English subjunctive has two (and only two) tenses:

1. the *present tense,* whose forms are for the most part identical with the past tense of the indicative.

2. the *past tense,* whose forms are identical with the past perfect indicative.

C. The German subjunctive: subjunctive II

As you can see from the following *if*-clauses, German and English follow essentially the same pattern in using the indicative and subjunctive moods in conditional sentences:

PRESENT INDICATIVE	If he *needs* it . . .
	Wenn er es braucht . . .
PRESENT SUBJUNCTIVE	If he *needed* it . . .
	Wenn er es brauchte . . .
PAST SUBJUNCTIVE	If he *had needed* it . . .
	Wenn er es gebraucht hätte . . .

The form of the German subjunctive used in these clauses is called subjunctive II. (Subjunctive I is a less common mood that will be treated in chapter 13.)

1. Word order

Wenn (*if*) is a subordinating conjunction: it forces the *conjugated verb form to the end of the clause:*

> Wenn er es brauchte, . . .
> Wenn er es gebraucht hätte, . . .

(For a detailed explanation of subordinating conjunctions, see p. 203, "Subordinating Conjunctions.")

2. Present tense forms of subjunctive II

The present tense of subjunctive II is derived from the *past tense of the indicative.*

a. Weak (regular) verbs

In the case of weak verbs, the present tense of subjunctive II is identical to the past tense of the indicative.

ich brauchte	wir brauchten
du brauchtest	ihr brauchtet
er brauchte	sie brauchten

Wenn ich es **brauchte**, . . .   (If I *needed* it, . . .)
Wenn es nicht so viel **kostete**, . . .   (If it *didn't cost* so much, . . .)

b. Strong (irregular) verbs

To form the present tense of subjunctive II of strong verbs:

1. take the past tense stem of the indicative:

> **war**
> **ging**
> **kam**

2. add an umlaut where possible (**a**, **o**, and **u**):

> **wär-**
> **ging-**
> **käm-**

3. and add the following subjunctive endings:

ich wär	**e**	wir wär	**en**
du wär	**est**	ihr wär	**et**
er wär	**e**	sie wär	**en**

Wenn er hier **wäre**, . . .   (If he *were* here, . . .)
Wenn wir jetzt **gingen**, . . .   (If we *went* now, . . .)

c. Exceptions

A few very commonly used verbs form the present tense of subjunctive II by simply adding an umlaut to the past tense indicative. These verbs are:

1. **haben** and **werden**

Infinitive	Past Indicative	Present Subjunctive II
haben	hatte	**hätte**
werden	wurde	**würde**

2. four of the modals and **wissen**

Infinitive	Past Indicative	Present Subjunctive II
wissen	wußte	wüßte
dürfen	durfte	dürfte
können	konnte	könnte
mögen	mochte	möchte
müssen	mußte	müßte
but sollen	sollte	sollte
wollen	wollte	wollte

NOTE: **Sollte** and **wollte** do *not* take an umlaut in subjunctive II. The past tense indicative and the present subjunctive II are identical.

Wenn ich einen Wagen hätte, . . .   (If I *had* a car, . . .)
Wenn sie es tun könnten, . . .   (If they *could* do it, . . .)
Wenn er kommen wollte, . . .   (If he *wanted* to come, . . .)

Two other verbs form the present tense of subjunctive II in the same way, but their present subjunctive II forms are becoming old-fashioned and less commonly used:

Infinitive	Past Indicative	Present Subjunctive II
bringen	brachte	brächte
denken	dachte	dächte

A third group of exceptions has present subjunctive II forms that are rarely heard in modern standard German. They are often used in older writing, however, and it is important to be able to recognize them:

Infinitive	Past Indicative	Present Subjunctive II
brennen	brannte	brennte
kennen	kannte	kennte
nennen	nannte	nennte
rennen	rannte	rennte
helfen	half	hülfe
stehen	stand	stünde
sterben	starb	stürbe
werfen	warf	würfe

■ FORM DRILLS

Present Subjunctive II of Weak Verbs

Put the following *wenn*-clauses into the present tense of subjunctive II.

> Example: Wenn er es kauft . . .
> Wenn er es *kaufte* . . .

1. Wenn er mich fragt . . .
2. Wenn der Anzug nicht zuviel kostet . . .
3. Wenn sie es braucht . . .
4. Wenn wir es jetzt abschicken . . .
5. Wenn du in der Stadt wohnst . . .
6. Wenn ich es morgen mache . . .
7. Wenn er das glaubt . . .
8. Wenn Sie ein Zimmer jetzt reservieren . . .

Express in German

Express the following *if*-clauses in German, using the present tense of subjunctive II.

1. If I did it tomorrow . . .
2. If he believed that . . .
3. If you lived downtown . . .
4. If she needed it . . .
5. If the suit didn't cost too much . . .
6. If we sent it off now . . .
7. If he asked me . . .
8. If you reserved a room now . . .

Present Subjunctive II of the Exceptions

Put the following *wenn*-clauses into the present tense of subjunctive II.

> Example: Wenn er kommen kann . . .
> Wenn er kommen *könnte* . . .

1. Wenn ich Zeit habe . . .
2. Wenn wir es finden können . . .
3. Wenn er es weiß . . .

4. Wenn ich fragen darf ...
5. Wenn sie dir helfen kann ...
6. Wenn du mit ihm sprechen willst ...
7. Wenn ich muß ...
8. Wenn er seinen Wagen hat ...

Express in German

Express the following *if*-clauses in German, using the present tense of subjunctive II.

1. If we could find it ...
2. If he knew it ...
3. If I had time ...
4. If she could help you ...
5. If you wanted to talk with him ...
6. If I had to ...
7. If he had his car ...

Present Subjunctive II of Strong Verbs

Put the following *wenn*-clauses into the present tense of subjunctive II.

> Example: Wenn er heute kommt ...
> Wenn er heute *käme* ...

1. Wenn er hier ist ...
2. Wenn du früher kommst ...
3. Wenn wir ins Restaurant gehen ...
4. Wenn ich den Schnellzug nehme ...
5. Wenn wir eine ganze Woche bleiben ...
6. Wenn die Ferien länger sind ...
7. Wenn sie fliegen ...
8. Wenn du länger schläfst ...
9. Wenn sie mich einlädt ...
10. Wenn wir in einer Gaststätte* essen ...

---

* A *Gaststätte* is a typical informal German restaurant. The word *Restaurant* is reserved for more formal and expensive places and for foreign restaurants.

3. Subjunctive II revisited

Look at the following examples:

English	German
If he *came* later,	Wenn er später käme, . . .
If he'd *come* later, . . .	Wenn er später kommen würde, . . .
(If he *would come* later, . . .)	

As you can see, both English and German have alternate forms for the present tense of subjunctive II:

a. a *one*-word form (*came* / **käme**) which is derived from the past tense of the indicative, and

b. a *two*-word form (*would come* / **würde . . . kommen**) which consists of:

ENGLISH	would + infinitive
GERMAN	würde + infinitive

All of the one-word subjunctive forms can be found in written German, particularly in older texts. Modern spoken German, however, replaces many of the one-word forms with the **würde** + *infinitive* construction.

a. The one-word form is used with:

weak verbs*	(e.g., brauchte)
sein and haben	(e.g., wäre, hätte)
wissen and *the modals*	(e.g., wüßte, könnte)

b. **Würde** + *infinitive* is used with all other verbs.[†]

▮ DRILLS

Present Subjunctive II of Strong Verbs: *Revisited*

Put the following *wenn*-clauses into the present tense of subjunctive II. With the exception of *wäre*, use the *würde* + *infinitive* construction.

---

* In modern colloquial German the **würde**-construction is frequently used even with weak verbs. Instructors who prefer to have their students use the **würde**-construction with weak verbs should feel free to do so.

† The one-word forms of **gehen** (**ginge**) and **kommen** (**käme**) are occasionally used in spoken German, but the **würde**-construction is far more common.

Example: Wenn er heute kommt . . .
            Wenn er heute *kommen würde* . . .

1. Wenn sie fliegen . . .
2. Wenn wir eine ganze Woche bleiben . . .
3. Wenn er hier ist . . .
4. Wenn ich den Schnellzug nehme . . .
5. Wenn wir ins Restaurant gehen . . .
6. Wenn du länger schläfst . . .
7. Wenn wir in einer Gaststätte essen . . .
8. Wenn die Ferien länger sind . . .
9. Wenn du früher kommst . . .
10. Wenn sie mich einlädt . . .

Express in German

Express the following *if*-clauses in German. With the exception of *wäre*, use the *würde* + *infinitive* construction.

1. If we stayed a whole week . . .
2. If you slept longer . . .
3. If he were here . . .
4. If we went to a (**ins**) restaurant . . .
5. If I took the express train . . .
6. If they flew . . .
7. If the vacation were longer . . . (plural in German)
8. If you came earlier . . .
9. If we ate in a *Gaststätte* . . .
10. If she invited me . . .

Present Subjunctive II: Mixed Drills

Put the following *wenn*-clauses into the present tense of subjunctive II.

1. Wenn du früher kommst . . .
2. Wenn sie es braucht . . .
3. Wenn die Ferien länger sind . . .
4. Wenn er seinen Wagen hat . . .
5. Wenn wir ins Restaurant gehen . . .
6. Wenn der Anzug nicht zuviel kostet . . .

7. Wenn er das glaubt . . .
8. Wenn wir eine ganze Woche bleiben . . .
9. Wenn ich muß . . .
10. Wenn du länger schläfst . . .
11. Wenn wir es jetzt abschicken . . .
12. Wenn er es weiß . . .
13. Wenn ich den Schnellzug nehme . . .
14. Wenn sie mich fragt . . .
15. Wenn wir es finden können . . .
16. Wenn sie fliegen . . .
17. Wenn du in der Stadt wohnst . . .
18. Wenn du mit ihm sprechen willst . . .
19. Wenn sie mich einlädt . . .
20. Wenn sie ein Zimmer jetzt reservieren . . .

Express in German: Mixed Drills

Express the following *if*-clauses in German, using the present tense of subjunctive II.

1. If she asked me . . .
2. If he had his car . . .
3. If they flew . . .
4. If you came earlier . . .
5. If they reserved a room now . . .
6. If we stayed a whole week . . .
7. If I had to . . .
8. If she needed it . . .
9. If we went to a restaurant . . .
10. If you lived downtown . . .
11. If he knew it . . .
12. If the suit didn't cost so much . . .
13. If you slept longer . . .
14. If I could find it . . .
15. If he believed that . . .
16. If the vacation were longer . . .
17. If she invited me . . .
18. If you wanted to talk with him . . .
19. If I took the express train . . .
20. If we sent it off now . . .

4. Past tense forms of subjunctive II

The past tense forms of subjunctive II are similar to the *past perfect forms of the indicative.*

Past Perfect Indicative	Past Subjunctive II
Er wargekommen.	Wenn er gekommen wäre . . .
(He had come.)	(If he had come, . . .)
Er hattees gemacht.	Wenn er es gemacht hätte . . .
(He had done it.)	(If he had done it, . . .)

a. Forms

The past tense of subjunctive II is made up of:

wäreor hätte+ *past participle*

hätte	gemacht
wäre	gekommen

b. Usage

First look at a sentence in the past perfect indicative:

Er war gekommen.   (He had come.)

This is a statement of fact. The person in question actually did come. But now look at a past tense subjunctive II clause:

Wenn er gekommen wäre, . . .   (If he had come, . . .)

This clause makes a contrary-to-fact statement. The implication is that the person in question did *not* come. In other words, the past tense of subjunctive II is used to talk about things that did not actually happen.

■ DRILLS

Past Subjunctive II of Verbs Taking *haben*

Put the following *wenn*-clauses into the past tense of subjunctive II.

Example: Wenn er es gefunden *hat* . . .
                  Wenn er es gefunden *hätte* . . .

1. Wenn sie Zeit gehabt haben . . .
2. Wenn er den Schnellzug genommen hat . . .
3. Wenn du länger geschlafen hast . . .
4. Wenn sie ein Zimmer reserviert haben . . .
5. Wenn er ihn gefragt hat . . .
6. Wenn sie mich eingeladen hat . . .

Past Subjunctive II of Verbs Taking *sein*

Put the following *wenn*-clauses into the past tense of subjunctive II.

Example: Wenn er gefahren *ist* . . .
Wenn er gefahren *wäre* . . .

1. Wenn sie früher gekommen ist . . .
2. Wenn sie ins Restaurant gegangen ist . . .
3. Wenn er geflogen ist . . .
4. Wenn sie eine ganze Woche geblieben sind . . .
5. Wenn es schön gewesen ist . . .
6. Wenn er Arzt geworden ist . . .

Past Subjunctive II: Mixed Drills

Put the following *wenn*-clauses into the past tense of subjunctive II.

1. Wenn er ihn gefragt hat . . .
2. Wenn er es gewußt hat . . .
3. Wenn sie ins Restaurant gegangen sind . . .
4. Wenn du länger geschlafen hast . . .
5. Wenn sie geflogen ist . . .
6. Wenn sie ein Zimmer reserviert haben . . .
7. Wenn er den Schnellzug genommen hat . . .
8. Wenn sie eine ganze Woche geblieben sind . . .
9. Wenn es schön gewesen ist . . .
10. Wenn sie in der Stadt gewohnt hat . . .

Express in German: Mixed Drills

Express the following *if*-clauses in German, using the past tense of subjunctive II.

1. If he had come earlier . . .
2. If they had reserved a room . . .

3. If I had known it . . .
4. If she had flown . . .
5. If he had taken the express train . . .
6. If they had stayed a whole week . . .
7. If you had asked him . . .
8. If he had slept longer . . .
9. If they had gone to a (ins) restaurant . . .
10. If you had lived downtown (in the city) . . .

Present and Past Subjunctive II: Mixed Drills

Put the wenn-clauses into the appropriate tenses of subjunctive II.

1. Wenn der Anzug nicht so viel kostet . . .
2. Wenn du ihn gefragt hast . . .
3. Wenn sie fliegen . . .
4. Wenn er früher gekommen ist . . .
5. Wenn wir es finden können . . .
6. Wenn du länger schläfst . . .
7. Wenn er in der Stadt gewohnt hat . . .
8. Wenn sie es braucht . . .
9. Wenn die Ferien länger sind . . .
10. Wenn das Wetter schön gewesen ist . . .
11. Wenn ich den Schnellzug nehme . . .
12. Wenn sie ein Zimmer reserviert haben . . .
13. Wenn wir es jetzt abschicken . . .
14. Wenn du mit ihm sprechen willst . . .
15. Wenn sie ins Restaurant gegangen sind . . .

Express in German: Mixed Drills

1. If she needed it . . .
2. If they had reserved a room . . .
3. If we could find it . . .
4. If I took the express train . . .
5. If they had gone to a restaurant . . .
6. If the suit didn't cost so much . . .
7. If he had lived downtown . . .
8. If you slept longer . . .
9. If you wanted to speak with him . . .
10. If he had come earlier . . .

11. If they flew . . .
12. If we sent if off now . . .
13. If the weather had been nice . . .
14. If the vacation were longer . . .
15. If you had asked him . . .

LEVEL TWO

I. COMPLETE CONDITIONAL SENTENCES: THE DANN-CLAUSE

Conditional sentences follow an *if-then* (**wenn-dann**) pattern. So far you have seen only **wenn**-clauses. Now look at some complete conditional sentences with **dann**-clauses (*then*-clauses):

PRESENT INDICATIVE

Wenn ich Zeit habe, (dann) *gehe* ich ins Kino.
If I have time, (*then*) *I'll go to the movies.*

PRESENT SUBJUNCTIVE II

Wenn ich Zeit hätte, (dann) *würde* ich ins Kino *gehen.*
(If I had time, (*then*) *I would go to the movies.*)

PAST SUBJUNCTIVE II

Wenn ich Zeit gehabt hätte, (dann) *wäre* ich ins Kino *gegangen.*
(If I'd had time, (*then*) *I would have gone to the movies.*)

A. Present indicative

1. Word order

Whenever a conditional sentence begins with a **wenn**-clause, the **dann**-clause will begin with a conjugated verb. (Only the word **dann** can come before the verb, but **dann** is almost always omitted.)

Wenn ich Zeit habe, **gehe** ich ins Kino.

2. Punctuation

Wenn-clauses and **dann**-clauses are always separated by commas.

B. Present subjunctive II

1. Word order

> Wenn ich Zeit hätte, würde ich ins Kino gehen.

The conjugated verb form (*here:* **würde**) is the first element of the **dann**-clause. If an infinitive (*here:* **gehen**) is used to complete the meaning of the clause, it must appear at the end of the sentence.

2. Usage

a. In **dann**-clauses the one-word subjunctive II form is used with:

the *modal auxiliaries* (e.g., **könnte**)

> Wenn ich Zeit hätte, könnte ich es machen.

and **sein** (e.g. **wäre**)*

> Wenn wir fliegen würden, wären wir in zwei Stunden da.

b. **Würde** + *infinitive* is used with all other verbs. (In contrast to **wenn**-clause usage, even **haben, wissen,** and *weak verbs* use the **würde**-construction in the **dann**-clause.)

> Wenn er das Geld hätte, würde er es kaufen.

C. Past subjunctive II

1. Word order

Look at the following conditional sentence:

> Wenn ich Zeit gehabt hätte, wäre ich ins Kino gegangen.

a. The conjugated verb form (**wäre**) is the first element in the **dann**-clause.

b. The past participle (**gegangen**) is the last element in the clause.

---

* Modern colloquial German frequently uses **würde . . sein** rather than **wäre** in the **dann**-clause:

> Wenn wir fliegen würden, würden wir in Zwei Stunden da sein.

II. INVERSION IN CONDITIONAL SENTENCES

Look at the following sentences:

PRESENT INDICATIVE   Ich komme mit, wenn ich das Geld habe.

PRESENT SUBJUNCTIVE II   Ich würde mitkommen, wenn ich das Geld hätte.

PAST SUBJUNCTIVE II   Ich wäre mitgekommen, wenn ich das Geld
gehabt hätte.

As you see, a conditional sentence can begin with a **dann**-clause. When this is the case:

a. The word **dann** is never used.

b. The **dann**-clause uses normal declarative word order (verb second).

III. MIXED TENSES IN CONDITIONAL SENTENCES

When the situation requires it, both English and German can mix tenses within a sentence. The logical pattern of such sentences is always:

If X *had happened* in the past, Y *would be* the case now.

PAST SUBJUNCTIVE II   PRESENT SUBJUNCTIVE II

Wenn du früher gekommen wärest,   hätten wir jetzt weniger zu tun.

(If you *had come* earlier,   we *would have* less to do now.)

IV. BEGINNING THE WENN-CLAUSE WITH A VERB

Kommt er heute nicht, (dann) kommt er morgen.
(If he doesn't come today, he'll come tomorrow.)

Hätte ich das gewußt, (dann) wäre ich zu Hause geblieben.
(Had I known that, I would have stayed home.)

Wenn-clauses can be introduced by a verb, in which case the word **wenn** disappears—and the word **dann** may be replaced by **so:**

Kommt er heute nicht, (so) kommt er morgen.

■ DRILLS

Present Tense Subjunctive II: the *dann*-clause

Form the suggested *dann*-clauses using the present tense of subjunctive II.

Example: Wenn ich Zeit hätte, ich / gehen / in / Kino
Wenn ich Zeit hätte, *würde* ich ins Kino *gehen*.

1. Wenn er mich fragte, ich / sagen / es ihm
2. Wenn die Ferien länger wären, wir / fahren / nach Europa
3. Wenn es wärmer wäre, wir / können / sitzen / draußen
4. Wenn ich den Schnellzug nehmen würde, ich / ankommen / früher
5. Wenn Sie ein Zimmer jetzt reservierten, Sie / haben / kein / Schwierigkeiten
6. Wenn du nicht hier wärest, ich / müssen / machen / es allein
7. Wenn ich Zeit hätte, ich / machen / es
8. Wenn er hier wäre, du / wissen / es
9. Wenn du früher kommen würdest, ich / abholen / dich
10. Wenn er seinen Wagen hätte, er / können / fahren / uns nach Hause
11. Wenn sie es brauchte, wir / geben / es ihr
12. Wenn du länger schlafen würdest, du / sein / nicht so müde

Express in German: the *dann*-clause

Form complete German sentences in the present tense of subjunctive II.

1. Wenn ich Zeit hätte, _____ .
   (I'd do it)

2. Wenn es wärmer wäre, _____ .
   (we could sit outside)

3. Wenn du früher kommen würdest, _____ .
   (I'd pick you up)

4. Wenn er hier wäre, _____ .
   (you'd know it)

5. Wenn die Ferien länger wären, _____ .
   (we'd go to Europe)

6. Wenn er seinen Wagen hätte, _____ .
                     (he could drive us home)

7. Wenn ich den Schnellzug nehmen würde, _____ .
                              (I'd arrive earlier)

8. Wenn du nicht hier wärest, _____ .
                    (I'd have to do it alone)

9. Wenn sie es brauchte, _____ .
                (we'd give it to her)

10. Wenn du länger schlafen würdest, _____ .
                       (you wouldn't be so tired)

11. Wenn er mich fragte, _____ .
              (I'd tell him)

12. Wenn Sie ein Zimmer jetzt reservierten, _____
                          (you wouldn't have any
_____ .
difficulties)

Past Tense Subjunctive II: the *dann*-clause

Form the suggested *dann*-clauses using the past tense of subjunctive II.

    Example: Wenn ich Zeit gehabt hätte, ich / gehen / in / Kino
                   Wenn ich Zeit gehabt hätte, *wäre* ich ins Kino *gegangen.*

1. Wenn er es gewußt hätte, er / sagen / es Ihnen.
2. Wenn der Anzug nicht so viel gekostet hätte, ich / kaufen / ihn
3. Wenn wir geflogen wären, wir / sein / in zwei Stunden da
4. Wenn du früher gekommen wärest, wir / haben / genug Zeit
5. Wenn die Ferien länger gewesen wären, ich / fahren / nach Europa
6. Wenn wir ins Restaurant gegangen wären, wir / verpassen / Zug
7. Wenn er das Geld gehabt hätte, er / nehmen / Mantel
8. Wenn du in der Stadt gewohnt hättest, du / brauchen / kein / Wagen
9. Wenn der Film nicht so lange gedauert hätte, wir / kommen / nicht
so spät nach Hause

Express in German: the *dann*-clause

Form complete German sentences in the past tense of subjunctive II.

1. Wenn du früher gekommen wärest, _____ .
                        (we would have had enough time)

2. Wenn er das Geld gehabt hätte, _____ .
                     (he would have taken the coat)

3. Wenn die Ferien länger gewesen wären, _____.
                                    (I would have gone to Europe)
4. Wenn wir ins Restaurant gegangen wären, _____
   _____.   (we would have
   missed the train)

5. Wenn der Anzug nicht so viel gekostet hätte, _____.
                                         (I would have bought it)
6. Wenn wir geflogen wären, _____.
                           (we would have been there in two hours)
7. Wenn er es gewußt hätte, _____.
                           (he would have told you)
8. Wenn du in der Stadt gewohnt hättest, _____.
                                    (you wouldn't have needed a car)
9. Wenn der Film nicht so lange gedauert hätte, _____
   _____.   (we wouldn't have
   come home so late)

Substitutions: Full Sentences

Put the following indicative sentences into present subjunctive II and past subjunctive II. Do all drills first in the present, then do them all in the past.

   Example: Wenn ich Zeit habe, gehe ich ins Kino.
              Wenn ich Zeit hätte, würde ich ins Kino gehen.
              Wenn ich Zeit gehabt hätte, wäre ich ins Kino gegangen.

1. Wenn er es weiß, sagt er es dir.
2. Wenn sie es braucht, geben wir es ihr.
3. Wenn du früher kommst, haben wir genug Zeit.
4. Wenn du in der Stadt wohnst, brauchst du keinen Wagen.
5. Wenn wir ins Restaurant gehen, verpassen wir den Zug.
6. Wenn ich Zeit habe, löse ich einen Reisescheck ein.
7. Wenn sie fliegen, sind sie in zwei Stunden da.
8. Wenn der Anzug nicht so viel kostet, kaufe ich ihn.
9. Wenn ich den Schnellzug nehme, komme ich früher an.
10. Wenn das Wetter schön ist, gehen wir schwimmen.

Synthetic Exercises: dann-clauses

These exercises include both present and past tense subjunctive II sentences as well as an occasional indicative sentence.

Form the suggested *dann*-clauses. These clauses must agree *logically* with the *wenn*-clauses.

> Example: Wenn ich Zeit hätte, (ich / gehen / Kino).
> Wenn ich Zeit hätte, *würde* ich ins Kino *gehen*.

1. Wenn Inge näher wohnte, (ich / besuchen / sie / öfter).
2. Wenn die Ferien länger wären, (wir / fahren / nach Europa).
3. Wenn ich es gefunden hätte, (ich / geben / es ihm).
4. Wenn es wärmer wäre, (wir / können / sitzen / draußen).
5. Wenn ich das gewußt hätte, (ich / weggehen / früher).
6. Wenn wir eine ganze Woche bleiben würden, (es / sein / billiger).
7. Wenn ich es finden kann, (ich / geben / es dir).
8. Wenn er hier wäre, (du / wissen / es).
9. Wenn wir ins Restaurant gegangen wären, (wir / verpassen / Zug).
10. Wenn er mich fragte, (ich / sagen / es ihm).
11. Wenn ich ihre Telefonnummer wüßte, (ich / anrufen / sie).
12. Wenn wir keine nette Wohnung finden, (wir / mieten / Haus).
13. Wenn sie geflogen wären, (sie / sein / in zwei Stunden da).
14. Wenn ich Zeit hätte, (ich / einlösen / Reisescheck).
15. Wenn du in der Stadt gewohnt hättest, (du / brauchen / kein / Wagen).
16. Wenn wir die Adresse wüßten, (wir / können / finden / Haus / leichter).
17. Wenn Sie ein Zimmer jetzt reservierten, (Sie / haben / kein / Schwierigkeiten).
18. Wenn du mir die Briefe gibst, (ich / einstecken / sie).
19. Wenn der Film nicht so lange gedauert hätte, (wir / kommen / nicht so spät / nach Hause).
20. Wenn du nicht hier wärest, (ich / müssen / machen / es allein).

Synthetic Exercises: *wenn*-clauses

Form the suggested *wenn*-clauses.

1. Es wäre leichter, (wenn / du / wohnen / in / Stadt).
2. Wir würden Tennis spielen, (wenn / es / sein / nicht so heiß).
3. Ich hätte das Buch bestellt, (wenn / ich / denken / daran).
4. Es wäre schneller, (wenn / Sie / nehmen / Zug).
5. Er würde kommen, (wenn / er / können).
6. Ich rufe dich an, (wenn / er / ankommen).
7. Sie wären mitgekommen, (wenn / sie / haben / Geld).

8. Ich würde diesen Mantel kaufen, (wenn / er / kosten / nicht so viel).
9. Wir hätten genug Zeit gehabt, (wenn / du / kommen / früher).
10. Sie würde es dir sagen, (wenn / sie / wissen / es).
11. Es wäre besser, (wenn / du / kommen / später).
12. Ich würde es nur machen, (wenn / ich / müssen).
13. Wir können ins Kino gehen, (wenn / du / wollen).
14. Ich hätte mehr verdient, (wenn / ich / werden / Arzt).
15. Wir wären schwimmen gegangen, (wenn / Wetter / sein / schön).
16. Sie würden es morgen bekommen, (wenn / wir / abschicken / es jetzt).
17. Ich sage es ihm, (wenn / ich / sehen / ihn).
18. Es wäre leichter, (wenn / wir / haben / Wagen).
19. Ich hätte dir geholfen, (wenn / du / anrufen / mich).

Synthetic Exercises: Mixed Tenses

Form the *second* clause of each sentence using the present tense subjunctive II.

1. Wenn ich geflogen wäre, (ich / sein / jetzt schon in Berlin).
2. Wenn Sie Ihre Arbeit gestern vorbereitet hätten, (Sie / haben / heute weniger zu tun).
3. Sie hätte es mir nicht gesagt, (wenn / es / sein / nicht wahr).
4. Wenn du später gegessen hättest, (du / sein / jetzt nicht so hungrig).

Synthetic Exercises: Mixed Tenses

Form the *first* clause of each sentence using the past tense of subjunctive II.

1. (Wenn / ich / fliegen), wäre ich jetzt schon in Berlin.
2. (Wenn / du / essen / später), wärest du jetzt nicht so hungrig.
3. (Wenn / Sie / vorbereiten / Arbeit / gestern), würden Sie heute weniger zu tun haben.
4. (Sie / sagen / es mir nicht), wenn es nicht wahr wäre.

Synthetic Exercises: *wenn*-clauses and *dann*-clauses

Form the suggested conditional sentences.

1. Wenn ich ihre Telefonnummer wüßte, (ich / anrufen / sie).
2. Ich würde den Mantel kaufen, (wenn / er / kosten / nicht so viel).
3. Es wäre schneller, (wenn / Sie / nehmen / Zug).

4. Wenn wir ins Restaurant gegangen wären, (wir / verpassen / Zug).
5. Ich würde es nur machen, (wenn / ich / müssen).
6. Wenn ich es finden kann, (ich / geben / es dir).
7. Wir hätten genug Zeit gehabt, (wenn / du / kommen / früher).
8. Wenn ich Zeit hätte, (ich / einlösen / Reisescheck).
9. Wenn es wärmer wäre, (wir / können / sitzen / draußen).
10. Ich hätte das Buch bestellt, (wenn / ich / denken / daran).
11. Es wäre leichter, (wenn / du / wohnen / in / Stadt).
12. Wenn ich geflogen wäre, (ich / sein / jetzt schon in Berlin).
13. Ich hätte mehr verdient, (wenn / ich / werden / Arzt).
14. Wir können ins Kino gehen, (wenn / du / wollen).
15. Wenn ich das gewußt hätte, (ich / weggehen / früher).
16. Wenn Inge näher wohnte, (ich / besuchen / sie öfter).
17. Ich hätte dir geholfen, (wenn / du / anrufen / mich).
18. Er würde kommen, (wenn / er / können).
19. Sie würden es morgen bekommen, (wenn / wir / abschicken / es jetzt).
20. Wenn ich es gefunden hätte, (ich / geben / es ihm).
21. Wenn er hier wäre, (du / wissen / es).
22. Ich rufe dich an, (wenn / er / ankommen).
23. Wenn du später gegessen hättest, (du / sein / jetzt nicht so hungrig).
24. Es wäre besser, (wenn / Sie / kommen / später).

Express in German

1. If I had time, I'd go to the movies.
2. It would be easier if you lived downtown.
3. If he were here, you'd know it.
4. I would have ordered the book if I had thought of it.
5. He'd come if he could.
6. If Inge lived closer, I'd visit her more often.
7. It would be better if you came later.
8. If I had found it, I would have given it to him.
9. If you had eaten later, you wouldn't be so hungry now.
10. I'd buy the coat if it didn't cost so much.
11. I'll call you up if he comes.
12. We would have had enough time if you had come earlier.
13. If it were warmer, we could sit outside.
14. I would have helped you if you had called me up.
15. If I had time, I'd cash a traveler's check.
16. It would be faster if you took the train.

17. I'd only do it if I had to.
18. They'd get it tomorrow if we sent it off now.
19. If I knew her telephone number, I'd call her up.
20. If we had gone to a (**ins**) restaurant, we would have missed the train.
21. If he can find it, he'll give it to you.
22. If I had known that, I would have left earlier.

LEVEL THREE

I. CONDITIONAL SENTENCES WITH MODAL AUXILIARIES

Look at the following conditional sentences that have modal expressions in the **dann**-clause:

PRESENT SUBJUNCTIVE II	Wenn du früher kommen würdest, könnte ich dich abholen.
PAST SUBJUNCTIVE II	Wenn du früher gekommen wärest, hätte ich dich abholen können.

A. Present tense of subjunctive II with modals

The **würde**-construction is not used with modal auxiliaries, not even in the **dann**-clause:

Wenn du früher kommen würdest, könnte ich dich abholen.

B. Past tense of subjunctive II with modals

1. *Double infinitive in the dann-clause*

Wenn du früher gekommen wärest, hätte ich dich abholen können.

Abholen können is a double infinitive construction. (For a complete explanation of double infinitives, see p. 157, "Compound Tenses of Modal Auxiliaries.")

2. Double infinitive in the wenn-clause

Look at a new sentence, one with a modal expression in the **wenn**-clause:

> Ich hätte ihn gefragt, wenn ich ihn hätte finden können.
> (I would have asked him if I could have found him.)

Normally the conjugated verb (e.g., **hätte**) is forced to the end of a **wenn**-clause. But the double infinitive has absolute claim on final position in a clause, which means that the conjugated verb has to come before it:

> . . . wenn ich ihn *hätte* finden können

This unusual word order occurs only with double infinitives in *subordinate clauses.*

3. Past subjunctive II of modals without dependent infinitives

> Ich hätte es gemacht, wenn ich gekonnt hätte.

When there is no dependent infinitive in a modal expression, the normal past participle is used in forming the past tense of subjunctive II:

> . . . wenn ich *gekonnt* hätte

C. Subjunctive II with modals in simple sentences

Up to this point you have seen subjunctive II with modals in conditional sentences, which are made up of two clauses. But modal expressions in subjunctive II are also common in simple sentences (sentences consisting of only one clause):

PRESENT SUBJUNCTIVE II   Du solltest wirklich nach Hause gehen.
                              (You really should go home.)

PAST SUBJUNCTIVE II   Du hättest wirklich nach Hause gehen sollen.
                              (You really should have gone home.)

D. Contrastive grammar

INDICATIVE	Du kannst es tun.	(You *can* do it.)
PRES. SUBJ. II	Du könntest es tun.	(You *could* do it.)
PAST SUBJ. II	Du hättest es tun können.	(You *could have done* it.)

Notice how differently English and German form the past tense of the subjunctive with modal auxiliaries:

> Du **hättest** es **tun können**.
> (You *could*   *have done* it.)

The German modal construction is "regular"; that is to say, the past tense of subjunctive II is formed in the usual way:

PRESENT TENSE	Du **könntest** es tun.
PAST TENSE	Du **hättest** es tun **können**.

But English does something unusual here. It leaves the modal alone and changes the dependent infinitive:

PRESENT TENSE	You could *do* it.
PAST TENSE	You could *have done* it.

■ DRILLS

Substitution Drills: Simple Sentences

Put the following indicative sentences into the present subjunctive II and the past subjunctive II.

> Example: Du sollst wirklich nach Hause gehen.
> Du solltest wirklich nach Hause gehen.
> Du hättest wirklich nach Hause gehen sollen.

1. Du kannst es machen.
2. Er soll um sieben Uhr vorbeikommen.
3. Dann müssen Sie es ihm sagen.
4. Sie können es vergessen.
5. Was sollen wir machen?

Substitution Drills: Conditional Sentences

Put the following indicative sentences into the present subjunctive II and the past subjunctive II.

1. Wenn sie ihren Wagen hat, kann sie uns nach Hause fahren.
2. Wenn es wärmer ist, können wir draußen sitzen.

3. Wenn du mit ihm sprechen willst, kannst du ihn zu Hause anrufen.
4. Wir können ins Kino gehen, wenn du willst.
5. Ich gebe es dir, wenn ich es finden kann.
6. Wenn wir Zeit haben, können wir noch ein Glas Wein trinken.
7. Ich mache es nur, wenn ich muß.
8. Wenn der Regen aufhört, können wir spazieren gehen.
9. Wenn er Karten haben will, muß er rechtzeitig schreiben.
10. Er kommt, wenn er kann.

Synthetic Exercises: *wenn*-clauses and *dann*-clauses

These exercises include both present and past tense subjunctive II sentences.

Form the suggested conditional sentences.

1. Wenn der Regen aufhörte, (wir / können) / spazierengehen).
2. Wenn es wärmer gewesen wäre, (wir / können / sitzen / draußen).
3. Ich hätte es nur gemacht, (wenn / ich / müssen).
4. Wir könnten ins Kino gehen, (wenn / du / wollen).
5. Es wäre nett gewesen, (wenn / Sie / können / kommen).
6. Wenn wir die Adresse wüßten, (wir / können / finden / Haus / leichter).
7. Er würde fragen, (wenn / er / wollen / wissen / es).
8. Wenn wir Zeit gehabt hätten, (wir / können / trinken / noch ein Glas Wein).
9. Es wäre besser, (wenn / Sie / können / erledigen / es früher).
10. Sie wäre gekommen, (wenn / sie / können).
11. Wenn du näher wohntest, (ich / können / besuchen / dich öfter).
12. Ich hätte es dir gegeben, (wenn / ich / können / finden / es).

Express in German

1. What should we do?
2. If we knew the address, we could find the house more easily.
3. You could have done it.
4. If it had been warmer, we could have sat outside.
5. If you lived closer, I could visit you more often.
6. She would have come if she could have.
7. I would have given it to you if I could have found it.
8. Then you would have to tell him.
9. He'd ask if he wanted to know (it).

10. If we had had time, we could have drunk another glass of wine.
11. It would be better if you could take care of it earlier.
12. He should have come by at seven o'clock.
13. I only would have done it if I had had to.
14. If the rain stopped, we could take a walk.
15. We could go to the movies if you wanted to.
16. It would have been nice if you could have come.

LEVEL FOUR

I. OTHER USES OF SUBJUNCTIVE II

A. Wishes

Look at the following sentences:

Wenn er nur hier wäre!	If he were only here!
Wenn er nur hier gewesen wäre!	If he had only been here!
Wenn er mir nur antworten würde!	If he would only answer me!
Wenn er mir nur geantwortet hätte!	If he had only answered me!
Wenn er nur kommen könnte!	If he could only come!
Wenn er nur hätte kommen können!	If he could only have come!

1. By their very nature, wishes are *contrary to facts* as they are now; for this reason, subjunctive II is used in expressing wishes.

The basic structure of such sentences is very simple; you just add **nur** (only, just) to a subjunctive II **wenn**-clause:

Wenn er kommen könnte . . .	If he could come . . .
Wenn er **nur** kommen könnte!	If he could only come!

Like **nicht** and **wohl**, **nur** comes after objects but before adverbs:

Wenn ich ihn **nur** heute sehen könnte!

2. In expressing wishes, the **würde**-construction is used with all verbs except:

haben, **sein**, **wissen**, and the *modal auxiliaries*

Note that the **würde**-construction is used even with weak verbs in wishes:

Wenn er mir nur antworten würde!

B. Polite forms

Kann ich mitkommen?	Can I come along?
Könnte ich mitkommen?	Could I come along?
Werden Sie mir helfen?	Will you help me?
Würden Sie mir helfen?	Would you help me?
Darf ich Sie stören?	May I disturb you?
Dürfte ich Sie stören?	Might I disturb you?
Sind Sie dagegen?	Are you against it?
Wären Sie dagegen?	Would you be against it?
Haben Sie jetzt Zeit?	Do you have time now?
Hätten Sie jetzt Zeit?	Would you have time now?

German, like English, uses the present tense of the subjunctive as a polite form. The use of the subjunctive makes a request or a question more tentative, less restrictive, which is a courtesy.

NOTE: In sentences of this kind the **würde**-construction is used with all verbs except:

sein ,haben , and the modals

C. ALS OB (ALS WENN) = as if (as though)

Als ob ich das nicht wüßte!   *As if* I didn't know that!

Als ob ich das nicht gewußt hätte!   *As if* I hadn't known that!

Als ob-constructions refer to contrary-to-fact situations and therefore require you to use subjunctive II. Like **wenn**-constructions, they require subordinate word order, that is, the conjugated verb comes at the end of the clause:

Als ob ich das nicht wüßte !

In **als ob**-clauses, the **würde**-construction is used with all verbs except:

sein ,haben ,wissen , and the modals

DRILLS

Subjunctive II: Wishes

Use the following elements to express wishes in both the present and the past subjunctive II.

> Example: Wenn / er / sein / nur / hier / !
> Wenn er nur hier wäre!
> Wenn er nur hier gewesen wäre!

1. Wenn / wir / haben / nur / Zeit / !
2. Wenn / sie / zurückkommen / nur / !
3. Wenn / ich / wissen / das / nur / !
4. Wenn / er / fragen / mich / nur / !
5. Wenn / ich / sein / nur / sicher / !
6. Wenn / wir / können / schlafen / nur / länger / !
7. Wenn / er / verkaufen / es / nur / !
8. Wenn / ich / können / tun / es / nur / !

Express in German

1. If I were only sure!
2. If he had only sold it!
3. If we only had time!
4. If I could only do it!
5. If he had only asked me!
6. If I had only known that!
7. If only she would come back!
8. If only we could have slept longer!

Subjunctive II: Polite forms

Put the following indicative sentences into subjunctive II to stress politeness.

1. Können wir länger bleiben?
2. Ist das Ihnen recht?
3. Werden Sie ihn fragen?
4. Haben Sie jetzt Zeit?

5. Darf ich etwas sagen?
6. Werden Sie mir einen Gefallen tun?
7. Kann ich Ihnen eine Tasse Kaffe bringen?
8. Werden Sie das für mich erledigen?

Express in German

1. Would you have time now?
2. Could I bring you a cup of coffee?
3. Would you do me a favor?
4. Might I say something?
5. Would you ask him?
6. Could you stay longer?
7. Would that be all right with you?
8. Would you take care of that for me?

Subjunctive II: *als ob*-expressions

Use the following elements to form subjunctive II sentences in the tenses indicated.

1. Als ob / ich / wissen / das / nicht / ! (*present* and *past*)
2. Als ob / sie / vergessen / das / ! (*present* and *past*)
3. Als ob / wir / tun / so etwas / ! (*present* and *past*)
4. Als ob / mein Zimmer / sein / zu warm / ! (*present* and *past*)
5. Als ob / ich / haben / eine Chance / ! (*present* and *past*)
6. Als ob / man / können / haben / zu viel Geld / ! (*present*)
7. Er sah aus // als ob / er schlafen / tagelang / nicht (*past*)
8. Es war // als ob / wir / sehen / es nie vorher (*past*)
9. Als ob / ich / denken / daran / nicht / ! (*past*)

Express in German

1. As if I didn't know that!
2. As if I had a chance!
3. As if I hadn't thought of that!
4. It was as if we had never seen it before.
5. As if one could have too much money!

6. He looked as if he hadn't slept for days.
7. As if we'd do something like that!

■ MIXED DRILLS (all levels)

Form the suggested sentences using subjunctive II. When the tense required
is not obvious, it is indicated in parentheses.

1. Wenn ich Zeit hätte // ich / einlösen / Reisescheck
2. Ich würde den Mantel kaufen // wenn / er / kosten / nicht so viel
3. Ich hätte das Buch bestellt // wenn / ich / denken / daran
4. Wenn wir ins Restaurant gegangen wären // wir / verpassen / Zug
5. Wenn / ich / können / tun / es / nur / ! (*present*)
6. Es wäre schneller // wenn / Sie / nehmen / Zug
7. Was / sollen / wir / machen (*present*)
8. Wir hätten genug Zeit gehabt // wenn / du / kommen / früher
9. Können / wir / bleiben / länger / ? (*present*)
10. Sie würde kommen // wenn / sie / können
11. Wenn du später gegessen hättest // du / sein / jetzt nicht so hungrig
12. Als ob / ich / wissen / das / nicht / ! (*present*)
13. Es wäre besser // wenn / du / wohnen / in / Stadt
14. Wenn wir Zeit gehabt hätten // wir / trinken / noch ein Glas Wein
15. Du / können / es / machen (*past*)
16. Sein / das / Ihnen / recht / ? (*present*)
17. Wenn ich ihre Telefonnummer wüßte // ich / anrufen / sie
18. Es wäre nett gewesen // wenn / Sie / können / kommen
19. Wir / sollen / besuchen / ihn / gestern (*past*)
20. Ich würde es nur machen // wenn / ich / müssen
21. Wenn der Film nicht so lange gedauert hätte // wir / kommen / nicht so spät nach Hause
22. Als ob / ich / denken / daran / nicht / ! (*past*)
23. Sie wäre gestern gekommen // wenn / sie / können
24. Wenn er hier wäre // du / wissen / es
25. Wenn / er / fragen / mich / nur / ! (*past*)
26. Tun / Sie / mir / ein / Gefallen / ? (*present*)
27. Wenn wir einen Stadtplan hätten // wir / können / finden / Haus / leichter

28. Sie wären mitgekommen // wenn / sie / haben / Geld
29. Wenn du näher wohntest // ich / können / besuchen / dich / öfter

Express in German

1. It would be faster if you took the train.
2. Could we stay longer?
3. If I knew her telephone number, I'd call her up.
4. We would have had enough time, if you had come earlier.
5. If we had a map, we could find the house easier.
6. What should we do?
7. If we had gone to a restaurant, we would have missed the train.
8. She'd come if she could.
9. As if I didn't know that!
10. I would have ordered the book if I had thought of it.
11. If we had had time, we could have drunk another glass of wine.
12. I'd buy the coat if it didn't cost so much.
13. If I could only do it!
14. If you had eaten later, you wouldn't be so hungry now.
15. I'd only do it if I had to.
16. Would you do me a favor?
17. We should have visited him yesterday.
18. It would have been nice if they could have come.
19. If I had time, I'd cash a traveler's check.
20. If he had only asked me!
21. As if I hadn't thought of that!
22. They would have come along if they had had the money.
23. If you lived closer, I could visit you more often.
24. You could have done it.
25. She would have come if she could have.
26. It would be easier if you lived downtown.
27. Would that be all right with you?
28. If he were here, you'd know it.
29. If the film hadn't lasted so long, we wouldn't have come home so late.

Infinitival
Constructions

11

A. Basic pattern: the infinitival clause

English and German treat infinitival clauses in essentially the same way:

> Er bat mich, ihm zu helfen.
> (He asked me *to help*.)

> Es ist Zeit, nach Hause zu gehen.
> (It's time *to go* home.)

In infinitival constructions, the English infinitive is preceded by the word *to* (*to* help) and the German infinitive is always preceded by **zu** (*zu* **helfen**). The basic difference between the languages is that the *German infinitive must stand at the end of its clause:*

> . . . , ihm zu helfen.
> (. . . , *to help* him.)

> . . . , nach Hause zu gehen.
> (. . . , *to go* home.)

In both English and German the infinitive can take an object (**ihm** zu helfen), and it can be used with prepositional phrases and other expressions of time, manner or place (e.g., **nach Hause** zu gehen).

NOTE 1: With separable-prefix verbs (e.g., **wieder·sehen**), the zu comes between the prefix and the basic verb:

> Es ist nett, Sie wieder**zu**sehen.
> (It's nice to see you again.)

NOTE 2: When an infinitival construction consists *only of an infinitive* + **zu** (e.g., **zu arbeiten**), it is no longer treated as a complete clause.

> Er fing an **zu arbeiten.**
> Er fing **zu arbeiten** an.
> (He started to work.)

You have the option of either incorporating it into the main clause (Er fing **zu arbeiten** an) or putting it after the main clause (Er fing an **zu arbeiten**). And unlike complete clauses, it is not set off from the main clause by a comma. But as soon as another element is added to the infinitival construction, it is considered to be a complete clause and it must be separated from the main clause by a comma:

> Er fing an, **bei der Bank** zu arbeiten.
> (He started to work at the bank.)

B. UM . . . ZU, OHNE . . . ZU, STATT . . . ZU

The prepositions **um, ohne,** and **statt*** often introduce infinitival clauses:

um . . . zu	Ich arbeite nachts, **um** mehr Geld **zu** verdienen. (I work nights [*in order*] *to* make more money.)
ohne . . . zu	Er hat es getan, **ohne** mich **zu** fragen. (He did it *without* ask*ing* me.)
statt . . . zu	**Statt** hier **zu** sitzen, sollten wir etwas tun. (*Instead of* sitt*ing* here, we should do something.)

---

* **Statt** and *an*statt mean exactly the same, but the shorter form **statt** is more common in conversational German.

1. **Um . . . zu** indicates purpose. It must be used (instead of just **zu**) when you can sensibly use *in order to* in the equivalent English sentence.

2. **Ohne . . . zu** and **statt . . . zu** are used with infinitives, whereas the equivalent English expressions use an –**ing** form of the verb:

. . . , ohne mich zu fragen	without *asking* me.
Statt hier zu sitzen, . . .	Instead of *sitting* here, . . .

C. SEIN + ZU + infinitive

Look at the following examples:

> Das ist leicht zu machen
> (That *is* easy *to do*.)
>
> So etwas ist nicht leicht zu finden
> (Something like that *isn't* easy *to find*.)

English and German both follow the same pattern, but it is far more common in German than it is in English. In fact, many German sentences of this type do not have exact English counterparts:

> Das ist nicht zu machen
> (That can't be done.)
>
> Das ist in jedem Kaufhaus zu finden
> (That can be found in any department store.)

When the pattern doesn't fit English usage, you usually find *can + a passive infinitive:*

> ist nicht zu machen = *can't be done*

The passive infinitive consists of *be + a past participle,* e.g., *be done.*

D. Contrastive grammar

There are certain circumstances in which English will use infinitival constructions and German will not. Note carefully three situations in which English and German go very different ways:

1. *when a subordinate clause is introduced by a question word*

I don't know *what* to do.	Ich weiß nicht, **was** ich machen sollte.*
who to see.	**wen** ich sehen sollte.
where to go.	**wohin** ich gehen sollte.
when to come.	**wann** ich kommen sollte.

In such circumstances English can choose between two constructions:

and
I don't know *what to do.*
I don't know *what I should do.*

German has no such choice. It always uses a construction similar to the second English example, that is, a full clause with a *subject* and a *conjugated verb:*

Ich weiß nicht, **was ich machen sollte.**

2. *when **sagen** is used in the introductory clause*

He *told* me *to do* it.
He *told* me *that I should do it.*   Er **sagte** mir, **daß ich es tun sollte.**

Here again, English has a choice, whereas German does not. After **sagen,** German always uses a full clause with a subject and a conjugated verb (most commonly a form of **sollen**).

But when another verb is substituted for *sagen,* an infinitival clause is used:

Er befahl mir, das **zu tun.**
(He ordered me *to do* that.)

3. *the special case of **wollen***

He wants <u>*her*</u> *to come along.*
Er will, **daß sie mitkommt.**

The English verb *wants* can take an object, in this case *her.* The object (*her*) also functions as *subject of the infinitive: she* is to come along. Such a construction is impossible in German. Instead, German uses a complete **daß**-clause with a *subject* and a *conjugated verb* (e.g., **daß sie mitkommt.**)

NOTE 1: **Er will *es* tun.**

---

* The subjunctive II form **sollte** is common in such expressions.

In this sentence, **es** is the object of **tun** (to do *it*), not of **wollen.** In such constructions the modal (**wollen**) cannot take an object, but the dependent infinitive (**tun**) can.

NOTE 2: **Möchten** is a polite form of **wollen** and it is used with the same constructions:

Er möchte, daß sie mitkommt.
(He *would like* her to come along.)

 DRILLS

Synthetic Exercises: Basic Infinitival Clauses

1. Es ist Zeit // gehen / nach Hause
2. Er hat versprochen // geben / es mir
3. Es ist nett // wiedersehen / dich
4. Er bat mich // helfen / ihm
5. Es hörte auf // regnen
6. Darf ich Sie bitten // nehmen / Platz
7. Es ist zu spät // gehen / heute abend / in / Kino
8. Wir haben vor // fahren / nächsten Sommer / nach Deutschland
9. Es ist sinnlos // warten / länger
10. Es ist fast unmöglich / kriegen / Karten / jetzt
11. Er bat mich // fahren / ihn / nach Hause

Express in German

1. He promised to give it to me.
2. It's time to go home.
3. He asked me to help him.
4. It stopped raining.
5. It's nice to see you again.
6. It's senseless to wait longer.
7. May I ask you to take a seat?
8. It's almost impossible to get tickets now.
9. We plan to go to Germany next summer.
10. It's too late to go to the movies tonight.
11. He asked me to drive him home.

Synthetic Exercises: Prepositions with Infinitival Clauses

1. Er hat es getan // ohne / fragen / mich
2. Ich bin gekommen // um / helfen / dir
3. Statt / fahren / nach Wien // blieben wir noch eine Woche in München
4. Sie kam // um / abholen / mich
5. Statt / essen / zu Hause // gehen wir ins Restaurant
6. Barbara ging weg // ohne / geben / mir / ihr- / Adresse

Express in German

1. She came to pick me up.
2. He did it without asking me.
3. Instead of driving to Vienna, we stayed another week in Munich.
4. Barbara left without giving me her address.
5. I came to help you.
6. Instead of eating at home, we're going to a restaurant.

Synthetic Exercises: *sein* + *zu* + infinitive

Example: Das / sein / leicht / sagen
Das ist leicht zu sagen.

1. Das / sein / schwer / glauben
2. Dieser Wagen / sein / leicht / fahren
3. Das / sein / nicht / machen
4. Sein Wagen / sein / nicht / reparieren (*past*)
5. So etwas / sein / nicht leicht / finden
6. Das / sein / schwer / sagen
7. Herr Kunz / sein / nicht / finden (*past*)

Express in German

1. That's hard to say.
2. That can't be done.
3. This car is easy to drive.
4. Mr. Kunz couldn't be found.
5. His car couldn't be repaired.
6. That's hard to believe.
7. Something like that isn't easy to find.

Synthetic Exercises: Subordinate Clauses

1. Wir wußten nicht // was / wir / sollen / tun
2. Ich sagte dir // daß / du / sollen / warten
3. Er will // daß / ich / machen / es
4. Ich weiß nicht // wann / ich / sollen / kommen
5. Er will nicht // daß / ich / helfen / ihm
6. Wissen Sie // wohin / wir / sollen / gehen / ?
7. Sie sagte uns // daß / wir / sollen / bleiben / hier
8. Wir wissen nicht // mit wem / wir / sollen / sprechen
9. Ich will // daß / du / mitnehmen / ihn
10. Er sagte mir // daß / ich / sollen / arbeiten / mehr

Express in German

1. I don't know when to come.
2. She told us to stay here.
3. We didn't know what to do.
4. He wants me to do it.
5. He said that I should work more.
6. We don't know who to talk to.
7. I want you to take him along.
8. Do you know where to go?
9. I told you to wait.
10. He doesn't want me to help him.

Synthetic Exercises: Mixed Drills

1. Es ist Zeit // gehen / nach Hause
2. Ich bin gekommen // um / helfen / dir
3. Wissen Sie // wohin / wir / sollen / gehen / ?
4. Er hat versprochen // geben / es mir
5. Das / sein / schwer / sagen
6. Ich sagte dir // daß / du / sollen / warten
7. Es ist nett // wiedersehen / dich
8. Er hat es getan // ohne / fragen / mich
9. Ich will // daß / du / mitnehmen / ihn
10. Er bat mich // fahren / ihn / nach Hause
11. Dieser Wagen / sein / leicht / fahren
12. Statt / fahren / nach Wien // blieben wir noch eine Woche in München
13. Es ist zu spät // gehen / heute abend / in / Kino

14. Wir wußten nicht // was / wir / sollen / tun
15. Sein Wagen / sein / nicht / reparieren (*past*)
16. Es ist sinnlos // warten / länger
17. Sie kam // um / abholen / mich
18. Er sagte mir // daß / ich / sollen / arbeiten / mehr
19. Wir haben vor // fahren / nächst- / Sommer / nach Deutschland
20. Er will nicht // daß / ich / helfen / ihm
21. Barbara ging weg // ohne / geben / mir / ihr- / Adresse
22. Darf ich Sie bitten // nehmen / Platz
23. Ich weiß nicht // wann / ich / sollen / kommen
24. So etwas / sein / nicht / leicht / finden
25. Es hörte auf // regnen
26. Sie sagte uns // daß / wir / sollen / bleiben / hier
27. Es ist fast unmöglich // kriegen / jetzt / Karten
28. Er will // daß / ich / machen / es
29. Das / sein / nicht / machen
30. Statt / essen / zu Hause // gehen wir ins Restaurant
31. Wir wissen nicht // mit wem / wir / sollen / sprechen
32. Er bat mich // helfen / ihm

Express in German

1. He asked me to help him.
2. That's hard to say.
3. He did it without asking me.
4. I don't know when to come.
5. It's time to go home.
6. I told you to wait.
7. He promised to give it to me.
8. I came to help you.
9. He wants me to do it.
10. This car is easy to drive.
11. We didn't know what to do.
12. It's nice to see you again.
13. Instead of eating at home, we're going to a restaurant.
14. She told us to stay here.
15. It stopped raining.
16. That can't be done.
17. He doesn't want me to help him.
18. It's too late to go to the movies this evening.
19. She came to pick me up.

20. It's senseless to wait longer.
21. We don't know who to talk to.
22. Something like that isn't easy to find.
23. It's almost impossible to get tickets now.
24. Barbara left without giving me her address.
25. He told me to work more.
26. We plan to go to Germany next summer.
27. Instead of driving to Vienna, we stayed another week in Munich.
28. I want you to take him along.
29. May I ask you to take a seat?
30. He asked me to drive him home.
31. His car couldn't be repaired.
32. Do you know where to go?

Relative Pronouns and Relative Clauses

12

LEVEL ONE

I. INTRODUCTION

Look at the following examples:

MAIN CLAUSE	RELATIVE CLAUSE
That's the man	*who bought our house.*
Here are the books	*that you wanted.*

Each of the sentences above has two parts: a *main clause* and a *relative clause*. The main clauses (That's the man *and* Here are the books) make sense when they stand alone. The relative clauses, however, are meaningful only when they are joined to the main clauses.

An English *relative clause* begins with a *relative pronoun*—normally a form of *who, that,* or *which*—that refers to an element in the main clause (the man *who,* the books *that*). The element in the main clause to which the relative pronoun refers is called its *antecedent* (*the man* who, *the books* that).

ANTECEDENT	RELATIVE PRONOUN
That's *the man*	*who* bought our house.
Here are *the books*	*that* you wanted.

A relative clause always tells us something new about its antecedent; it defines or specifies it more fully.

That's the man

is a grammatically complete simple sentence, but only a fuller context can specify *which* man. Adding a relative clause is one way to create such a context:

That's the man *who bought our house.*

Relative pronouns and relative clauses can be looked at another way:

That's *the man.* He (*the man*) bought our house.
That's *the man who* bought our house.

When two simple sentences have a common element, they may be combined to form a compound sentence by making one of the sentences a relative clause. The common element appears as a noun in the main clause (e.g., *the man*) and as a relative pronoun in the relative clause (e.g., *who*).

II. RELATIVE PRONOUNS

A. English relative pronouns

English has two sets of relative pronouns: one for people, another for things.

	People	**Things**
SUBJECT	who	that (which)
OBJECT	who(m)	that (which)
POSSESSIVE	whose	whose (of which)

If the antecedent is a *person,* the relative pronoun is *who:*

the *man, who*

If the antecedent is a *thing,* the relative pronoun is *that* or *which:*

the *books, that*

B. German relative pronouns

Where English uses *natural gender* to distinguish people from things (the woman = *she;* the film = *it*), German uses *grammatical gender* (**der** Anzug = **er; das** Hemd = **es; die** Jacke = **sie**).

And since German *relative pronouns* also reflect grammatical gender, the same forms are used for both people and things.

1. *Gender and number are determined by the antecedent.*

If its antecedent is masculine, a relative pronoun is also masculine; if its antecedent is plural, a relative pronoun is also plural, and so on. For this reason, German has masculine, neuter, feminine and plural relative pronouns.

Wie heißt **der Mann,** *der* gestern hier war?
(What's the name of the man *who* was here yesterday?)

Wo ist **der Brief,** *der* heute morgen ankam?
(Where is the letter *that* came this morning?)

As you can see from the examples, German uses the relative pronoun **der** to refer to both a person (**der Mann**) and a thing (**der Brief**). English chooses between *who* and *that* in such situations.

2. *Case is determined by the function in the relative clause.*

While the gender and number of a relative pronoun are determined by its antecedent, its *case* depends solely on how it is used in the relative clause.

NOMINATIVE   Das ist der Mann, **der** gestern hier war.
                        Der is the subject of the relative clause.

ACCUSATIVE   Das ist der Mann, **den** ich meine.
                        Den is the direct object of **meinen.**

C. Table of German relative pronouns

Most of the forms of the relative pronoun are identical to those of the definite article. But pay particular attention to *the five forms in boldface;* they are *unlike* the definite article.

	Masc.	*Neut.*	*Fem.*	*Pl.*
NOMINATIVE	der	das	die	die
ACCUSATIVE	den	das	die	die
DATIVE	dem	dem	der	**denen**
GENITIVE	**dessen**	**dessen**	**deren**	**deren**

NOTE: In older works, forms of **welcher** (*which*) were often used as relative pronouns. These forms are now archaic.

III. RULES

A. Word order

Relative clauses are *subordinate* clauses: therefore they require subordinate word order. This means that the *conjugated verb form comes at the end of the clause.*

> Das ist der Mann, der unser Haus gekauft hat.

B. Gender and number

The gender and number of a relative pronoun are the same as the gender and number of the noun to which the relative pronoun refers (its antecedent). If the antecedent is masculine singular, the pronoun must also be masculine singular; if it is plural, the pronoun must be plural, and so on.

> Das ist der Mann, der unser Haus gekauft hat.
> Das sind die Leute, die unser Haus gekauft haben.

C. Case

The case of a relative pronoun depends on its *function in the relative clause.*

The following examples are all in the masculine singular:

> NOM.   Das ist der Mann, der unser Haus gekauft hat.
> (who bought our house.)

ACC.   Das ist der Mann, **den** wir gestern gesehen haben.
            (we saw yesterday *or*
            whom we saw yesterday.)

            Das ist der Mann, an **den** ich gedacht habe.
            (I was thinking of *or*
            of whom I was thinking.)

DAT.   Das ist der Mann, **dem** wir es gegeben haben.
            (we gave it to *or*
            to whom we gave it.)

            Das ist der Mann, **dem** du danken solltest.
            (you should thank *or*
            whom you should thank.)

            Das ist der Mann, nach **dem** Sie gefragt haben.
            (you were asking about *or*
            about whom you were asking.)

GEN.   Das ist der Mann, **dessen** Hilfe du brauchst.
            (whose help you need.)

As the above examples show, a relative pronoun can have various functions within its clause. It can be:

NOM. Subject: Der Mann, **der** unser Haus gekauft hat.

ACC. Object of verb: Der Mann, **den** wir gestern gesehen haben.

      Object of prep.:   Der Mann, an **den** ich gedacht habe.

DAT. Indirect object: Der Mann, **dem** wir es gegeben haben.

      Object of verb: Der Mann, **dem** du danken solltest.

      Object of prep.:   Der Mann, nach **dem** Sie gefragt haben.

GEN. Possessive pron.:   Der Mann, **dessen** Hilfe du brauchst.

NOTE: **Dessen** and **deren,** like all other personal pronouns, take their gender and number from the person(s) or thing(s) they refer to (their antecedent[s]).

MASC.	Der Mann, dessen Tochter . . .
NEUT.	Das Land, dessen Grenze . . .
FEM.	Die Stadt, deren Bürgermeister . . .
PLURAL	Die Leute, deren Sohn . . .

D. Position and punctuation

Der Mann, den Sie suchen, ist gerade weggegangen.
(The man you're looking for just left.)

1. A German relative clause comes immediately after its antecedent in the main clause. The only exception to this is in sentences in which *only one word would follow the relative clause.* For example:

Hast du den Mann gesehen, der gerade hier war?

2. German relative clauses are always set off by commas.

3. A German relative pronoun is normally the first element in its clause. The *only* exception to this rule is when the relative pronoun is the object of a preposition. In this case the *preposition* is the first element in the clause:

Das ist der Mann, an den ich gedacht habe.

E. No omission of German relative pronouns

Relative pronouns are often omitted from English sentences. But *relative pronouns may never be omitted from German sentences:*

Das ist der Mann, den ich meine.
(That's the man I mean *or* whom I mean.)

Das ist der Mann, für den ich arbeite.
(That's the man I work for *or* for whom I work.)

NOTE 1: When a preposition is used, it normally appears at the end of an English relative clause:

the man I work *for*

In German, the preposition must always precede the relative pronoun:

der Mann, für den ich arbeite

In other words, the German pattern is the same as the more formal English pattern:

the man, *for whom* I work

NOTE 2: When a progressive verb form is used (e.g. *is standing*), English often omits both the relative pronoun *and* the form of the verb *to be* (e.g., *is*). Such omissions are not possible in German:

The man who is standing over there is my boss.
The man standing over there is my boss.

but: Der Mann, der da drüben steht, ist mein Chef.

Since most of the sentences in the following drills are in conversational German, the Express in German drills will be cued with the colloquial English relative forms—unless clarity demands otherwise.

DRILLS

Fill-ins: By Case

Supply the correct forms of the relative pronoun.

NOMINATIVE

	Masc.	*Neut.*	*Fem.*	*Pl.*
NOM.	der	das	die	die

1. Hier ist ein Buch, _____ mich interessiert.
   (that)

2. Kennst du die Leute, _____ heute abend kommen?
   (who)

3. Die Suppe, _____ so gut war, steht nicht mehr auf der
   (that)
   Speisekarte.

4. Wo ist der Mann, _____ gerade hier war?
   (who)

5. Sehen Sie die Dame, _____ gerade aus dem Laden kommt?
   (who)

6. Wo ist das Lokal, _____ früher hier war?
                          (that)

7. Die Rotweine, _____ mir am besten gefallen, kommen aus
                     (that)
Frankreich.

8. Das ist der Herr, _____ mit Ihnen sprechen will.
                         (who)

9. Wo hält der Bus, _____ zur Universität fährt?
                        (that)

10. Wer war die Frau, _____ neben ihm saß?
                          (who)

ACCUSATIVE

	Masc.	Neut.	Fem.	Pl.
ACC.	den	das	die	die

1. Die Arbeit, _____ er geschrieben hat, war sehr gut.
                   (that)

2. Das ist das Haus, _____ wir kaufen wollten.
                          (that)

3. Sind das die Bücher, _____ Sie meinen?
                             (that)

4. Der Wein, _____ ich kaufen wollte, war nicht mehr da.
                 (that)

5. Das ist die Marke, an _____ ich gedacht habe.
                              (which)

6. Das ist der Mann, für _____ ich arbeite.
                              (whom)

7. Vielen Dank für die Karte, _____ Sie uns geschickt haben.
                                   (that)

8. Das Hemd, _____ ich kaufen wollte, war zu teuer.
                 (that)

9. Hier sind die Briefe, auf _____ du gewartet hast.
                                 (which)

10. Das war eine Nacht, _____ ich nie vergessen werde.
                            (that)

11. Ich warte noch auf das Paket, _____ er mir geschickt hat.
   (that)

12. Wir haben Freunde da, _____ wir besuchen wollen.
   (whom)

13. Ich zeige dir den Brief, _____ er mir geschrieben hat.
   (that)

DATIVE

	Masc.	Neut.	Fem.	Pl.
DAT.	dem	dem	der	**denen**

1. Das Zimmer, in _____ ich wohne, ist viel zu klein.
   (which)

2. Das ist die Universität, an _____ er studiert hat.
   (which)

3. Der Arzt, zu _____ ich ging, war wirklich sehr gut.
   (whom)

4. Das sind die Leute, _____ wir unser Haus verkauft haben.
   (to whom)

5. Das ist kein Haus, in _____ ich wohnen möchte.
   (which)

6. Ist das die Tasse, aus _____ ich getrunken habe?
   (which)

7. Kennst du das Mädchen, mit _____ er ausgeht?
   (whom)

8. Die Familie, bei _____ er wohnt, spricht nur Deutsch.
   (which)

9. Das ist der Mann, _____ du danken solltest.
   (whom)

10. Die Bücher, nach _____ Sie gefragt haben, sind noch nicht da.
   (which)

GENITIVE

	Masc.	Neut.	Fem.	Pl.
GEN.	**dessen**	**dessen**	**deren**	**deren**

1. Der Mann, _____ Gepäck da steht, kommt gleich zurück.
   (whose)

2. Die Jacke, _____ Farbe mir gefiel, war nicht mehr da.
   (whose)

3. Die Leute, _____ Haus wir mieten, sind in Innsbruck.
   (whose)

4. Ist das das Lokal, _____ Weine so gut sind?
   (whose)

5. Ich kenne viele Studenten, _____ Eltern in Europa wohnen.
   (whose)

6. Hier ist ein Mantel, _____ Farbe mir gefällt.
   (whose)

7. Das ist das Mädchen, für _____ Vater ich arbeite.
   (whose)

8. Die Dame, _____ Pakete da liegen, ist vor einer Stunde
   (whose)
   weggegangen.

Fill-ins: by gender

Supply the correct forms of the relative pronoun.

MASCULINE

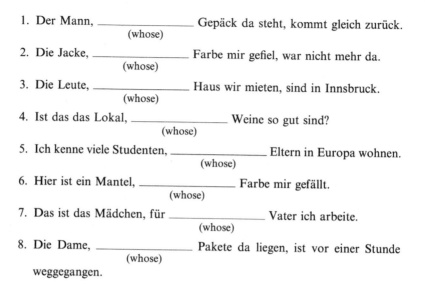

	Masc.
NOM.	der
ACC.	den
DAT.	dem
GEN.	**dessen**

1. Wo ist der Mann, _____ gerade hier war?
   (who)

2. Ich zeige dir den Brief, _____ er uns geschrieben hat.
   (that)

3. Das ist der Mann, _____ du danken solltest.
   (whom)

4. Hier ist ein Mantel, _____ Farbe mir gefällt.
   (whose)

5. Der Wein, _____ ich kaufen wollte, war nicht mehr da.
   (that)

6. Wo hält der Bus, _____ zur Universität fährt?
   (that)

7. Der Mann, _____ Gepäck da steht, kommt gleich zurück.
   (whose)

8. Der Arzt, zu _____ ich ging, war wirklich sehr gut.
   (whom)

9. Das ist der Mann, für _____ ich arbeite.
   (whom)

10. Der Laden, an _____ ich gedacht habe, ist nicht weit von hier.
    (whom)

NEUTER

	Neut.
NOM.	das
ACC.	das
DAT.	dem
GEN.	**dessen**

1. Wo ist das Lokal, _____ früher hier war?
   (that)

2. Das Zimmer, in _____ ich wohne, ist viel zu klein.
   (which)

3. Ich warte noch auf das Paket, _____ er mir geschickt hat.
   (that)

4. Das ist das Mädchen, für _____ Vater ich arbeite.
   (whose)

5. Das ist das Haus, _____ wir kaufen wollten.
   (that)

6. Kennst du das Mädchen, mit _____ er ausgeht?
   (whom)

7. Hier ist ein Buch, _____ mich interessiert.
   (that)

8. Ist das das Lokal, _____ Weine so gut sind?
   (whose)

9. Das Hemd, _____ ich kaufen wollte, war zu teuer.
   (that)

10. Das ist kein Haus, in _____ ich wohnen möchte.
    (which)

FEMININE

	Fem.
NOM.	die
ACC.	die
DAT.	der
GEN.	**deren**

1. Wer war die Frau, _____ neben ihm saß?
   (who)

2. Das ist die Marke, an _____ ich gedacht habe.
   (which)

3. Die Dame, _____ Pakete da liegen, kommt gleich zurück.
   (whose)

4. Das ist die Universität, an _____ er studiert hat.
   (which)

5. Die Suppe, _____ so gut war, steht nicht mehr auf der
   (that)
   Speisekarte.

6. Ist das die Tasse, aus _____ ich getrunken habe?
   (which)

7. Die Arbeit, _____ er geschrieben hat, war sehr gut.
   (that)

8. Die Jacke, _____ Farbe mir gefiel, war nicht mehr da.
   (whose)

9. Die Familie, bei _____ er wohnte, sprach nur Deutsch.
   (which)

10. Das war eine Nacht, _____ ich nie vergessen werde.
    (that)

PLURAL

	Pl.
NOM.	die
ACC.	die
DAT.	**denen**
GEN.	**deren**

1. Kennst du die Leute, _____ heute abend kommen?
   (who)

2. Hier sind die Briefe, auf _____ du gewartet hast.
   (which)

3. Die Bücher, nach _____ Sie gefragt haben, sind noch nicht da.
   (which)

4. Die Leute, _____ Haus wir mieten, sind in Innsbruck.
   (whose)

5. Wir haben Freunde da, _____ wir besuchen wollen.
   (whom)

6. Sind das die Bücher, _____ Sie meinen?
   (that)

7. Ich kenne viele Studenten, _____ Eltern in Europa wohnen.
   (whose)

8. Was kosten die Zigarren, _____ er raucht?
   (that)

9. Das sind die Leute, _____ wir unser Haus verkauft haben.
   (to whom)

10. Die Rotweine, _____ mir am besten gefallen, kommen aus
    (that)
    Frankreich.

Mixed Drills

1. Das ist das Haus, _____ wir kaufen wollten.
   (that)

2. Wo hält der Bus, _____ zur Universität fährt?
   (that)

3. Ist das die Tasse, aus _____ ich getrunken habe?
   (which)

4. Die Arbeit, _____ er geschrieben hat, war sehr gut.
   (that)

5. Ist das das Lokal, _____ Weine so gut waren?
   (whose)

6. Das ist der Mann, _____ du danken solltest.
   (whom)

7. Kennst du die Leute, _____ heute abend kommen?
   (who)

8. Ich zeige dir den Brief, _____ er mir geschrieben hat.
   (that)

9. Das Zimmer, in _____ ich wohne, ist viel zu klein.
   (which)

10. Die Leute, _____ Haus wir mieten, sind in Innsbruck.
    (whose)

11. Hier ist ein Buch, _____ mich interessiert.
    (that)

12. Das ist die Marke, an _____ ich gedacht habe.
    (which)

13. Wir haben Freunde da, _____ wir besuchen wollen.
    (whom)

14. Der Arzt, zu _____ ich ging, war wirklich sehr gut.
    (whom)

15. Das sind die Leute, _____ wir unser Haus verkauft haben.
    (to whom)

16. Die Suppe, _____ so gut war, steht nicht mehr auf der
    (that)
    Speisekarte.

17. Hier ist ein Mantel, _____ Farbe mir gefällt.
    (whose)

18. Das ist kein Haus, in _____ ich wohnen möchte.
    (which)

19. Wer war die Frau, _____ neben ihm saß?
    (who)

20. Der Wein, _____ ich kaufen wollte, war nicht mehr da.
    (that)

21. Die Dame, _____ Pakete da liegen, kommt gleich zurück.
    (whose)

22. Sind das die Bücher, _____ Sie meinen?
    (that)

23. Die Familie, bei _____ er wohnte, sprach nur Deutsch.
    (which)

24. Ich warte noch auf das Paket, _____ er mir geschickt hat.
    (that)

25. Das war eine Nacht, _____ ich nie vergessen werde.
    (that)

26. Das ist das Mädchen, für _____ Vater ich arbeite.
                                  (whose)

27. Wo ist der Mann, _____ gerade hier war?
                    (who)

28. Die Bücher, nach _____ Sie gefragt haben, sind noch nicht da.
                 (which)

29. Hier sind die Briefe, auf _____ du gewartet hast.
                       (which)

30. Kennst du das Mädchen, mit _____er ausgeht?
                         (whom)

Express in German

1. Where is the man who was just here?
2. The paper he wrote was very good.
3. The room I'm living in is much too small.
4. We have friends there we want to visit.
5. Here's a book that interests me.
6. Is that the cup I was drinking out of?
7. That's the man you should thank.
8. Is that the place whose wines were so good?
9. Here are the letters you were waiting for.
10. I'll show you the letter he wrote me.
11. Those are the people we sold our house to.
12. Who was the woman sitting next to him?
13. Do you know the girl he goes out with?
14. The lady whose packages are lying there is coming right back.
15. That's the house we wanted to buy.
16. Are those the books you mean?
17. The family he lived with only spoke German.
18. Here's a coat whose color I like.
19. The doctor I went to was really very good.
20. The books you were asking about aren't here yet.
21. The wine I wanted to buy wasn't there any more.
22. Do you know the people who are coming this evening?
23. That's the girl whose father I work for.
24. That's not a house I'd like to live in.
25. The soup that was so good isn't on the menu any more.
26. I'm still waiting for the package he sent me.
27. That was a night that I'll never forget.

28. The people whose house we're renting are in Innsbruck.
29. Where does the bus stop that goes to the university?
30. That's the brand I was thinking of.

LEVEL TWO

I. SPECIAL RELATIVE CONSTRUCTIONS

A. The relative adverb WO

> Er wohnt jetzt in Wien (in Deutschland).
> Es geht ihm dort sehr gut.

> Er wohnt jetzt in Wien (in Deutschland),
>   wo es ihm sehr gut geht.

Wo *must* be used, instead of a relative pronoun, when referring to place names (e.g., of cities, states, countries, continents).

NOTE 1: Like relative pronouns, the relative adverb **wo** requires subordinate word order: the inflected verb must be at the end of the clause.

NOTE 2: The relative adverb **wo** *may* be used when referring to other expressions of place. In such cases, it is an alternate form which *may* be used in place of a preposition and a relative pronoun:

> Ist das das Restaurant, wo du gearbeitet hast?*
> (Is that the restaurant, *where* you worked?)

> or: Ist das das Restaurant, in dem du gearbeitet hast?
> (Is that the restaurant, *in which* you worked?
>   *that* you worked *in*?)

B. The relative pronoun WER
(unnamed antecedents with persons)

Look at the following sentences:

> NOM.   Wissen Sie, wer das ist?
>   (Do you know *who* that is?)

---

* This use of **wo,** however, is quite informal and colloquial.

ACC.   Ich weiß nicht, wen Sie meinen.
(I don't know *who* you mean.)

Ja, ich weiß ganz genau, an wen er gedacht hat.
(Yes, I know exactly *who* he was thinking *of*.)

DAT.   Hast du gesehen, wem er es gegeben hat?
(Did you see *who* he gave it to?)

Wissen Sie, nach wem er gefragt hat?
(Do you know *who* he was asking about?)

GEN.   Ich bin nicht sicher, wessen Buch das ist.
(I'm not sure *whose* book that is.)

In none of these sentences is there an *antecedent* with which the pronoun can agree in gender and number. The antecedent (the *person* referred to) may be known to the speaker (e.g., Ich weiß ganz genau, an wen er gedacht hat.), *but it is not named in the sentence.* When the unnamed antecedent is a *person,* the appropriate form of the interrogative pronoun **wer (wen, wem, wessen)** must be used.

The relative pronoun **wer** is also used where the English language uses *whoever* (*he who*):

Wer zu spät kommt, wird den Zug verpassen.
(*Whoever* comes too late will miss the train.)

C. The relative pronoun WAS
(unnamed antecedents with things)

Look at the following sentences:

NOM.   Wissen Sie, was das ist?
(Do you know *what* that is?)

ACC.   Ich weiß nicht, was Sie meinen.
(I don't know *what* you mean.)

Ja, ich weiß ganz genau, woran er gedacht hat.
(Yes, I know exactly *what* he was thinking *of*.)

DAT.   Wissen Sie, wonach er gefragt hat?
(Do you know *what* he was asking about?)

As in the sentences with **wer,** these sentences have no expressed antecedent with which the relative pronoun can agree. Here, however, things, rather

than persons, are being referred to. When the unnamed antecedent is a
thing, the appropriate form of the interrogative pronoun **was** must be used.

NOTE: *prepositional usage with the relative pronouns* **wer** *and* **was:**

PERSONS	THINGS
Ich weiß, **an wen** er gedacht hat. Wissen Sie, **nach wem** er gefragt hat?	Ich weiß, **woran** er gedacht hat. Wissen Sie, **wonach** er gefragt hat?
With *persons* one uses: *preposition + appropriate form of* **wer**	With *things* one uses: **wo(r)– +** *preposition* **wor–** is used if the preposition begins with a vowel (e.g., **woran**). Otherwise, **wo–** is used (e.g., **wonach**).

The relative pronoun **was** also has the meaning *what,* in the sense of *that
which:*

> Was er sagte, war sehr interessant.
> (*What* [*that which*] he said was very interesting.)

D. Special uses of *was*

The relative pronoun **was** *must* be used when the antecedent is:

1. *a superlative adjective used as a noun**

> Das ist das Beste, was wir haben.
> (That's the best [that] we have.)

2. *a neuter pronoun indicating quantity*

alles	everything	etwas	something
vieles	much, a lot	wenig	little
manches	much, many a thing	nichts	nothing

> Alles (vieles, etc.), was er sagte, war interessant.
> (*Everything* [*much,* etc.] that he said was interesting.

* See p. 322: Adjectival Nouns.

3. *a clause*

Herr von Wiese geht jeden Tag spazieren, was ihm gar nicht schadet.
(Mr. von Wiese goes walking every day, *which* doesn't hurt him at all.

Karl will nicht mitkommen, was höchst ungewöhnlich ist.
(Karl doesn't want to come along, *which* is highly unusual.)

In these sentences the antecedent is not a single element in the main clause,
but *rather the whole clause itself*. (What doesn't hurt Mr. von Wiese is the
fact that he goes walking every day. What is highly unusual is *the fact* that
Karl doesn't want to come along.)

E. No omission of German relative pronouns

As was previously pointed out, relative pronouns can never be omitted from
German relative clauses:

Das ist das Beste, was wir haben.

On the other hand, they are often omitted in English:

That's the best we have.

■ DRILLS

Fill-ins: the Relative Pronoun *wer*

Supply the correct forms of the pronoun and, where necessary, the preposition.

1. Haben Sie gehört, _____ heute abend kommt?
   (who)

2. Weißt du, _____ sie meint?
   (whom)

3. Ich bin nicht sicher, _____ er es gesagt hat.
   (to whom)

4. Ich möchte wissen, _____ Idee das war.
   (whose)

5. Weißt du, _____ er wartet?
   (for whom)

6. Ich weiß nicht, _____ ich glauben sollte.
                                (whom)

7. _____ mitkommen will, muß fünfzig Mark zahlen.
      (Whoever)

8. Wissen Sie, _____ er gefragt hat?
                        (about whom)

9. Können Sie mir sagen, _____ Wagen das ist?
                                    (whose)

10. Ich weiß nicht, _____ er ausgegangen ist.
                          (with whom)

11. Er hat vergessen, _____ er es gegeben hat.
                            (to whom)

12. Ich weiß nicht, _____ es getan hat.
                            (who)

13. Wissen Sie, _____ er gedacht hat?
                      (of whom)

Fill-ins: the Relative Pronoun *was*

Supply the correct pronoun or *wo(r)*-compound.

1. Ich weiß nicht, _____ er meinte.
                            (what)

2. Das ist alles, _____ ich weiß.
                          (that)

3. Er will nicht mitkommen, _____ sehr ungewöhnlich ist.
                                    (which)

4. Haben Sie gehört, _____ sie gesprochen haben?
                            (about what)

5. Das ist das Beste, _____ wir haben.
                            (that)

6. Er hatte nichts, _____ uns interessierte.
                          (that)

7. Ich weiß nicht, _____ er gedacht hat.
                        (of what)

8. Hast du ihn gefragt, _____ er machen will?
                              (what)

9. Wissen Sie, _____ er wartet?
                    (for what)

10. Das ist das Nächste, _____ wir tun müssen.
    (that)

11. Wissen Sie, _____ er gefragt hat?
    (about what)

12. Das ist etwas, _____ ich nicht verstehen kann.
    (that)

Fill-ins: Mixed Drills

1. Ich weiß nicht, _____ es getan hat.
   (who)

2. Das ist alles, _____ ich weiß.
   (that)

3. Weißt du, _____ sie meint?
   (whom)

4. Ich weiß nicht, _____ er gedacht hat.
   (*what* he was thinking *of*)

5. Er hat vergessen, _____ er es gegeben hat.
   (to whom)

6. Können Sie mir sagen, _____ Wagen das ist?
   (whose)

7. Das ist das Beste, _____ wir haben.
   (that)

8. Er will nicht mitkommen, _____ sehr ungewöhnlich ist.
   (which)

9. Wissen Sie, _____ er gefragt hat?
   (*who* he was asking *about*)

10. Haben Sie gehört _____ heute abend kommt?
    (who)

11. Ich weiß nicht, _____ er meinte.
    (what)

12. Wissen Sie, _____ er wartet?
    (*what* he's waiting *for*)

13. Ich bin nicht sicher, _____ ich es gesagt habe.
    (to whom)

14. Er hatte nichts, _____ uns interessierte.
    (that)

15. Ich weiß nicht, _____ er ausgegangen ist.
    (*who* he went out *with*)

16. _____ mitkommen will, muß fünfzig Mark zahlen.
    (Whoever)

17. Das ist das Nächste, _____ wir tun müssen.
    (that)

18. Wissen Sie, _____ ich gedacht habe?
    (*who* I was thinking *of*)

19. Haben Sie gehört, _____ sie gesprochen haben?
    (*what* they were talking *about*)

20. Ich möchte wissen, _____ Idee das war.
    (whose)

21. Hast du ihn gefragt, _____ er machen will?
    (what)

22. Wissen Sie, _____ er gefragt hat?
    (*what* he was asking *about*)

23. Ich weiß nicht, _____ ich glauben sollte.
    (whom)

24. Das ist etwas, _____ ich nicht verstehen kann.
    (that)

25. Weißt du, _____ er wartet?
    (*who* he's waiting *for*)

26. Karl ist in Stuttgart, _____ er Freunde besucht.
    (where)

Express in German

1. I don't know what he meant.
2. He forgot who he gave it to.
3. That's something I can't understand.
4. Do you know who I was thinking of?
5. Have you heard who's coming this evening?
6. I'd like to know whose idea that was.
7. That's the best we have.
8. Do you know what he's waiting for?
9. I don't know who I should believe.
10. He didn't have anything that interested us.
11. Do you know what he was asking about?
12. Did you ask him what he wants to do?

13. Do you know who she means?
14. Did you hear what they were talking about?
15. I'm not sure who he told it to.
16. He doesn't want to come along, which is very unusual.
17. I don't know who he went out with.
18. That's the next thing we have to do.
19. Can you tell me whose car that is?
20. Do you know who he's waiting for?
21. I don't know who did it.
22. That's all I know.
23. Karl is in Stuttgart visiting friends.
24. Do you know who he was asking about?
25. I don't know what he was thinking of.
26. Whoever wants to come along has to pay fifty marks.

■ MIXED DRILLS (Both Levels)

Fill-ins

1. Sind das die Bücher, _____ Sie meinen?
                              (that)

2. Das ist das Beste, _____ wir haben.
                          (that)

3. Das Zimmer, _____ ich wohne, ist viel zu klein.
                (*that* I'm living *in*)

4. Ich weiß nicht, _____ es getan hat.
                        (who)

5. Die Arbeit, _____ er geschrieben hat, war sehr gut.
                    (that)

6. Ist das die Tasse, _____ ich getrunken habe?
                        (*that* I was drinking *from*)

7. Haben Sie gehört, _____ sie gesprochen haben?
                          (*what* they talking *about*)

8. Hier ist ein Mantel, _____ Farbe mir gefällt.
                              (whose)

9. Der Wein, _____ ich kaufen wollte, war nicht mehr da.
                  (that)

10. Wissen Sie, _____ er gefragt hat?
   (*who* he was asking *about*)

11. Das ist alles, _____ ich weiß.
   (that)

12. Wo ist der Mann, _____ gerade hier war?
   (who)

13. Das sind die Leute, _____ wir unser Haus verkauft
   (*who* we sold our house *to*)
   haben.

14. Weißt du, _____ sie meint?
   (whom)

15. Wissen Sie, _____ ich gedacht habe?
   (*who* I was thinking *of*)

16. Kennst du die Leute, _____ heute abend kommen?
   (who)

17. Die Leute, _____ Haus wir mieten, sind in Innsbruck.
   (whose)

18. Hier sind die Briefe, _____ Sie gewartet haben.
   (*that* you were waiting *for*)

19. Hier ist ein Buch, _____ mich interessiert.
   (that)

20. Das ist der Mann, _____ du danken solltest.
   (whom)

21. Ich weiß nicht, _____ er gedacht hat.
   (*what* he was thinking *of*)

22. Karl ist in Stuttgart, _____ er Freunde besucht.
   (where)

23. Ich weiß nicht, _____ er meinte.
   (what)

24. Ist das das Lokal, _____ Weine so gut waren?
   (whose)

25. Wissen Sie, _____ er gefragt hat?
   (*what* he was asking *about*)

26. Der Arzt, _____ ich ging, war wirklich sehr gut.
   (*who* I went *to*)

27. Das ist das Nächste, _____ wir tun müssen.
   (that)

28. Wissen Sie, _____ er wartet?
    (*what* he's waiting *for*)

29. Das war eine Nacht, _____ ich nie vergessen werde.
    (that)

30. Die Bücher, _____ Sie gefragt haben, sind noch
    (*that* you were asking *about*)
    nicht da.

31. Das ist kein Haus, _____ ich wohnen möchte.
    (*that* I'd like to live *in*)

32. Er hatte nichts, _____ uns interessierte.
    (that)

33. Das ist das Mädchen, _____ Vater ich arbeite.
    (*whose* father I work *for*)

34. Weißt du, _____ er wartet?
    (*who* he's waiting *for*)

35. Ich zeige dir den Brief, _____ er mir geschrieben hat.
    (that)

36. Die Familie, _____ er wohnte, sprach nur Deutsch.
    (*that* he was living *with*)

37. Das ist das Haus, _____ wir kaufen wollten.
    (that)

38. Die Suppe, _____ so gut war, steht nicht mehr auf der
    (that)
    Speisekarte.

39. Ich möchte wissen, _____ Idee das war.
    (whose)

40. Er hat vergessen, _____ er es gegeben hat.
    (*who* he gave it *to*)

Express in German

1. That's the house we wanted to buy.
2. The doctor I went to was really very good.
3. Do you know who he's waiting for?
4. That's the best that we have.
5. Who was the man who was just here?

6. I don't know what he was thinking of.
7. Is that the place whose wines are so good?
8. Are those the books you mean?
9. Do you know who he was asking about?
10. That was a night I'll never forget.
11. I don't know what he meant.
12. The room I'm living in is much too small.
13. Karl is in Stuttgart visting friends.
14. Do you know the people who are coming this evening?
15. The books you were asking about aren't here yet.
16. Did you hear what they were talking about?
17. The people whose house we're renting are in Innsbruck.
18. I don't know who did it.
19. The paper he wrote was very good.
20. Is that the cup I was drinking out of?
21. The wine I wanted to buy wasn't there anymore.
22. Do you know what he's waiting for?
23. He didn't have anything that interested us.
24. Here's a coat whose color I like.
25. That's not a house I'd like to live in.
26. The soup that was so good isn't on the menu anymore.
27. Do you know who she meant?
28. I'd like to know whose idea that was.
29. The family he lived with only spoke German.
30. I'll show you the letter he wrote me.
31. Those are the people we sold our house to.
32. That's all I know.
33. That's the man you should thank.
34. Do you know who I was thinking of?
35. Here's a book that interests me.
36. That's the girl whose father I work for.
37. He forgot who he gave it to.
38. Do you know what he was asking about?
39. Here are the letters you were waiting for.
40. That's the next thing we have to do.

Subjunctive I:
Indirect Speech
13

I. INTRODUCTION

There are essentially two ways of reporting what another person has said or written. The easier way is to use direct quotation:

> Die Münchner sagen: „Unser Bier ist das beste."
> (People from Munich say, "Our beer is best.")
>
> Der Finanzminister sagte: „Höhere Steuern sind notwendig."
> The minister of finance said, "Higher taxes are necessary."

As you can see, German and English treat direct quotations in essentially the same manner: the speaker's exact words are reproduced and enclosed in quotation marks. The introductory statement that identifies the speaker **(Die Münchner sagen, Der Finanzminister sagte)** is separated from the quotation by a colon in German, by a comma in English.

It is much more common, however, to use *indirect quotation*. Indirect quotation reproduces what the speaker says, but not necessarily in the speaker's exact words. Sometimes changes have to be made to keep the meaning straight:

DIRECT QUOTATION	*"I'm* satisfied with it."
INDIRECT QUOTATION	He says *he's* satisfied with it.

Indirect quotation is essentially the same in German—with one exception. When quoting indirectly, the German speaker can choose one of three verb forms (or *moods*), depending on his *attitude* toward the original quotation. The three forms (moods) are:

subjunctive I

indicative

subjunctive II

A. Subjunctive I

Subjunctive I is used in formal, impartial reporting:

Der Finanzminister sagte, höhere Steuern seien notwendig.

Seien is the subjunctive I counterpart of **sind.** By choosing this form of the verb, the reporter shows that he is maintaining an objective distance from the finance minister's words. He is neither agreeing nor disagreeing with them, but merely attributing the statement to its source.

B. Indicative

If the same person were to write:

Der Finanzminister sagte, höhere Steuern sind notwendig.

one might infer that the reporter agrees with the finance minister's statement. **Sind** is in the indicative mood; it implies a statement of fact.

C. Subjunctive II

The choice of subjunctive II:

Der Finanzminister sagte, höhere Steuern wären notwendig.

implies skepticism on the reporter's part. He is suggesting that the finance minister's statement is not necessarily true and he is using the subjunctive II form **wären** (a form used with contrary-to-fact statements) to indicate this.

D. Usage

Subjunctive I is usually reserved for careful reporting—television newscasts, newspaper articles, magazines, books, essays, term papers (!). In everyday conversation the tendency is to avoid subjunctive I and to choose instead between the indicative and subjunctive II.

II. FORMS OF SUBJUNCTIVE I

A. Present tense

The present tense of subjunctive I is formed by adding the following subjunctive endings to the stem of the verb:

−e	−en
−est	−et
−e	−en

Note that subjunctive I verb forms never have the stem-vowel change found in their present indicative counterparts.

PRESENT INDICATIVE		SUBJUNC-TIVE I	PRESENT INDICA-TIVE	SUBJUNC-TIVE I	PRESENT INDICA-TIVE	SUBJUNC-TIVE I
ich	sehe	sehe	kann	könne	werde	werde
du	siehst	sehest	kannst	könnest	wirst	werdest
er	sieht	sehe	kann	könne	wird	werde
wir	sehen	sehen	können	können	werden	werden
ihr	seht	sehet	könnt	könnet	werdet	werdet
sie	sehen	sehen	können	können	werden	werden

The only exception is the verb **sein**, which has no endings in the 1st and 3rd persons singular:

ich	**sei**	wir	seien
du	seiest	ihr	seiet
er	**sei**	sie	seien

Contrast a present tense subjunctive I quotation and its indicative counter-part:

PRESENT TENSE INDICATIVE   Er sagt, daß er es nicht tun kann.

PRESENT TENSE SUBJUNCTIVE I   Er sagt, daß er es nicht tun könne.

Both sentences are translated as:

He says that he can't do it.

B. Past tense

The past tense of subjunctive I is derived from the present perfect tense of the indicative:

PRESENT PERFECT INDICATIVE   PAST SUBJUNCTIVE I
Er ist gekommen.   Er sei gekommen.
Er hat es gemacht.   Er habe es gemacht.

RULE: The past tense of subjunctive I is composed of:

> **sei** or **habe** + *a past participle*

C. Future tense

The future tense of subjunctive I is analogous to the future tense of the indicative. The only difference is that the auxiliary **werden** *uses subjunctive I forms:*

ich werde	wir werden
du werdest	ihr werdet
er werde	sie werden

FUTURE INDICATIVE   FUTURE SUBJUNCTIVE I

Er wird es versuchen.   Er werde es versuchen.

D. Tense usage

In general the tense used in an indirect quotation is dependent upon the tense used in the direct quotation that underlies it.

1. If the direct quotation is in the present tense indicative, the indirect quotation must be in the present tense of subjunctive I:

PRESENT INDICATIVE   PRESENT SUBJUNCTIVE I

„Es ist notwendig.“   Er sagte, es sei notwendig.

2. If the direct quotation is in any tense referring to *past time*, the indirect quotation is in the past tense of subjunctive I:

PAST TIME INDICATIVE   PAST SUBJUNCTIVE I

„Es war notwendig.“
„Es ist notwendig gewesen.“ } Er sagte, es sei notwendig gewesen.
„Es war notwendig gewesen.“

NOTE: Whereas the indicative has three tenses to use in referring to past time (past, present perfect, and past perfect), *subjunctive I has only one.*

3. If the direct quotation is in the future tense, the auxiliary **werden** is put into the present tense of subjunctive I:

FUTURE INDICATIVE   „Ippendorf wird eines Tages berühmt sein.“

PRESENT SUBJUNCTIVE I   Er sagte, Ippendorf werde eines Tages berühmt sein.

E. Mandatory substitution of subjunctive II for subjunctive I

Except for the verb **sein,** subjunctive I forms and indicative forms are identical in the plural. Whenever subjunctive I and indicative forms are identical, *subjunctive II must be used:*

„Wir haben etwas gefunden.“
Sie behaupten, sie (haben) hätten etwas gefunden.

F. Subjunctive II stays subjunctive II

If the original quotation is in subjunctive II, the indirect quotation will also be in subjunctive II:

„Ich wäre damit zufrieden.“
("I'd be satisfied with that.")

Er sagt, er wäre damit zufrieden.

„Man könnte das auch anders machen.“
("One could also do that another way.")

Er sagte, man könnte das auch anders machen.

DRILLS

Direct to Indirect Statements

Put the following sentences into subjunctive I. If *daß* is used, the conjugated
verb form must be put at the end of the clause.

Examples: Ich habe nichts davon gehört.
               Er sagte, daß . . .
               Er sagte, daß er nichts davon gehört *habe.*

               Wir waren nicht da.
               Sie sagten, sie . . .
               Sie sagten, sie *seien* nicht da *gewesen.*

1. Der Mercedes ist der beste Wagen.
   Herr Benz meint, der Mercedes . . .
2. Wir haben zuviel zu tun.
   Alle Studenten behaupten, sie . . .
3. Er ist daran schuld.
   Man sagt, er . . .
4. Er hat nichts gegen unseren Plan.
   Er versicherte uns, er . . .
5. Wir haben etwas gefunden.
   Sie riefen, daß . . .
6. Herr Stern war immer ein vorsichtiger Fahrer.
   Im Bericht stand, daß . . .
7. Ich habe mich geirrt.
   Herr Hausmann behauptet, daß er . . .
8. Wir waren da, aber wir konnten nichts finden.
   Sie sagen, sie . . .
9. Es geht mir in Wien sehr gut.
   Er schreibt, es . . .
10. England könnte wieder eine Weltmacht werden.
    Der Minister meinte, England . . .
11. Ich habe vor, ein Buch darüber zu schreiben.
    Herr Karst sagt, er . . .
12. Er wurde ermordet.
    Man sagt, er . . .
13. Die Königin hat sich erkältet.
    Es wurde berichtet, daß die Königin . . .

14. Herr Schmidt ist nicht im Büro.
Die Sekretärin sagt, Herr Schmidt . . .
15. Ich kenne keinen besseren Wagen.
Er hat gesagt, daß er . . .
16. Wir sind nie in Amsterdam gewesen.
Sie behaupten, sie . . .
17. Ein Kompromiß käme nicht in Frage.
Diesem Artikel nach . . .

Direct to Indirect Reports

Put the following sentences into subjunctive I.
1. Das Europäische Parlament wird in der Zeit vom 14. bis zum 17. Juni
gewählt. Das entschieden gestern die Außenminister der Europäischen
Gemeinschaft in Brüssel.

   In Brüssel wurde gestern bekanntgegeben, daß . . .

2. Ein Hubschrauber ist in der Nähe von Augsburg abgestürzt. Alle fünf
Insassen kamen mit dem Leben davon.

   Aus München wurde berichtet, daß . . .

3. Marseilles wurde am Dienstag von der Polizei „abgeriegelt". An allen
größeren Straßen hatten die Beamten Sperren errichtet. Sie kontrollierten
alle vorbeigehenden Wagen. Mehrere Personen wurden festgenommen,
aber die Gesuchten waren nicht dabei. Es handelte sich um die Männer,
die in der vorigen Woche einen Geldtransport überfallen und 450.000
Franc erbeutet hatten.

   Unser Korrespondent in Frankreich berichtet, daß . . .

4. Die Zeit arbeitet wieder für den Markenartikel. Nach einer Phase der
Angst und des Sparens will der Bundesbürger sich jetzt wieder „was
leisten". Marken, die im Preisgerangel der letzten Jahre Charakter und
Kompetenz nicht verloren haben und damit begehrenswert geblieben
sind, werden davon profitieren.

   Mehrere Wirtschaftswissenschaftler meinen, daß . . .

5. In den USA ist etwas Undenkbares geschehen: ein Minister entschuldigte
sich bei einem Journalisten für eine Taktlosigkeit. Nachdem ein
Korrespondent eine etwas scharfe Frage an den Verteidigungsminister

gestellt hatte, verlor der Minister seine Beherrschung. Er gestikulierte wild, schlug mit der Faust auf den Tisch und rief: „Ich habe die Nase voll von diesen Andeutungen." Einen Tag später bat er den Reporter in sein Büro und entschuldigte sich für seinen Wutanfall.

Man sagt, daß in den USA . . .

6. Die Konjunktur in der Bundesrepublik erholt sich weiter—wenn auch unter Schwankungen. Man erwartet deshalb im Frühjahr erstmals seit längerer Zeit wieder eine positive Wachstumsrate, die freilich noch nicht auf einen Arbeitsmarkt durchschlägt, wo bislang hauptsächlich saisonale Gründe für Erleichterung sorgten. Die deutsche Außenhandelsbilanz ist weiter positiv, der Überschuß hat sich jedoch im April leicht abgeschwächt.

Das Bundeswirtschaftsministerium meint, daß . . .

7. Mit Tränengas und Schlagstöcken ging die Bonner Polizei gegen Studenten vor, die beim Sommerfest der Universität zwei Feuer entzündet hatten. Die Feuerwehr ist von Randalierern behindert worden. Beamte, die man darauf eingesetzt hat, sind mit Flaschen beworfen worden.

Folgendes wurde uns heute mitgeteilt: . . .

Reconstruction of indirect discourse

In Adalbert Stifter's "Brigitta," the narrator presents the following information as indirect quotation. Reconstruct Stifter's original text by putting the excerpt into subjunctive I.

Der Major ist nicht in der Gegend geboren. Er stammt von einer sehr reichen Familie. Er ist seit seiner Jugend fast immer auf Reisen gewesen, man weiß eigentlich nicht recht wo, so wie man auch nicht weiß, in welchen Diensten er sich den Majorsrang verdient hat.

Special
Problems
14

I. BASIC SENTENCE STRUCTURE

A. Order of direct and indirect objects

1. Introduction

Many German and English verbs can take both a *direct object* (D.O.) and an *indirect object* (I.O.):

	I.O.	D.O.
Ich schicke	meiner Freundin	eine Karte.
(I'm sending	my friend	a card.)

The *direct object* is the person or thing immediately acted upon and it is in the *accusative case.* In our example it shows:

> *what* is being sent (eine Karte)

The *indirect object* shows the "destination" of the direct object and it is in the *dative case.* Since the indirect object is almost always a person, it tells us *whom* the direct object is intended for:

> D.O.   I.O.
> *The postcard* is intended for *my friend.*

2. Order of nouns and pronoun objects

Ich bringe dem Chef die Liste.

In the example above, both the direct object and the indirect object are *nouns*. But either one—or both—can be replaced by *personal pronouns*. German arranges these objects in a certain order, depending on whether the *direct* object is a noun or a pronoun.

RULES:

1. *If the direct object is a noun, it follows the indirect object.*

I.O.   D.O.

Ich bringe dem Chef die Liste.

Ich bringe ihm   die Liste.

2. *If the direct object is a personal pronoun, it precedes the indirect object.*

D.O.   I.O.

Ich bringe sie dem Chef.

Ich bringe sie ihm.

NOTE: It is the *direct* object that determines the order. If it is a pronoun, it comes first; if it is a noun it comes last. Whether the *indirect* object is a noun or a pronoun has no effect on the order of objects.

3. Indefinite pronouns

Words like **nichts, alles,** and **etwas** are called *indefinite pronouns*. As far as word order is concerned, *they behave like nouns*. This means that they follow an indirect object.

I.O.   D.O.

Ich bringe dem Chef etwas.

Ich bringe ihm   etwas.

4. *Agreement of nouns and pronouns*

If a personal pronoun is substituted for a noun, it must agree with the noun it replaces. That is, it must reflect the same gender, number, and case. The following table shows the agreement of nouns and the 3rd person pronouns that can replace them.

	Singular		
	MASCULINE	NEUTER	FEMININE
NOM.	der Mann, der Tisch: **er**	das Kind, das Buch: **es**	die Dame, die Zeitung: **sie**
ACC.	den Mann, den Tisch: **ihn**	das Kind, das Buch: **es**	die Dame, die Zeitung: **sie**
DAT.	dem Mann, dem Tisch: **ihm**	dem Kind, dem Buch: **ihm**	der Dame, der Zeitung: **ihr**
	Plural ALL GENDERS		
NOM.	die Männer, Tische, Kinder, Bücher, Damen, Zeitungen: **sie**		
ACC.	die Männer, etc.		**sie**
DAT.	den Männern, etc.		**ihnen**

The 1st and 2nd person pronouns are as follows:

NOM.	ich	du	wir	ihr	Sie
ACC.	mich	dich	uns	euch	Sie
DAT.	mir	dir	uns	euch	Ihnen

5. *Ein-words*

The **ein**-words are **ein, kein,** and the possessive adjectives (**mein, dein,** etc.). The following table gives the nominative, accusative and dative endings for the **ein**-words.

	Singular			Plural
	MASCULINE	NEUTER	FEMININE	ALL GENDERS
NOM.	mein☐	mein☐	meine	meine
ACC.	meinen	mein☐	meine	meine
DAT.	meinem	meinem	meiner	meinen

 DRILLS

Replacement Drill: Indirect Objects

Replace the noun indirect object with a personal pronoun.

> Example: Ich schicke *meinem Bruder* eine Karte.
> Ich schicke *ihm* eine Karte.

1. Sagen Sie meiner Sekretärin die Adresse!
2. Ich kaufe den Kindern etwas.
3. Ich sage es meinem Chef.
4. Zeigen Sie es der Kellnerin!
5. Gibst du Hans den Schlüssel?
6. Sag es deinen Freunden!
7. Ich kaufe meiner Schwester etwas.

Replacement Drills: Direct Objects

Replace the noun direct object with a personal pronoun.

> Example: Ich schicke meinem Bruder *eine Karte.*
> Ich schicke *sie* meinem Bruder.

1. Bring mir die Post!
2. Ich zeige dir meinen Computer.
3. Sag meiner Freundin die Adresse.
4. Bitte, geben Sie mir das Buch.
5. Schicken Sie mir die Bücher?
6. Wir zeigen unseren Freunden das Haus.
7. Ich bringe dir die Zeitung.
8. Geben Sie ihm den Brief!

■ MIXED DRILLS

Complete the sentences by putting the objects in their correct order.

1. Ich bringe _____. die Zeitung
   dir

   Ich bringe _____. sie
   dir

2. Gibst du _____? den Schlüssel
   Hans

   Gibst du _____? den Schlüssel
   ihm

3. Wir zeigen _____. das Haus
   ihnen

   Wir zeigen _____. es
   ihnen

4. Ich kaufe _____. etwas
   den Kindern

   Ich kaufe _____. etwas
   ihnen

5. Ich sage _____. es
   meinem Chef

   Ich sage _____. es
   ihm

6. Ich zeige _____. meinen Computer
   dir

   Ich zeige _____. ihn
   dir

7. Schicken Sie _____? die Bücher
   mir

   Schicken Sie _____? sie
   mir

8. Ich sage _____. nichts
   ihm

9. Sag _____! es
   deinen Freunden

   Sag _____! es
   ihnen

10. Geben Sie _____! den Brief
    ihm

    Geben Sie _____! ihn
    ihm

11. Ich kaufe _____. ein Bier
    dir

12. Wir bringen _____. etwas
    dir

13. Bitte, geben Sie _____! das Buch
    mir

    Bitte, geben Sie _____! es
    mir

14. Sagen Sie _____! die Adresse
    meiner Sekretärin

    Sagen Sie _____! die Adresse
    ihr

    Sagen Sie _____! sie
    meiner Sekretärin

    Sagen Sie _____! sie
    ihr

Express in German

1. I'll show you my computer.
   I'll show it to you.

2. I'm going to buy the children something.
   I'm going to buy them something.

3. We're going to show them the house.
   We're going to show it to them.

4. Tell it to your friends.
   Tell it to them.

5. Are you going to send me the books?
   Are you going to send them to me?

6. We'll bring you something.

7. Are you going to give Hans the key?
   Are you going to give him the key?

8. I'll buy you a beer.

9. Give him the letter.
   Give it to him.

10. I'll bring you the newspaper.
    I'll bring it to you.

11. I won't tell them anything.

12. Tell my secretary the address.
    Tell her the address.
    Tell it to my secretary.
    Tell it to her.

B. Order of adverbs

When a German sentence contains two or more adverbial expressions, they occur in the following order:

TIME	MANNER	PLACE
wann / *when*	**wie** / *how*	**wo** / *where*

	WANN	**WIE**	**WO**
Ich fahre	immer	langsam.	
Ich fahre	sehr oft		nach Berlin.
Ich fahre		schnell	nach Hause.
Ich fahre	in zwei Wochen		nach Deutschland.

NOTE: As you can see from the prepositional phrases **nach Berlin, nach Hause, in zwei Wochen,** and **nach Deutschland,** entire phrases can function as adverbs.

■ DRILLS

Word Order with Adverbial Expressions

Put the adverbial expressions into their proper order. (This drill does *not* require the use of case endings.)

1. Ich fahre   (nach Stuttgart
                   morgen).
2. Er arbeitet   (immer
                   zu Hause).
3. Er bleibt   (hier
                   zehn Tage).
4. Ich gehe   (nach Hause
                   sehr selten).
5. Wir sind   (da
                   bald).
6. Machst du das   (immer
                   so)?
7. Wir bleiben   (in Amerika
                   zwei Jahre).
8. Ich gehe   (zu Hans
                   später).
9. Er spricht   (meistens
                   zu laut).
10. Man ißt   (in Frankreich
                   sehr gut).

Express in German

1. He's staying here ten days.
2. One eats very well in France.
3. We'll be there soon.
4. I'm going to Hans' later.
5. He always works at home.

6. I'm going to Stuttgart tomorrow.
7. We're staying there two years.
8. Do you always do it that way?
9. He usually talks too loud.
10. I very rarely go home.

Word Order with Adverbial Expressions

(This drill *requires* the use of case endings.)

1. Wir gehen   (ins Theater
                  am Freitag).
2. Wir kommen   (morgen
                  zu euch).
3. Er fährt   (aufs Land
                im Juli).
4. Ich arbeite   (im Büro
                  allein).
5. Er bleibt   (bei uns
                 zwei Wochen).
6. Sie gehen   (nach Hause
                  nach dem Konzert).
7. Ich fahre   (nach Deutschland
                  nächstes Jahr).
8. Hans fährt   (mit dem Wagen
                  in die Stadt).
9. Er kommt   (mit dem Zug
                 morgen).
10. Ich fahre   (nach Mainz
                  im August).

Express in German

1. We're going to the country in July.
2. I'm going to the theater on Friday.
3. I'm going to Germany next year.
4. He's working alone in his office.
5. He's staying at our place for two weeks.
6. He's coming on the train tomorrow.
7. I'm going to Mainz in August.
8. We're going home after the concert.

C. Position of NICHT (and NIE) in the simple sentence

In a simple sentence **nicht** comes

after subject, verb, + all objects:

> Ich gebe es ihm nicht.
> Gibst du es mir nicht?

before everything else:

> Ich sehe ihn nicht oft.   (before time expression)
> Er ist nicht zu Hause.   (before expression of place)
> Er läuft nicht schnell.   (before expression of manner)
> Das ist nicht schön.   (before predicate adjective)
> Sie geht nicht weg.   (before separable prefix)
> Er will nicht bleiben.   (before infinitive)
> Wir haben ihn nicht gesehen.   (before past participle)

EXCEPTIONS:

1. *specific time expressions*

> Ich arbeite heute (diese Woche) nicht.

Nicht comes *after specific* time expressions, but *before general* time expressions (e.g., Ich sehe ihn nicht oft.).

2. *special stress*

Nicht can come before an object that is being given special emphasis:

> Ich gab es nicht Karl (sondern Hans).

This implies a contrast, e.g., *not* to Karl *but rather* to Hans.

 DRILLS

Introductory Drills on Negative Constructions

Negate the following statements and questions.
1. Siehst du ihn?
2. Ich verstehe ihn.
3. Bleibt er hier?
4. Ich finde das Buch sehr interessant.

5. Er ist immer hier.
6. Gehst du heute abend nach Hause?
7. Arbeitet er zu Hause?
8. Fährt er zu schnell?
9. Machst du das immer so?
10. Ich sehe ihn sehr oft.
11. Er ist jetzt da.
12. Ich komme aus Berlin.
13. Werden Sie müde?
14. Ich sag's dir.

Express in German

1. I don't understand him.
2. Aren't you going home this evening?
3. He isn't there now.
4. Aren't you getting tired?
5. Don't you see him?
6. I don't find that book very interesting.
7. Isn't he driving too fast?
8. I don't come from Berlin.
9. Doesn't he work at home?
10. Don't you always do it that way?
11. I don't see him very often.
12. He isn't always here.
13. I won't tell you.
14. Isn't he staying here?

Advanced Drills on Negative Constructions

Negate the following statements and questions.

1. Warum fährst du mit dem Zug?
2. Sie arbeitet allein im Büro.
3. Alwin ist heute in die Stadt gegangen.
4. Kurt ist gestern gekommen.
5. Können Sie das für mich machen?
6. Er ist heute vorbeigekommen.
7. Das ist sehr interessant.
8. Das Hotel liegt neben dem Bahnhof.
9. Laufen Sie gern ski?
10. Das ist leicht zu machen.

11. Ich kann es heute machen.
12. Er hat uns sehr gut unterhalten.

Express in German

1. I can't do it today.
2. Kurt didn't come yesterday.
3. That isn't very interesting.
4. Why didn't you take the train?
5. Don't you like to ski?
6. She isn't working at the office.
7. That isn't easy to do.
8. Can't you do that for me?
9. Alwin didn't go downtown today.
10. He didn't come by yesterday.
11. He didn't entertain us very well.
12. The hotel isn't next to the railroad station.

II. NOUNS

A. Nouns and gender

1. Introduction

The best way to learn the gender of a German noun is to learn its definite article when you learn the noun. Think of the noun and its article as a unit: not **Tisch** or **Lampe** or **Sofa,** but *der* **Tisch,** *die* **Lampe,** *das* **Sofa.** There are a few simple rules, however, that will let you predict the gender of some of the most common groups of nouns you will meet.*

2. Predictably masculine nouns

1. Nouns referring to male persons, including their *nationalities* and *professions.*

---

* We have limited ourselves to a manageable set of rules that govern a meaningful number of nouns. There are so many rules and exceptions concerning noun gender that to learn them all would be more difficult than learning the gender of each noun by rote.

der Mann   der Arzt   der Amerikaner
der Bruder   der Lehrer   der Schweizer

2. Nouns with the suffix –er added to the stem of a verb.

der Sprecher   der Wecker

NOTE: When the stem vowel of the verb changes from **a** to **ä** or from **au** to **äu** in the 3rd person singular, the changed stem is normally, but not always, used in forming the noun.

	backen	der Bäcker
	laufen	der Läufer
but:	fahren	der Fahrer

3. Nouns referring to days, parts of days, months, and seasons.

der Montag   der September
der Abend   der Herbst

3. Predictably feminine nouns

1. Nouns referring to female persons, including their *nationalities* and *professions*.

die Frau   die Ärztin*   die Amerikanerin
die Schwester   die Lehrerin   die Schweizerin

2. Nouns with the following suffixes:

–ei   die Bäckerei, die Metzgerei

–heit   die Freiheit, die Gesundheit

–keit   die Freundlichkeit, die Einsamkeit

–schaft   die Freundschaft, die Gesellschaft

–ung   die Zeitung, die Wohnung

* **die Ärztin,** etc. The suffix –**in** changes a masculine noun into its female counterpart. If the vowel in the syllable immediately preceding the suffix is **a, o, u,** or **au** it is normally umlauted, e.g., **der Arzt,** but **die Ärztin.**

3. Most nouns ending in **–e**

<blockquote>die Suppe, die Liebe, die Garage</blockquote>

Common exceptions: **der Junge, das Ende**

4. Predictably neuter nouns

1. Nouns with the suffixes:

–chen	das Mädchen, das Märchen
–lein	das Fräulein, das Büchlein

NOTE: The vowel of the preceding syllable is umlauted if possible, that is, if it is **a, o, u,** or **au.**

2. Infinitives used as nouns:

<blockquote>das Essen, das Laufen, das Schwimmen</blockquote>

NOTE: The English equivalents of these nouns normally end in –ing, e.g., *running, swimming*. But this is not always the case: **Essen** can mean both *eating* and *meal*.

3. Proper names of towns and cities, and most states, countries, and continents.

<blockquote>

das Berlin der zwanziger Jahre
the Berlin of the twenties

das schöne Italien
beautiful Italy

das Europa von heute
the Europe of today

</blockquote>

NOTE: Articles are normally only used with modifiers, that is, with words which give some additional information, such as the adjective **schön** or the prepositional phrase **von heute.**

But even when there is no modifier present, it is necessary to know the gender:

<blockquote>Kennst du Italien?   Es ist großartig!</blockquote>

DRILLS

Gender Identification

Read the following words, preceding each of them by **der, das,** or **die** to indicate its gender.

Examples: Schönheit
die Schönheit

Lautsprecher
der Lautsprecher

a. 1. Sprecher
2. Krankheit
3. Hoffnung
4. Gehen
5. Dezember
6. Hamburg
7. Landschaft
8. Reise
9. Freitag
10. Bäckerei

b. 1. Morgen
2. Ärztin
3. Städtchen
4. Freund
5. Dankbarkeit
6. Schweden
7. Absender
8. Schönheit
9. Geschichte
10. Ingenieur

c. 1. Ordnung
2. Tochter
3. Europa
4. Norweger
5. Heidelberg
6. Küche
7. Onkel
8. Schneiderei
9. Herbst
10. Wissen

d. 1. Italienerin
2. Tennisschläger
3. Fräulein
4. Tante
5. Frankreich
6. Gewerkschaft
7. Pferderennen
8. Anwalt
9. Mittwoch
10. Müdigkeit

e. 1. Briefträger
2. Häuschen
3. Vorlesung
4. Frühling
5. Kindheit
6. Fahren
7. Fehler
8. Engländerin
9. März
10. Schweinerei

f. 1. Leidenschaft
2. Spanier
3. Bächlein
4. Fahrer
5. Lehrerin
6. Sommer
7. Südamerika
8. Laufen
9. Juli
10. Götterdämmerung

B. Formation of noun plurals

There are a limited number of plural forms that are commonly used in German. Although one can't usually predict the plural form of a given noun, familiarity with the seven basic plural patterns is highly useful.

	Singular	Plural	Changes from Singular
1.	Brief	Briefe	−e
2.	Mantel	Mäntel	¨
3.	Anzug	Anzüge	¨e
4.	Kleid	Kleider	−er (see NOTE 1)
	Buch	Bücher	¨er
5.	Adresse	Adressen	−n (see NOTE 2)
	Hemd	Hemden	−en
6.	Wagen	Wagen	− (no change)
7.	Auto	Autos	−s

NOTE 1: ¨**er**

Kleid	Kleider	−er
Buch	Bücher	¨er

This group always takes an −**er** ending and takes an umlaut if possible (that is, if the stem vowel of the noun is a vowel that can take an umlaut: **a, o, u,** and **au**).

NOTE 2: −**(e)n**

Adresse	Adressen	−n
Hemd	Hemden	−en

The plural forms of this group always end in −**en.** If the singular form ends in an −**e,** then only an −**n** ending is added.

 DRILLS

Plural Forms

Put the noun phrases in boldface into the plural. (In some cases, you will also have to change the verb form.)

Example: Was kostet **das Buch?**
            Was **kosten die Bücher?**

a. −e

1. Ich schreibe **den Brief** morgen.
2. **Dieser Tisch** ist hübsch.
3. **Mein Freund** kommt heute abend.
4. **Der Abend** ist kühl.
5. **Mein Bein** tut weh.

b. ¨

1. **Der Laden** ist geschlossen.
2. **Dieser Mantel** ist zu teuer.
3. Kennen Sie **meine Tochter?**
4. **Dieser Apfel** ist gut.
5. **Mein Bruder** studiert in Frankfurt.

c. ¨e

1. **Welcher Zug** fährt nach Köln?
2. Ich nehme **meinen Sohn** mit.
3. **Dieser Platz** ist belegt.
4. **Welchen Anzug** meinst du?
5. **Die Nacht** ist sehr schön.

d. ⁽¨⁾er

1. Ich nehme **dieses** Buch.
2. **Ihr Kleid** ist sehr hübsch.
3. Wer ist **der Mann** da drüben?
4. Ich habe **dieses Bild** gern.
5. **Das Haus** ist sehr alt.

e. −(e)n

1. Weißt du **die Adresse?**
2. **Die Prüfung** ist morgen.
3. Wo ist **meine Krawatte?**
4. **Meine Schwester** wohnt in Berlin.
5. Ich finde **dieses Hemd** hübsch.
6. Kaufst du **die Zeitung?**

f. –

1. Mach **das Fenster** zu!
2. **Das Zimmer** ist zu klein.
3. Wo ist **mein Koffer?**
4. Gib mir **den Teller,** bitte.
5. **Dieser Wagen** kostet zu viel.

g. –s

1. **Dieses Auto** ist schnell.
2. Was kostet **dieses Radio?**
3. **Das Hotel** ist zu teuer.
4. Ich nehme **diesen Pulli.**
5. **Das Büro** ist geschlossen.

Mixed Drills

1. **Welcher Zug** fährt nach Köln?
2. **Dieser Mantel** ist zu teuer.
3. Ich schreibe **den Brief** morgen.
4. Mach **das Fenster** zu!
5. **Die Prüfung** ist morgen.
6. Ich nehme **dieses Buch.**
7. **Das Büro** ist geschlossen.
8. **Mein Freund** kommt heute abend.
9. Weißt du **die Adresse?**
10. Wo ist **mein Koffer?**
11. Was kostet **dieses Radio?**
12. **Der Laden** ist geschlossen.
13. **Ihr Kleid** ist sehr hübsch.
14. **Meine Schwester** wohnt in Berlin.
15. **Dieser Platz** ist belegt.
16. **Das Zimmer** ist sehr klein.
17. **Dieses Hotel** ist zu teuer.
18. **Mein Bein** tut weh.
19. **Welchen Anzug** meinst du?
20. Ich finde **dieses Hemd** hübsch.
21. **Mein Bruder** studiert in Mainz.
22. Wer ist **der Mann** da drüben?
23. Gib mir **den Teller,** bitte.

24. **Dieses Auto** ist schnell.
25. Ich nehme **meinen Sohn** mit.
26. **Der Abend** ist kühl.
27. **Das Haus** ist sehr alt.
28. Wo ist **meine Krawatte?**

Express in German

1. My friends are coming this evening.
2. I'll take these books.
3. Where are my suitcases?
4. The stores are closed.
5. Which suits do you mean?
6. These hotels are too expensive.
7. The tests are tomorrow.
8. Which trains go to Cologne?
9. My legs hurt.
10. Her dresses are very pretty.
11. Close the windows!
12. These cars are fast.
13. I'll write the letters tomorrow.
14. Who are the men over there?
15. These coats are too expensive.
16. Do you know the addresses?
17. The rooms are very small.
18. The offices are closed.
19. Where are my ties?
20. These seats are taken.

C. Weak nouns*

1. The basic pattern

A few German nouns take endings in the *singular* as well as the plural. Almost all of these nouns are *masculine* and have the ending **–en** in all cases

---

* This section should be done after the final genitive patterns in Chapter 2, "Adjective Endings," p. 80.

except the *nominative singular:*

	SINGULAR	PLURAL
NOM.	der Student	die Studenten
ACC.	den Studenten	die Studenten
DAT.	dem Studenten	den Studenten
GEN.	des Studenten	der Studenten

If the nominative singular already ends in −e (for example, **der Junge, der Kunde**), all you do is add an −n to get the −en ending:

	SINGULAR	PLURAL
NOM.	der Junge	die Jungen
ACC.	den Jungen	die Jungen
DAT.	dem Jungen	den Jungen
GEN.	des Jungen	der Jungen

EXCEPTION:

	SINGULAR	PLURAL
NOM.	der Herr	die Herren
ACC.	den Herrn	die Herren
DAT.	dem Herrn	den Herren
GEN.	des Herrn	der Herren

As you can see, **Herr** takes only an −n ending in the singular.

2. The subgroup of the basic pattern

There is a subgroup of weak nouns that takes an −**ens** ending (rather than −**en**) in the genitive singular. Except for this difference, these nouns behave like other weak nouns:

	SINGULAR	PLURAL
NOM.	der Name	die Namen
ACC.	den Namen	die Namen
DAT.	dem Namen	den Namen
GEN.	des Namens	der Namen

Members of this group include **der Gedanke, der Glaube, der Name** and **der Wille.**

 DRILLS

Fill-ins

Supply the missing noun endings and adjective endings.

1. Sagen Sie mir Ihr____ Name____, bitte.
2. Sie muß zu ein____ Spezialist____ gehen.
3. Er hilft ein____ Kunde____.
4. Rufen Sie ein____ Polizist____!
5. Um Gottes Wille____!
6. All____ Student____ brauchen Geld.
7. Sie haben ein____ neu____ Präsident____.
8. Trotz sein____ deutsch____ Name____ spricht er kein Deutsch.
9. Er hat nie ein____ originell____ Gedanke____ gehabt.
10. Es ist eine Frage d____ Glaube____. (a question of faith)
11. Zeigen Sie dies____ Herr____ (*sing.*) einen Anzug.
12. Ich habe ihn als Patient____ gehabt.
13. Das ist der Wagen mein____ Junge____. (*lit.* "of my boy")
14. Er hilft viel____ Mensch____.

Express in German

1. All students need money.
2. Show this gentlemen a suit.
3. Call a policeman!
4. That's my boy's car.
5. He helps a lot of people. (*Use* **Mensch.**)
6. Tell me your name, please.
7. It's a question of faith.

8. She has to go to a specialist.
9. He never had an original thought.
10. In spite of his German name he doesn't speak any German.
11. I had him as a patient.
12. For God's sake!
13. He's helping a customer.
14. They have a new president.

III. SETZEN / SITZEN, LEGEN / LIEGEN, HÄNGEN / HÄNGEN*

German and English have three pairs of look-alike verbs that are also related in meaning:

setzen / sitzen	*to set / to sit*
legen / liegen	*to lay / to lie*
hängen / hängen	*to hang / to hang*

1. **Setzen, legen,** and **hängen** are *transitive* (i.e., can take a direct object):

SUBJECT	VERB	D.O.	ADVERBIAL PHRASE
Die Gäste	legen	ihre Mäntel	auf das Bett.

Sitzen, liegen, and **hängen** are *intransitive* (cannot take a direct object):

	SUBJECT	VERB	ADVERBIAL PHRASE
	Die Mäntel	liegen	auf dem Bett.

No direct object is possible in this last sentence.

2. When *adverbs of place* are used with the *transitive verbs* **setzen, legen,** and **hängen,** there is *motion* involved and the adverbs answer the question **wohin** / *where (to).*†

When adverbs of place are used with the *intransitive verbs* **sitzen, liegen,** and **hängen,** there is *no motion* involved and the adverbs answer the question **wo** / *where.*

---

* This special problem should be done after two-way prepositions.

† For a discussion of the distinction between **wo** and **wohin,** see p. 110, Two-way Prepositions.

MOTION   Die Gäste legen ihre Mäntel auf *das* Bett.   (wohin + acc.)

NO MOTION   Die Mäntel liegen auf *dem* Bett.   (wo + dat.)

3. **Setzen, legen, hängen** (*transitive*) are *weak* (regular) verbs.
Sitzen, liegen, hängen (*intransitive*) are *strong* (irregular) verbs.

The following table compares the principal parts of these verbs with those of their English counterparts:

Comparison of Principal Parts

Transitive			Intransitive		
INFINITIVE	PAST	PRESENT PERFECT	INFINITIVE	PAST	PRESENT PERFECT
setzen	**setzte**	**hat gesetzt**	**sitzen**	**saß**	**hat gesessen**
to set	set	has set	to sit	sat	has sat
legen	**legte**	**hat gelegt**	**liegen**	**lag**	**hat gelegen**
to lay	laid	has laid	to lie	lay	has lain
hängen	**hängte**	**hat gehängt**	**hängen**	**hing**	**hat gehangen**
to hang	hung	has hung*	to hang	hung	has hung

DRILLS

Substitution Drills: Past and Present Perfect Tenses

Put the following present tense sentences into the past tense and the present perfect tense.

1. Er hängt seine Jacke an den Haken.
2. Die Jacke hängt an den Haken.
3. Sie setzt das Kind auf das Sofa.
4. Das Kind sitzt auf dem Sofa.
5. Er legt das Buch auf den Tisch.
6. Das Buch liegt auf dem Tisch.

---

* English has a regular transitive verb: *to hang   hanged   has hanged,* but it is reserved for the specific case of *to execute by hanging.*

Synthetic Exercises

Form complete sentences in the present tense, past tense, and present perfect tense, unless otherwise indicated.

1. Wir / sitzen / an / Fenster
2. Erich / hängen / sein- / Jacke / an / Haken
3. Warum / liegen / du so lange / in / Bett / ?
4. Frau / setzen / Kind / auf / Sofa
5. Wir / hängen / das Schild / über / Tür
6. Zeitung / liegen / auf / Tisch
7. Schlüssel / hängen / an / Tür
8. Er / legen / Zeitung / auf / Stuhl
9. Kinder / sitzen / auf / Sofa
10. Bild / hängen / über / Bett
11. Ich / legen / Mäntel / auf / Bett
12. Er / setzen / Radio / Fußboden

Express in German

1. We were sitting at the window.
2. I laid the coats on the bed.
3. Erich hung his jacket on the hook.
4. Why did you lie in bed so long? (*present perfect*)
5. The children were sitting on the sofa.
6. He laid the newspaper on the chair.
7. We hung the sign over the door.
8. The key is hanging on the door.
9. The newspaper is lying on the table.
10. He set the radio on the floor.

IV. *HIN* AND *HER*

A. Introduction

Hin and **her** are used to show whether something is moving towards the speaker (**her**) or away from the speaker (**hin**). For example, if you were standing on the first floor and someone came downstairs *towards you,* you would say:

> Er kommt die Treppe herunter.
> (He's coming downstairs.)

If you were upstairs and the person were going downstairs, *away from you,* you would say:

> Er geht die Treppe hinunter.
> (He's going downstairs.)

B. *Hin* and *her* as verbal compliments

Both **hin** and **her** can be used by themselves as verbal complements:

> Kommen Sie her!*   (Come here!)
> Ich fahre morgen hin.*   (I'm driving there tomorrow.)

NOTE: When used by themselves, **her** is normally translated as English *here* and **hin** corresponds to English *there.*

C. *Hin* and *her* used with verb prefixes

Hin and **her** are often found preceding some verb prefixes:

herunter	hinunter	(down)
herauf	hinauf	(up)
heraus	hinaus	(out)
herein	hinein	(in)

The sets of **hin** and **her** compounds above are by far the most commonly used.

D. *Wohin/Woher* *

Hin and **her** are often *suffixed* to the question word **wo:**

> Wohin? (Where to?)   Woher? (Where from?)

When used with **wo, hin** and **her** can either remain suffixed to **wo:**

> Wohin gehen Sie?   (Where are you going [to]?)

or they can separate and go to the end of the sentence:

> Wo gehen Sie hin?   (Where are you going [to]?)

---

* As the examples show, **her** is almost always used with the verb **kommen,** while **hin** is used with **gehen, fahren,** and other verbs which imply motion *away from* the speaker. (One would say: "*Come* to me," but: "*Go* away!".)

Both forms are correct but the separated forms are much more common in spoken German.

NOTE the following common idiom:

Wo kommen Sie *her?*   (*Where* do you come *from?*)

■ DRILLS

Supply the appropriate forms of **hin** or **her.**
1. Kommen Sie ___ein, bitte.
2. Sie ist gerade ___ausgegangen.
3. Er kam die Treppe ___unter.
4. Können Sie in einer Stunde ___aufkommen?
5. Wo fahren Sie denn morgen ___?
6. Sie ist in den Keller ___untergegangen.
7. Kannst du einen Moment ___auskommen?
8. Er ging die Treppe ___auf und in sein Zimmer ___ein.
9. Wo kommen Sie ___?

Express in German

1. Where are you going tomorrow?
2. He came down the stairs.
3. Can you come out for a moment?
4. She went down into the cellar.
5. Come in, please.
6. He went up the stairs and into his room.
7. She just went out.
8. Where do you come from?
9. Can you come up in an hour?

V. ADJECTIVAL NOUNS

A. Introduction

Look at the following two sentences:

> Hans is a German exchange student.
> Hans is a German.

In the first sentence, *German* is an adjective: it modifies the noun *student*. In the second sentence, however, *German* is a noun.

Adjectives can also function as nouns in German. In fact, this is far more common in German than it is in English.

B. General rules

1. Capitalization

Adjectives functioning as nouns are capitalized (as are all German nouns):

der Deutsche

2. Adjective endings

German adjectives take the same adjective endings when they function as nouns as they do when functioning as adjectives:

Er ist ein junger deutscher Student.
Er ist ein junger Deutscher.

Similarly: Sie ist eine junge deutsche Studentin.
Sie ist eine junge Deutsche.

with **der**-words	MASCULINE		FEMININE		PLURAL	
NOM.	der	Deutsche	die	Deutsche	die	Deutschen
ACC.	den	Deutschen	die	Deutsche	die	Deutschen
DAT.	dem	Deutschen	der	Deutschen	den	Deutschen
GEN.	des	Deutschen	der	Deutschen	der	Deutschen
with **ein**-words						
NOM.	ein	Deutscher	eine	Deutsche	keine	Deutschen
ACC.	einen	Deutschen	eine	Deutsche	keine	Deutschen
DAT.	einem	Deutschen	einer	Deutschen	keinen	Deutschen
GEN.	eines	Deutschen	einer	Deutschen	keiner	Deutschen

after **wenige, einige, andere, mehrere, viele**	
NOM.	viele Deutsche
ACC.	viele Deutsche
DAT.	vielen Deutschen
GEN.	vieler Deutscher

> when not preceded by a limiting word
> _____
> Er ist Deutscher.*
> Sie ist Deutsche.
> Sie sind Deutsche.

a. Common adjectival nouns

der/die Angestellte	employee
der/die Arme	poor man, woman
der Beamte	official, government employee
(die Beamtin, –nen	
is a normal [not	
adjectival] noun)	
der/die Bekannte	acquaintance
der/die Blonde	blond
der/die Deutsche	German
der/die Fremde	tourist, stranger
der/die Tote	dead man, woman

3. Gender

a. *Masculine* and *feminine* adjectival nouns usually refer to people:

der Verwandte   relative (male)

die Verwandte   relative (female)

b. *Neuter* adjectival nouns refer to things, qualities, or characteristics:

Das ist das Gute (Schlechte, Dumme) daran.
(That's *the good thing* [*bad thing, stupid thing*] about it.)

_____

* When not preceded by an adjective, nationalities (**Deutscher**) and professions (**Beamter**) are used without the indefinite article in the nominative case:

Er ist Deutscher.   (He's *a* German.)
Er ist Beamter.   (He's *a* government employee.)

But when the expression includes an adjective, the indefinite article *is* used:

Er ist **ein junger** Deutscher.
Er ist **ein hoher** Beamter.

Neuter adjectival nouns are commonly found after **etwas, nichts, viel, wenig,** and **alles:**

> Er hat nichts Interessantes gesagt.
> (He didn't say anything interesting.)

> Ich brauche etwas Größeres.
> (I need something larger.)

Adjectives following etwas, nichts, viel, and wenig take *strong endings.*

    etwas anderes*
    nichts Besonderes
    viel Gutes (*lit.*: much that is good)
    wenig Neues (*lit.*: little that is new)

Adjectives following alles take *weak* endings.

    alles mögliche*

DRILLS

Adjectival Nouns: Masculine and Feminine

Supply the correct endings.
1. Sie ist ein____ Verwandt____ von mir.
2. Er ist ein Fremd____.
3. Sie haben viel____ Bekannt____ in dieser Stadt.
4. Der Brief ist von ein____ Verwandt____ (*masculine*).
5. Sie ist Angestellt____ bei einem Reisebüro.
6. Beamt____ (*plural*) verdienen nicht viel.
7. Er ist ein alt____ Bekannt____ von mir.
8. Sie kennt viel____ Deutsch____.
9. Ich habe es von ein____ Verwandt____ (*feminine*) bekommen.
10. Ist er Beamt____?
11. Ich kenne einig____ Angestellt____ bei der Deutschen Bank.
12. Ach Hans. Du Arm____!
13. Mein____ Verwandt____ wohnen alle in Süddeutschland.
14. Er hat ein____ Tot____ (*masculine*) in der Badewanne gefunden.
15. Viel____ Fremd____ besuchen diese Stadt.

---

* Note that **andere(s)** and **mögliche(s)** are *not* capitalized.

16. Sie ist ein___ alt___ Bekannt___ von mir.
17. Gehen Sie zu d___ Beamt___ (*masculine*) da vorne.
18. Siehst du d___ Blond___ (*masc. or fem.*) da drüben?

Adjectival Nouns: Neuter

Supply the correct endings.

1. Es ist nichts Wichtig___.
2. Haben Sie etwas Neu___ gehört?
3. Wir versuchen alles möglich___.
4. Ich brauche etwas Größer___.
5. Das Schlecht___ daran ist, daß ich mehr arbeiten muß.
6. Es ist nichts Besonder___.
7. Ich möchte etwas Kalt___ trinken.
8. Das war das Gut___ daran.
9. Haben Sie nichts ander___?
10. Das Nett___ daran ist, daß Renate da sein wird.
11. Ich möchte eine Jacke, bitte. Etwas Dunkl___.
12. Alles Gut___! (*a wish:* "All the best to you!")
13. Er hat nichts Interessant___ gesagt.

Adjectival Nouns: Mixed Drills

Supply the correct endings.

1. Mein___ Verwandt___ wohnen alle in Süddeutschland.
2. Er hat nichts Interessant___ gesagt.
3. Haben Sie nichts ander___?
4. Er ist ein alt___ Bekannt___ von mir.
5. Das war das Gut___ daran.
6. Viel___ Fremd___ besuchen diese Stadt.
7. Haben Sie etwas Neu___ gehört?
8. Sie ist ein___ Verwandt___ von mir.
9. Alles Gut___!
10. Es ist nichts Wichtig___.
11. Sie kennt viel___ Deutsch___.
12. Ist sie Beamt___?
13. Ich brauche etwas Größer___.
14. Ist er ein Verwandt___ von dir?
15. Wir versuchen alles möglich___.
16. Sie ist Angestellt___ bei einem Reisebüro.
17. Siehst du d___ Blond___ da drüben?

18. Das Nett___ daran ist, daß Renate da sein wird.
19. Gehen Sie zu d___ Beamt___ (*masculine*) da vorne.
20. Sie haben viel___ Bekannt___ in dieser Stadt.
21. Es ist nichts Besonder___.
22. Ich möchte eine Jacke, bitte. Etwas Dunkl___.
23. Der Brief ist von mein___ Verwandt___ (*plural*) in Mainz.
24. Beam___ (*plural*) verdienen nicht viel.

Express in German

1. It's nothing important.
2. Is he a relative of yours?
3. They have a lot of friends (acquaintances) in this city.
4. He didn't say anything interesting.
5. She's an employee at a travel agency.
6. We're trying everything possible.
7. She knows a lot of Germans.
8. She's a relative of mine.
9. I need something bigger.
10. That was the good thing about it.
11. Government employees don't earn much.
12. It's nothing special.
13. A lot of tourists visit this city.
14. All the best!
15. The letter is from my relatives in Mainz.
16. Don't you have anything else (different)?
17. He's an old friend (acquaintance) of mine.
18. Do you see the blond over there?
19. The nice thing about it is that Renate will be there.
20. Have you heard anything new?
21. My relatives all live in South Germany.

VI. *EIN*-WORDS AS PRONOUNS

A. Introduction

The ein-words (**ein, kein,** and the possessive adjectives) are most often found in noun phrases: *ein* **Tisch,** *kein* **Geld,** *mein* **Löffel.** Once a noun has been used, however, it is usually not repeated, but rather replaced by a pronoun— either a normal personal pronoun or, if necessary, an **ein**-word used as a pronoun:

> Ich habe keinen Löffel.   Hier, nehmen Sie meinen.
> (I don't have a spoon.)   (Here, take mine.)

There is an important difference in form between **ein**-words in their normal usage and **ein**-words used as pronouns: in the three instances where **ein**-words don't take strong endings in noun phrases, *they do take strong endings when used as pronouns:*

MASC. NOM. SING.   Kein☐ Brief ist gekommen.   Keiner ist gekommen.

NEUT. NOM. SING.   Kein☐ Buch ist gekommen.   Keines* ist gekommen.

NEUT. ACC. SING.   Ich habe kein☐ Geld.   Ich habe keines.

B. The special case of *man*

The pronoun **man** (*one*) doesn't carry its own stem into the accusative and dative. Instead, it uses **einen** and **einem** as its accusative and dative forms:

> NOMINATIVE   Man sagt das nicht.
> (*One*† doesn't say that.
> You don't say that.)

> ACCUSATIVE   Das kann einen enttäuschen.
> (That can disappoint *one*.
> That can disappoint you.)

> DATIVE   Das kann einem weh tun.
> (That can hurt *one*.
> That can hurt you.)

NOTE: **Man** stays **man**. Once you've started a train of thought using the pronoun **man,** you have to continue with **man.** You can't shift to the pronoun **er,** as the following example shows:

> Zuerst liest man die Speisekarte. Dann bestellt man sein Essen.
> (First you read the menu. Then you order your meal.)

---

* In conversational German the **e** is dropped from **keines** and it becomes **keins.**

† The pronoun **man** is frequently used in conversational German, whereas its English counterpart *one* has become stuffy and overformal. Spoken English normally uses "you" where German uses **man.**

▇ DRILLS

Supply the appropriate form of **man** or the necessary endings for the **ein**-words used as pronouns.

1. Hast du einen Schlüssel? Nein, ich habe kein____.
2. Kann ich dein Buch leihen? Ich habe mein____ vergessen.
3. So etwas kauft man nicht, wenn es ein____ zu teuer ist.
4. Hast du einen Kuli? Mein____ ist kaputt.
5. Leg deinen Mantel auf mein____.
6. Leihst du mir dein Auto? Mein____ ist bei der Reparatur.
7. Wenn man ein Zimmer mietet, muß____ eine Kaution zahlen.

Express in German

1. Will you lend me your car? Mine is in the shop.
2. Do you have a key? No, I don't have one.
3. When you rent a room, you have to pay a deposit. (*Use* **man.**)
4. Do you have a ballpoint? Mine's broken.
5. Lay your coat on top of mine.
6. You don't buy something like that if it is too expensive for you. (*Use* **man.**)
7. Can I borrow your book? I forgot mine.

VII. THE PRESENT PARTICIPLE

A. Formation

> *infinitive* + **d**
> koch**end**   boiling
> führ**end**   leading

The German present participle is formed by adding the ending **–d** to the infinitive form of the verb.

B. Usage

German present participles usually function as *adjectives* and take the usual adjective endings:

> kochend es Wasser   boiling water
> die führend en Kritiker   the leading critics

Occasionally, one finds them in other environments:

„In die Hütte tretend hatte er den Todgeweihten beim Abendessen am Tisch sitzend vorgefunden, in Hemdsärmeln mit beiden Backen kauend "

Bertolt Brecht, „Der Augsburger Kreidekreis"

(*Stepping* into the cottage he had found the doomed man at dinner, *sitting* at the table in his shirt-sleeves, *chewing* with both cheeks.)

Such constructions are rare, however, and almost never occur in *spoken* German.

C. Contrastive usage

The German present participle should never be confused with progressive forms of English verbs.

> Er sitzt am Tisch.   He *is sitting* at the table.
> Er saß am Tisch.   He *was sitting* at the table.

German has *no* progressive verb forms.

 DRILLS

Present Participles

Change the infinitives into present participles, and supply the correct adjective endings.

1. Kein denken____ Mensch tut so etwas.
2. Das ist ein brennen____ Problem.

3. Aber er ist doch ein zahlen____ Gast.
4. Ich möchte ein Zimmer mit fließen____ Wasser.
5. In kommen____ Jahren machen wir das anders.
6. Das war eine überraschen____ Antwort.
7. Er sagte es mit ein____ wohlwollen____ Lächeln.
8. Das ist ein____ wachsen____ Firma.
9. Vorsicht vor d____ fahren____ Zug! (*dative*)
10. Das ist ein stören____ Lärm.
11. Es war ein erschrecken____ Erlebnis.
12. Sie sagte es mit zittern____ Stimme.
13. Ja, Heidi, es gibt doch fliegen____ Untertassen.
14. Das ist kein überzeugen____ Argument.
15. Er ist ein hervorragen____ Physiker.

Express in German

1. That was a surprising answer.
2. That's a burning problem.
3. But he's a paying guest.
4. She said it with (a) trembling voice.
5. That's a disturbing noise.
6. He's an outstanding physicist.
7. I'd like a room with running water.
8. That's not a convincing argument.
9. It was a frightening experience.
10. It's a growing firm.
11. He said it with a well-meaning smile.
12. In coming years we'll do that differently.
13. Yes, Heidi, there really are flying saucers.
14. Watch out for (**Vorsicht vor**) the moving train.
15. No thinking person does something like that.

VIII. FUTURE PERFECT

A. Formation

The future perfect, like the future, consists of **werden** + *infinitive*. The only difference is that in this case the infinitive is a so-called *perfective infinitive*.

The perfective infinitive consists of the *past participle of a verb* followed by the *infinitive of its perfect auxiliary* (i.e., **haben** or **sein**)

REGULAR INFINITIVE	PRESENT PERFECT	PERFECTIVE INFINITIVE
vergessen (to forget)	hat vergessen (has forgotten)	vergessen haben (to have forgotten)
nehmen (to take)	hat genommen (has taken)	genommen haben (to have taken)
sein (to be)	ist gewesen (has been)	gewesen sein (to have been)
gehen (to go)	ist gegangen (has gone)	gegangen sein (to have gone)
werden (to become)	ist geworden (has become)	geworden sein (to have become)

Note that the perfect auxiliary can be either **sein** or **haben** depending upon the verb in question and that consequently the *perfect infinitive* will end in either **sein** or **haben**.

B. Comparison

		INFINITIVE
FUTURE	Ich werde es	nehmen .
	I *will*	*take* it.

		PERFECT INFINITIVE
FUTURE PERFECT	Ich werde es	genommen haben .
	I *will*	*have taken* it.

		INFINITIVE
FUTURE	Er wird	gehen .
	He *will*	*go.*

		PERFECT INFINITIVE
FUTURE PERFECT	Er wird	gegangen sein .
	He *will*	*have gone.*

As in all compound tenses, only the auxiliary (**werden** in this instance) can change; the infinitive is a constant:

	AUXILIARY	INFINITIVE
Ich	werde	gegangen sein.
Du	wirst	gegangen sein.
Er, sie, es	wird	gegangen sein.

C. Usage

The future perfect (like the future) has both a literal and a figurative meaning.

1. Literal meaning

The future perfect deals with the future as if it were already past time. This tense is to the future tense what the present perfect is to the present.

PRESENT	He's doing it (now).
PRESENT PERFECT	He *has done* it (by now).
FUTURE	He will do it (tomorrow).
FUTURE PERFECT	He *will have done* it (by tomorrow).

Both the present perfect and the future perfect imply that an action is *finished* (i.e., past) as of a certain point in time. In one instance that point is *now* (i.e., the present instant); in the other, the point is sometime in the future, e.g., *tomorrow*.

2. Figurative meaning: probability

In English as well as German, the future and the future perfect can be used to imply probability. The *future* connotes *present probability*. The *future perfect* connotes *past probability*. For example, if you hear a door slam, you might say:

> „Das wird wohl Rudi sein." (future tense)
> ("That *will be* Rudi." *or* "That *is probably* Rudi.")

If you heard the door slam last night, you might now say:

> „Das wird wohl Rudi gewesen sein." (future perfect)
> ("That *will have been* Rudi." *or* "That *was probably* Rudi.")

NOTE: **Wohl** reinforces the notion of *probably*.

DRILLS

Substitution Drills

Put the following *present perfect* sentences into the *future perfect.*

Example: Das *ist* Rudi *gewesen.*
Das *wird* Rudi *gewesen sein.*

1. Anna ist wohl zu Hause geblieben.
2. Onkel Franz ist wohl längst eingeschlafen.
3. Bald haben wir unser ganzes Geld ausgegeben.
4. Bis Montag habe ich meine letzte Seminararbeit eingereicht.
5. Sie ist wohl nach Mitternacht angekommen.
6. Dieser Mantel hat wohl über tausend Mark gekostet.
7. Bis Freitag sind wir eine ganze Woche hier gewesen.
8. Bis morgen hast du seinen Namen vergessen.

Fill-ins: The Perfective Infinitive

1. Dieser Mantel wird wohl über tausend Mark _____.
   (have cost)

2. Bis Freitag werden wir eine ganze Woche hier _____.
   (have been)

3. Bis morgen wirst du seinen Namen _____.
   (have forgotten)

4. Sie werden wohl nach Mitternacht _____.
   (have arrived)

5. Bald werden wir unser ganzes Geld _____.
   (have spent)

6. Anna wird wohl zu Hause _____.
   (have stayed)

7. Bis Montag werde ich meine letzte Seminararbeit _____.
   (have handed in)

8. Onkel Franz wird längst _____.
   (have fallen asleep)

Synthetic Exercises

Form complete sentences in the future perfect.

Example: Das / werden / Rudi / gewesen
Das wird Rudi gewesen sein.

1. Sie / werden / wohl / nach Mitternacht / angekommen
2. Onkel Franz / werden / wohl / längst / eingeschlafen
3. Bis morgen / du / werden / seinen Namen / vergessen
4. Dieser Mantel / werden / wohl / über tausend Mark / gekostet
5. Bis Montag / ich / werden / meine letzte Seminararbeit / eingereicht
6. Anna / werden / wohl / zu Hause / geblieben
7. Bald / wir / werden / unser ganzes Geld / ausgegeben
8. Bis Freitag / wir / werden / eine ganze Woche / hier / gewesen

Express in German

1. Soon we will have spent all our money.
2. By tomorrow you will have forgotten his name.
3. This coat probably cost over a thousand marks.
4. Anna probably stayed home.
5. By Friday we will have been here a whole week.
6. They probably arrived after midnight.
7. Uncle Franz has probably long since fallen asleep.
8. By Monday I will have handed in my last seminar paper.

IX. MODALS WITH PERFECTIVE INFINITIVES

A. Introduction

As the following examples show, this is a very common and useful
construction:

Sie muß es gefunden haben.
(She *must have found* it.)

Wer kann es getan haben?
(Who *can have done* it?)

Sie müssen einen Fehler gemacht haben.
(You *must have made* a mistake.)

B. Formation

Sentences of this type consist of a *modal auxiliary* and a *perfective infinitive**:

MODAL		PERFECTIVE INFINITIVE
Sie muß	es	gefunden haben.
Wer kann	es	gemacht haben.

C. Sentence structure

1. *Modals with perfective infinitives*

Sentences using *modals* with *perfective infinitives* are based upon underlying facts. Look at the following statement of fact:

Kurt hat den Brief geschrieben.

This sentence states that a letter has been written and positively identifies who wrote it.

When the modal **kann** is added to it, the following changes take place:

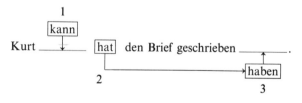

Kurt kann den Brief geschrieben haben.
(Kurt *can have written* the letter.)
(Kurt *may have written* the letter.)

  1. **Kann** (the conjugated form of the modal) must occupy the second (or verb) position in the sentence.

  2. **Hat,** which was in the second position before, moves to the end of the sentence.

---

* A *perfective infinitive* consists of a *past participle* (e.g., **gefunden**) followed by the *infinitive of its perfect auxiliary* (i.e., either **haben** or **sein**). Also see p. 24.

3. Since a simple sentence cannot have *two* conjugated verbs, **hat** appears at the end of the sentence *as an infinitive*.

The resulting sentence still deals with facts (the letter *is* written), but now we are *speculating* about something (in this case, *who* wrote the letter).

D. Usage

The modals used in expressions of this type are, for all practical purposes, limited to **können, müssen,** and **sollen.** And for the most part, they are only used in the present tense.

The English equivalents of the German sentences vary depending upon the modal auxiliary.

1. Können

> Wer kann es getan haben?
> (Who *can* have done it?)
> (Who *could* have done it?)*

English can use either the present tense indicative (*can*) or the past tense indicative (*could*) in these expressions.

CAUTION: "Who *could have done* it?" has two possible German equivalents:

> Wer kann es gemacht haben?

and   Wer hätte es machen können?

The second sentence is in the past tense of subjunctive II, which is used *only in contrary-to-fact situations*. (See pp. 219–21, 230, and 242–44.)

2. Müssen

> Sie muß es gefunden haben.
> (She *must* have found it.)

With **müssen** (*must*), both English and German use the present tense.

---

* Colloquial English commonly uses *could* instead of *can,* but the meaning is the same.

3. Sollen

Was soll er gesagt haben?
(What *is* he *supposed to have said?*)
(What did he *supposedly say?*)

In the case of **sollen,** there are two possible English equivalents.

a. First, there is the combination of the present tense of *supposed to* (e.g., *is supposed to*) and a perfective infinitive (e.g., *have said*). This is basically the same way that German forms the construction.

b. Or one can express one's speculation with the adverb *supposedly* and use the simple past tense (*did say*) rather than the perfective infinitive (*have said*):

What *did* he *supposedly say?*

 DRILLS

Replacement Drills

Insert the modal auxiliaries into the following sentences, making the necessary changes in the verb forms.

Example: Sie hat es gefunden. (müssen)
Sie muß es gefunden haben.

1. Er hat es gewußt. (müssen)
2. Wer hat den Brief geschrieben? (können)
3. Sie haben einen Fehler gemacht. (müssen)
4. Sie hat ihn gesehen. (müssen)
5. Er hat es vergessen. (können)
6. Wer hat es gemacht? (sollen)
7. Wer ist es gewesen? (können)
8. Sie hat es ihm gesagt. (müssen)
9. Er hat es von einem Freund bekommen. (sollen)
10. Sie sind später gekommen. (können)
11. Wem hat er es gegeben? (können)
12. Sie hat es zu Hause gelassen. (müssen)

Fill-ins

1. Sie muß ihn _____.
(have seen)

2. Wem kann er es _____?
(have given)

3. Sie müssen einen Fehler _____.
(have made)

4. Er soll es von einem Freund _____.
(to have gotten)

5. Sie muß es zu Hause _____.
(have left)

6. Wer kann es _____?
(have been)

7. Er kann es _____.
(have forgotten)

8. Sie muß es _____.
(have known)

9. Wer soll es _____?
(to have done)

10. Sie können später _____.
(have come)

11. Wer kann den Brief _____?
(have written)

12. Sie muß es ihm _____.
(have told)

Synthetic Exercises

Make complete sentences in the present tense using modals with perfective infinitives.

Example: Er / müssen / es / gefunden
Er muß es gefunden haben.

1. Er / müssen / es / gewußt
2. Sie / müssen / es ihm / gesagt
3. Wer / können / Brief / geschrieben / ?
4. Er / sollen / es / von / ein- / Freund / bekommen
5. Wem / können / er es / gegeben / ?

6. Sie / müssen / Fehler / gemacht
7. Wer / können / es / gewesen / ?
8. Er / können / es / vergessen
9. Sie / müssen / es zu Hause / gelassen
10. Wer / sollen / es / gemacht / ?
11. Sie / können / später / gekommen
12. Sie / müssen / ihn / gesehen

Express in German

1. She must have known it.
2. He can have forgotten it.
3. Who can it have been?
4. She must have left it at home.
5. Who is supposed to have done it?
6. You must have made a mistake.
7. Who can have written the letter?
8. They can have come later.
9. She must have seen him.
10. Who can he have given it to?
11. They must have told him.
12. He supposedly got it from a friend.

Strong and Irregular Verbs

INFINITIVE (*3rd sing.* *pres.*)	PAST (*3rd sing. pres.* *subj. II*)	PAST PARTICIPLE	MEANING
backen (bäckt)	buk *or* backte (büke *or* backte)	gebacken	to bake
befehlen (befiehlt)	befahl (beföhle)	befohlen	to command
beginnen	begann (begänne)	begonnen	to begin
beißen	biß	gebissen	to bite
bergen (birgt)	barg (bärge)	geborgen	to hide
bersten (birst)	barst (bärste)	ist geborsten	to burst
bewegen	bewog (bewöge)	bewogen	to induce[1]

---

[1] **Bewegen** meaning *to move* is weak.

biegen	bog	gebogen	to bend
	(böge)		
bieten	bot	geboten	to offer
	(böte)		
binden	band	gebunden	to bind
	(bände)		
bitten	bat	gebeten	to request
	(bäte)		
blasen	blies	geblasen	to blow
(bläst)			
bleiben	blieb	ist geblieben	to remain
braten	briet	gebraten	to roast
(brät or			
bratet)			
brechen	brach	gebrochen	to break
(bricht)	(bräche)		
brennen	brannte	gebrannt	to burn
	(brennte)		
bringen	brachte	gebracht	to bring
	(brächte)		
denken	dachte	gedacht	to think
	(dächte)		
dingen	dingte or dang	gedungen	to engage,
	(dänge)		hire
dringen	drang	ist, hat gedrungen	to press
	(dränge)		
dünken	dünkte or deuchte	gedünkt or	to seem
(impers.)		gedeucht	
(dünkt or			
deucht)			
dürfen	durfte	gedurft	to be allowed
(darf)	(dürfte)		
einladen	lud . . . ein or	eingeladen	to invite
	ladete . . . ein		
	(lüde . . . ein or		
	(ladete . . . ein)		
empfehlen	empfahl	empfohlen	to
(empfiehlt)	(empfähle)		recommend
erbleichen	erblich	ist erblichen	to die
erlöschen	erlosch	erloschen	to go out
(erlischt)	(erlösche)		(of light)

erschrecken[1]	erschrak	ist **erschrocken**	to become
(erschrickt)	(erschräke)		frightened
essen	aß	**gegessen**	to eat
(ißt)	(äße)		(*of people*)
fahren	fuhr	ist, hat **gefahren**	to drive
(fährt)	(führe)		
fallen	fiel	ist **gefallen**	to fall
(fällt)			
fangen	fing	**gefangen**	to catch
(fängt)			
fechten	focht	**gefochten**	to fight
(ficht)	(föchte)		
finden	fand	**gefunden**	to find
	(fände)		
flechten	flocht	**geflochten**	to braid
(flicht)	(flöchte)		
fliegen	flog	ist, hat **geflogen**	to fly
	(flöge)		
fliehen	floh	ist **geflohen**	to flee
	(flöhe)		
fließen	floß	ist **geflossen**	to flow
	(flösse)		
fressen	fraß	**gefressen**	to eat (*of*
(frißt)	(fräße)		*animals*)
frieren	fror	**gefroren**	to freeze
	(fröre)		
gebären	gebar	**geboren**	to bear
(gebiert *or*	(gebäre)		
gebärt)			
geben	gab	**gegeben**	to give
(gibt)	(gäbe)		
gedeihen	gedieh	**gediehen**	to thrive
gehen	ging	ist **gegangen**	to go
gelingen	gelang	ist **gelungen**	to succeed
	(gelänge)		
gelten	galt	**gegolten**	to be worth
(gilt)	(gälte)		
genesen	genas	ist **genesen**	to recover
	(genäse)		

---

[1] **Erschrecken** used transitively is weak.

genießen	genoß		genossen	to enjoy
	(genösse)			
geschehen	geschah	ist	geschehen	to happen
(*impers.*)	(geschähe)			
(geschieht)				
gewinnen	gewann		gewonnen	to win
	(gewönne)			
gießen	goß		gegossen	to pour
	(gösse)			
gleichen	glich		geglichen	to resemble
gleiten	glitt	ist	geglitten	to glide
glimmen	glomm *or* glimmte		geglommen *or*	to gleam
	(glömme)		geglimmt	
graben	grub		gegraben	to dig
(gräbt)	(grübe)			
greifen	griff		gegriffen	to seize
haben	hatte		gehabt	to have
(du hast,	(hätte)			
er hat)				
halten	hielt		gehalten	to hold
(hält)				
hängen	hing		gehangen	to hang
				(*intrans.*)
heben	hob		gehoben	to lift
	(höbe)			
heißen	hieß		geheißen	to be called
helfen	half		geholfen	to help
(hilft)	(hülfe)			
kennen	kannte		gekannt	to know
	(kennte)			
klimmen	klomm	ist	geklommen	to climb
	(klömme)			
klingen	klang		geklungen	to sound
	(klänge)			
kneifen	kniff		gekniffen	to pinch
kommen	kam	ist	gekommen	to come
	(käme)			
können	konnte		gekonnt	to be able
(kann)	(könnte)			
kriechen	kroch	ist	gekrochen	to creep
	(kröche)			

laden	**lud**	**geladen**	to load; invite
(lädt)	(lüde)		
lassen	**ließ**	**gelassen**	to let
(läßt)			
laufen	**lief**	ist **gelaufen**	to run
(läuft)			
leiden	**litt**	**gelitten**	to suffer
leihen	**lieh**	**geliehen**	to lend
lesen	**las**	**gelesen**	to read
(liest)	(läse)		
liegen	**lag**	**gelegen**	to lie, recline
	(läge)		
lügen	**log**	**gelogen**	to (tell a) lie
	(löge)		
mahlen	**mahlte**	**gemahlen**	to grind
meiden	**mied**	**gemieden**	to avoid
melken	**molk** *or* **melkte**	**gemolken**	to milk
(melkt)	(mölke)	*or* **gemelkt**	
messen	**maß**	**gemessen**	to measure
(mißt)	(mäße)		
mögen	**mochte**	**gemocht**	to like; may
(mag)	(möchte)		
müssen	**mußte**	**gemußt**	must
(muß)	(müßte)		
nehmen	**nahm**	**genommen**	to take
(nimmt)	(nähme)		
nennen	**nannte**	**genannt**	to name
	(nennte)		
pfeifen	**pfiff**	**gepfiffen**	to whistle
preisen	**pries**	**gepriesen**	to praise
quellen	**quoll**	ist **gequollen**	to gush
(quillt)	(quölle)		
raten	**riet**	**geraten**	to advise
(rät)			
reiben	**rieb**	**gerieben**	to rub
reißen	**riß**	ist, hat **gerissen**	to rip
reiten	**ritt**	ist, hat **geritten**	to ride
rennen	**rannte**	ist **gerannt**	to run
	(rennte)		
riechen	**roch**	**gerochen**	to smell
	(röche)		

ringen	rang (ränge)	gerungen	to struggle, wrestle; wring
rinnen	rann (ränne)	ist geronnen	to run
rufen	rief	gerufen	to call
salzen	salzte	gesalzen	to salt
saufen (säuft)	soff (söffe)	gesoffen	to drink (of animals)
saugen	sog (söge)	gesogen	to suck
schaffen[1]	schuf (schüfe)	geschaffen	to create
scheiden	schied	ist geschieden	to separate
scheinen	schien	geschienen	to seem; shine
schelten (schilt)	schalt (schälte)	gescholten	to scold
schieben	schob (schöbe)	geschoben	to shove
schießen	schoß (schösse)	geschossen	to shoot
schlafen (schläft)	schlief	geschlafen	to sleep
schlagen (schlägt)	schlug (schlüge)	geschlagen	to strike
schleichen	schlich	ist geschlichen	to sneak
schließen	schloß (schlösse)	geschlossen	to close
schmeißen	schmiß	geschmissen	to fling, throw
schmelzen (schmilzt)	schmolz (schmölze)	ist, hat geschmolzen	to melt (intrans.)
schneiden	schnitt	geschnitten	to cut
schreiben	schrieb	geschrieben	to write
schreien	schrie	geschrieen	to cry
schreiten	schritt	ist geschritten	to stride
schweigen	schwieg	geschwiegen	to be silent
schwellen (schwillt)	schwoll (schwölle)	ist geschwollen	to swell (intrans.)

---

[1] **Schaffen** meaning *to work, to be busy* is weak.

schwimmen	schwamm (schwämme)	ist, hat **geschwommen**	to swim
schwinden	schwand (schwände)	ist **geschwunden**	to disappear
schwingen	schwang (schwänge)	**geschwungen**	to swing
schwören	schwor (schwüre)	**geschworen**	to swear
sehen (sieht)	sah (sähe)	**gesehen**	to see
sein (ist)	war (wäre)	ist **gewesen**	to be
senden	sandte *or* sendete (sendete)	**gesandt** *or* **gesendet**	to send
sieden	sott (sötte)	ist, hat **gesotten**	to boil
singen	sang (sänge)	**gesungen**	to sing
sinken	sank (sänke)	ist **gesunken**	to sink
sinnen	sann (sänne)	**gesonnen**	to think
sitzen	saß (säße)	**gesessen**	to sit
sollen (soll)	sollte	**gesollt**	shall
speien	spie	**gespieen**	to spit
spinnen	spann (spänne)	**gesponnen**	to spin
sprechen (spricht)	sprach (spräche)	**gesprochen**	to speak
sprießen	sproß (sprösse)	ist **gesprossen**	to sprout
springen	sprang (spränge)	ist **gesprungen**	to spring
stechen (sticht)	stach (stäche)	**gestochen**	to prick
stecken	stak (stäke)	**gesteckt**	to stick (*intrans.*)
stehen	stand (stünde)	**gestanden**	to stand

stehlen	stahl	gestohlen	to steal
(stiehlt)	(stähle)		
steigen	stieg	ist gestiegen	to ascend
sterben	starb	ist gestorben	to die
(stirbt)	(stürbe)		
stieben	stob	ist gestoben	to scatter
	(stöbe)		
stinken	stank	gestunken	to stink
	(stänke)		
stoßen	stieß	gestossen	to push
(stößt)			
streichen	strich	ist, hat gestrichen	to stroke
streiten	stritt	gestritten	to argue
tragen	trug	getragen	to carry
(trägt)	(trüge)		
treffen	traf	getroffen	to meet; hit
(trifft)	(träfe)		
treiben	trieb	getrieben	to drive
treten	trat	ist, hat getreten	to step
(tritt)	(träte)		
triefen	troff	getroffen	to drip
	(tröffe)		
trinken	trank	getrunken	to drink
	(tränke)		
trügen	trog	getrogen	to deceive
	(tröge)		
tun	tat	getan	to do
(tut)	(täte)		
verderben	verdarb	ist, hat verdorben	to spoil
(verdirbt)	(verdürbe)		
verdrießen	verdroß	verdrossen	to annoy
	(verdrösse)		
vergessen	vergaß	vergessen	to forget
(vergißt)	(vergäße)		
verlieren	verlor	verloren	to lose
	(verlöre)		
verlöschen	verlosch	ist verloschen	to extinguish
(verlischt)	(verlösche)		
verschlingen	verschlang	verschlungen	to wind; devour
	(verschlänge)		

verschwinden	verschwand (verschwände)	ist verschwunden	to disappear
verzeihen	verzieh (verziehe)	verziehen	to pardon
wachsen (wächst)	wuchs (wüchse)	ist gewachsen	to grow
wägen	wog (wöge)	gewogen	to weigh (*fig.*)
waschen (wäscht)	wusch (wüsche)	gewaschen	to wash
weichen	wich	ist gewichen	to yield
weisen	wies	gewiesen	to show
wenden	wandte *or* wendete	gewandt *or* gewendet	to turn
werben (wirbt)	warb (würbe)	geworben	to apply (for)
werden (wird)	wurde (würde)	ist geworden	to become
werfen (wirft)	warf (würfe)	geworfen	to throw
wiegen	wog (wöge)	gewogen	to weigh (*lit.*)
winden	wand (wände)	gewunden	to wind
wissen (weiß)	wußte (wüßte)	gewußt	to know
wollen (will)	wollte	gewollt	will
wringen	wrang (wränge)	gewrungen	to wring
ziehen	zog (zöge)	ist, hat gezogen	to pull, move
zwingen	zwang (zwänge)	gezwungen	to force

Vocabulary

Nominative singular and plural forms are indicated; unusual genitive singular endings are also supplied. Principal parts, as well as the 3rd person singular present tense form, of strong and irregular verbs are given; weak verbs appear in the infinitive form only. The following symbols are used:

    * strong verb
    · separable prefix
  (s) verb with auxiliary **sein**

ab (+ *acc*). from (*a point in time*) on, beginning with
der **Abend, -e** evening
aber but
ab · fahren* to leave (fährt . . . ab), fuhr . . . ab, ist abgefahren
ab · holen to pick up

ab · riegeln to cordon off
ab · schicken to send off
sich **ab · schwächen** to weaken
der **Absender, —** sender (*of a letter or package*)
ab · stürzen (s) to crash (*airplane*)
acht eight

die **Adresse, -n**   address
der **Agent, -en, -en**   agent
   ähnlich   similar
die **Algebra**   algebra
   alle   all
   allein   alone
   alles   everything
die **Alpen** (*pl.*)   the Alps
   als   when; than
   als ob   as though, as if
   alt, älter, ältest-   old
der **Amerikaner, —**   American
die **Amerikanerin, -nen**
   American (female)
   amerikanisch (*adj.*)
   American
sich **amüsieren**   to have a good
   time
   an (*two-way prep.*)   on (*with
   vertical surfaces*), at, to
   ander-   other
   ändern   to change
   anders   otherwise, another
   way
die **Andeutung, -en**   allusion,
   insinuation
der **Anfang, ⁼e**   beginning
   an·fangen*   to begin
   (fängt . . . an), fing . . . an,
   angefangen
der **Angestellte, -n** (*adj. noun*)
   employee
die **Angst, ⁼e**   fear, anxiety
   an·kommen*   to arrive
   (kommt . . . an),
   kam . . . an, ist
   angekommen
   an·rufen*   to call up
   (ruft . . . an), rief . . . an,
   angerufen
   an·sehen*   to look at

(sieht . . . an), sah . . . an,
   angesehen
sich **an·sehen*** (etwas)   to take
   a look at, look over
   anstatt   instead of
   antworten (auf + *acc.*)   to
   answer (*with things*)
   antworten (+ *dat.*)   to
   answer (*with people*)
der **Anwalt, ⁼e**   lawyer
   an·ziehen*   to put on
   (zieht . . . an), zog . . . an,
   angezogen
sich **an·ziehen***   to get dressed
der **Anzug, ⁼e**   suit
der **Apfel, ⁼**   apple
die **Apotheke, -n**   pharmacy,
   drugstore
der **April**   April
die **Arbeit, -en**   work; (term)
   paper
   arbeiten (an + *dat.*)   to work
   (on)
der **Arbeitsmarkt, ⁼e**   labor
   market
das **Argument, -e**   argument
der **Arm, -e**   arm
   arm, ärmer, ärmst-   poor
die **Armee, -n**   army
die **Art und Weise**   way, way of
   doing things
der **Artikel, —**   article
der **Arzt, ⁼e**   doctor
die **Ärztin, -nen**   doctor,
   physician (female)
der **Atem**   breath
   auf (*two-way prep.*)   on (*with
   horizontal surfaces*)
   auf und ab   back and forth;
   up and down
   auf·halten*   to hold up

(hält . . . auf), hielt . . . auf,
aufgehalten
auf · hören to stop, cease
auf · machen to open
auf · räumen to clean up,
straighten up
der **Aufsatz, ⸚e** essay, paper
auf · stehen* to get up;
stand up
(steht . . . auf),
stand . . . auf, ist
aufgestanden
auf · wachen (s) to wake up
das **Auge, -n** eye
der **August** August
aus (+ *dat.*) from; out of
die **Außenhandelsbilanz** foreign
trade balance
der **Außenminister, —** foreign
minister
die **Außenpolitik** foreign policy
außer (+ *dat.*) besides
aus · geben* to spend
(gibt . . . aus), gab . . . aus,
ausgegeben
aus · gehen* to go out
(geht . . . aus), ging . . . aus,
ist ausgegangen
aus · machen to turn out
aus · sehen* to look
(*appearance*)
(sieht . . . aus), sah . . . aus,
ausgesehen
aus · steigen* to get out,
climb out
(steigt . . . aus),
stieg . . . aus, ist
ausgestiegen
aus · suchen to select
ausverkauft sold out
aus · ziehen* to take off;

move out
(zieht . . . aus), zog . . . aus,
hat (ist) ausgezogen
sich **aus · ziehen*** to get
undressed
das **Auto, -s** car
der **Automat, -en, -en**
coin-operated machine
der **Autor, -en** author
der **Autoschlosser, —**
automobile mechanic

das **Bächlein, —** little brook
die **Backe, -n** cheek
der **Bäcker, —** baker
die **Bäckerei, -en** bakery
die **Badewanne, -n** bathtub
der **Bahnhof, ⸚e** railroad station
bald soon
der **Ball, ⸚e** ball
die **Banane, -n** banana
die **Bank, -en** bank
der **Bart, ⸚e** beard
bauen to build
der **Baum, ⸚e** tree
Bayern Bavaria
bayrisch Bavarian
der **Beamte, -n** (*adj. noun*)
official, government
employee
die **Beamtin, -nen** official,
government employee
(*female*)
bedeutend significant,
important
bedienen to serve
sich **bedienen** to serve oneself
sich **beeilen** to hurry
befehlen* to order
(befiehlt), befahl, befohlen

begegnen (s) + *dat.* to meet, run into
begehrenswert desirable
beginnen* to begin (beginnt), begann, begonnen
begraben* to bury (begräbt), begrub, begraben
behandeln to treat
behaupten to assert, maintain, say
die **Beherrschung** control
behindern to obstruct, hinder
bei (+ *dat.*) near; at (*a person's house*)
das **Bein, -e** leg
beiseite aside, to the side
das **Beispiel, -e** example
bekannt known, well-known
der **Bekannte** (*adj. noun*) acquaintance, friend
bekannt · geben* to announce (gibt . . . bekannt), gab . . . bekannt, bekanntgegeben
bekommen* to get, receive (bekommt), bekam, bekommen
belegen to occupy
beleidigen to insult
das **Benzin** gasoline
beobachten to observe
bequem comfortable
bereuen to regret
der **Berg, -e** mountain
der **Bericht, -e** report
berichten to report
berühmt famous

besichtigen to look at (*sightseeing*)
die **Besitzung, -en** estate
besonder- (*adj.*) special
besonders especially
besprechen* to discuss (bespricht), besprach, besprochen
besser better
bestellen to order (*food, etc.*)
am **besten** best
bestimmt certainly, for certain, for sure
der **Besuch, -e** visit
besuchen to visit
außer Betrieb out of order
das **Bett, -en** bed
beugen to bend
sich **beugen** (**über** + *acc.*) to bend (over)
bevor (*conj.*) before
beworfen thrown, plastered (**Sie wurden mit Flaschen beworfen.** Bottles were thrown at them.)
bezahlen to pay (for)
die **Bibliothek, -en** library
das **Bier, -e** beer
das **Bild, -er** picture
billig cheap
die **Birne, -n** pear
bis (*conj.*) until (*prep.* + *acc.*) until; as far as; to; by
bislang up until now
bitte please
die **Bitte, -n** request
bitten* (**um** + *acc.*) to ask (for) (bittet), bat, gebeten

bleiben* to stay, remain
(bleibt), blieb, ist geblieben
der **Bleistift, -e** pencil
der **Blonde** (*adj. noun*) blond
die **Blume, -n** flower
die **Bluse, -n** blouse
die **Bombe, -n** bomb
böse angry, mad
brauchen to need; use
braun brown
brechen* to break
(bricht), brach, gebrochen
brennen* to burn
(brennt), brannte, gebrannt
der **Brief, -e** letter
die **Briefmarke, -n** postage
stamp
der **Briefträger, —** letter carrier,
mailman
die **Brille, -n** (eye) glasses
bringen* to bring, take
(bringt), brachte, gebracht
das **Brot** bread
die **Brücke, -n** bridge
der **Bruder, ⁒** brother
das **Buch, ⁒er** book
das **Büchlein, —** little book
der **Bundesbürger, —** citizen of
the Federal Republic of
Germany
das **Bundeswirtschaftsministerium**
Federal Ministry of
Commerce
der **Bürgermeister, —** mayor
das **Büro, -s** office
der **Bus, -se** bus

die **Cassette, -n** cassette
die **Chance, -n** chance
der **Charakter, -e** character

der **Chef, -s** boss
(das) **China** China
die **Cola, -s** cola
der **Computer, —** computer

da (*adv.*) there
(*conj.*) since, because
da drüben over there
dabei sein* to be there, be
present
dagegen against it
die **Dame, -n** lady
damit so that
dankbar grateful
die **Dankbarkeit** gratitude,
thankfulness
danken (+ *dat.*) to thank
dann then
daß that
dauern to last
davon · kommen* to get
away, escape
(kommt . . . davon),
kam . . . davon, ist
davongekommen
(**mit dem Leben**
davonkommen* to escape
with one's life)
die **Decke, -n** blanket
decken to set (a table)
dein your (*familiar singular*)
denken* (**an** + *acc.*) to think
(about)
(denkt), dachte, gedacht
sich **denken*** (etwas) to imagine
(something)
denn (*conj.*) for, because
derselbe, dasselbe, dieselbe
the same
deshalb for this (that) reason

deutsch German
der **Deutsche** (*adj. noun*)
German
(das) **Deutschland** Germany
der **Dezember** December
der **Dialekt, -e** dialect
der **Dichter, —** poet; writer
dick fat
die **Dienerschaft, -en** staff
(*of servants*)
der **Dienst, -e** service
der **Dienstag, -e** Tuesday
dieser, dieses, diese this
das **Ding, -e** thing
direkt direct(ly)
der **Direktor, -en** director
doch but
der **Donnerstag, -e** Thursday
draußen outside
drei three
dritt- third
drohen (+ *dat.*) to threaten
drüben over there
dumm, dümmer, dümmst-
stupid
dunkel, dunkler, dunkelst-
dark
durch (+ *acc.*) through
durch · schlagen* (**auf**) to
have an effect on, affect
(schlägt . . . durch),
schlug . . . durch,
durchgeschlagen
durchsuchen to search
dürfen* may, to be
allowed to
(darf), durfte, gedurft

die **Ecke, -n** corner
die **Ehe, -n** marriage

ehrlich honest, honorable
eigentlich actually, really
einfach simple, simply
der **Einfluß, ⁻sse** influence
ein · führen to introduce
einige some, several
Einkäufe machen to do
(some) shopping
ein · kaufen to shop
ein · kaufen gehen* to go
shopping
das **Einkommen** income
ein · laden* to invite
(lädt . . . ein), lud . . . ein,
eingeladen
ein · lösen to cash (a check)
einmal once
ein · reichen to hand in
die **Einsamkeit** loneliness
ein · schlafen* to fall asleep
(schläft . . . ein),
schlief . . . ein, ist
eingeschlafen
ein · setzen to put into
action
ein · stecken to mail (e.g., a
letter in a mailbox)
ein · steigen* to get in,
climb in
(steigt . . . ein),
stieg . . . ein, ist
eingestiegen
die **Eltern** (*pl.*) parents
empfehlen* to recommend
(empfiehlt), empfahl,
empfohlen
das **Ende, -n** end
endlich at last, finally
die **Energie** energy
(das) **England** England
der **Engländer, —** Englishman

die **Engländerin, -nen**
Englishwoman
das **Enkelkind, -er** grandchild
entdecken to discover
entscheiden* to decide
(entscheidet), entschied,
entschieden
sich **entschließen*** to decide
(entschließt), entschloß,
entschlossen
sich **entschuldigen** (**bei** + *dat.*)   to
apologize (to)
enttäuschen to disappoint
entzünden to ignite, light
sich **erholen** to recover
erinnern to remind
sich **erinnern** to remember
sich **erinnern an** (+ *acc.*)   to
remember
sich **erkälten** to catch cold
erkennen* to recognize
(erkennt), erkannte,
erkannt
erklären to explain
das **Erlebnis, -se** experience
erledigen to take
care of
die **Erleichterung, -en** relief
ermordern to murder
die **Ernte, -n** harvest
erschrecken* to become
frightened
(erschrickt), erschrak, ist
erschrocken
erst- first
erstmals first, for the first
time
erwarten to expect
erzählen to tell, relate
essen* to eat
(ißt), aß, gegessen

das **Essen, —** meal
etwas something
etwas langsamer a little
slower
euer your (*familiar plural*)
(das) **Europa** Europe
europäisch European
die **Europäische Gemeinschaft**
The European Community
das **Experiment, -e** experiment

das **Fahren** driving
fahren* to drive
(fährt), fuhr, ist gefahren
der **Fahrer, —** driver
der **Fahrplan, ̈-e** timetable
fallen* to fall
(fällt), fiel, ist gefallen
die **Familie, -n** family
fangen* to catch
(fängt), fing, gefangen
die **Farbe, -n** color
fast almost
die **Faust, ̈-e** fist
der **Februar** February
fehlen to be missing, absent,
or lacking
der **Fehler, —** mistake
das **Fenster, —** window
die **Ferien** (*pl.*) vacation
das **Fernsehen** television
im **Fernsehen** on television
fertig ready; finished
sich **fertig · machen** to get ready
fest · nehmen* to detain,
arrest
(nimmt . . . fest),
nahm . . . fest,
festgenommen

das **Feuer,** — fire
die **Feuerwehr** fire department
der **Film, -e** film
der **Finanzminister,** — minister
of finance
finden* to find
(findet), fand, gefunden
der **Finger,** — finger
die **Firma, die Firmen** firm,
company
der **Fisch, -e** fish
flach flat
die **Flasche, -n** bottle
fliegen* to fly
(fliegt), flog, ist geflogen
fließen* to flow
(fließt), floß, ist geflossen
der **Flughafen,** ⸚ airport
die **Flugnummer, -n** flight
number
der **Fluß,** ⸚sse river
folgen (+ *dat.*) to follow
Folgendes the following
das **Foto, -s** photo
die **Frage, -n** question
fragen (**nach** + *dat.*) to ask
(about)
der **Franc,** — franc
(das) **Frankreich** France
französisch French
die **Frau, -en** woman; wife; Mrs.
das **Fräulein,** — young woman,
Miss
die **Freiheit, -en** freedom
freilich to be sure
der **Freitag, -e** Friday
der **Fremde** (*adj. noun*) stranger
sich **freuen** (**auf** + *acc.*) to look
forward to
(**über** + *acc.*) to be
happy about

der **Freund, -e** friend
die **Freundlichkeit, -en**
friendliness, kindness
die **Freundschaft, -en** friendship
frisch fresh
der **Friseur, -e** barber
froh happy, glad
fröhlich merry
früh, früher, frühst- early
das **Frühjahr** spring
der **Frühling, -e** spring
das **Frühstück, -e** breakfast
frühstücken to breakfast,
eat breakfast
sich **fühlen** to feel
führen to lead
fünf five
fünfzig fifty
für (+ *acc.*) for
die **Furcht** fear
fürchten (+ *dir. obj.*) to be
afraid of
sich **fürchten** (**vor** + *dat.*) to be
afraid (of)
der **Fuß** ⸚e foot
der **Fußboden,** ⸚ floor

ganz whole, entire, all,
complete(ly)
gar nicht not at all
die **Garage, -n** garage
der **Garten,** ⸚ garden
der **Gast,** ⸚e guest
die **Gaststätte, -n** informal
German restaurant
das **Gebäude,** — building
geben* to give
(gibt), gab, gegeben
geboren sein* to be born
gebrauchen to use; need

der **Geburtstag, -e** birthday
der **Gedanke, -ns, -n** thought
die **Gefahr, -en** danger
gefallen* (+ *dat.*) to please
(gefällt), gefiel, gefallen
(**Es gefällt mir.** I like it;
lit.: It pleases me.)
der **Gefallen, —** favor
gegen (+ *acc.*) against, into
die **Gegend, -en** area,
neighborhood, region
gegenüber (+ *dat.*)
opposite, across from
gehen* to go
(geht), ging, ist gegangen
gehören (+ *dat.*) to belong
(to)
das **Geld, -er** money
der **Geldtransport, -e** a
"Brink's" truck
gelegen situated
gemeinsam common,
mutual
die **Gemeinschaft, -en**
community
genau exact(ly)
der **Generaldirektor, -en**
director (of a firm)
sich **genieren** to be embarrassed
genug enough
das **Gepäck** luggage
gerade just; right now
geradeaus straight ahead
gern, lieber, am liebsten
gladly, willingly
**etwas gern (lieber, am liebsten)
tun** to like (prefer, like
best) to do something
der **Geruch, ̈e** smell
das **Geschäft, -e** business
geschehen* to happen

(geschieht), geschah, ist
geschehen
das **Geschenk, -e** present
die **Geschichte, -n** story; history
geschlossen closed
geschult schooled, trained
die **Gesellschaft, -en** society
gestern yesterday
gestikulieren to gesticulate
der **Gesuchte** (*adj. noun*) person
being hunted for
gesund healthy
die **Gesundheit** health
die **Gewerkschaft, -en** labor
union
sich **gewöhnen** (**an** + *acc.*) to
get used (to)
die **Gewohnheit, -en** habit
gewöhnlich usual(ly)
das **Glas, ̈er** glass
der **Glaube, -ns, -n** faith, belief
glauben (+ *acc. with things*)
(+ *dat. with persons*)
to believe
gleich right now,
immediately
glücklich happy; lucky
das **Gold** gold
der **Goldfisch, -e** goldfish
die **Götterdämmerung** twilight
of the gods
das **Gras** grass
gratulieren (+ *dat.*) to
congratulate
die **Grenze, -n** border, edge
grob, gröber, gröbst- coarse,
crude
groß, größer, größt- large
großartig great (*colloquial*)
der **Großvater, ̈** grandfather
grün green

der **Grund, ⸚e**   reason, cause
grüßen   to greet
gut, besser, best-   good, well

das **Haar, -e**   hair
haben*   to have
(hat), hatte, gehabt
haften für   to be responsible
for
das **Hähnchen, —**   (fried)
chicken
der **Haken, —**   hook
halb   half
halten*   to hold
(hält), hielt, gehalten
halten* von   (+ *dat.*)   to
think of (*opinion*)
der **Hammer, ⸚**   hammer
die **Hand, ⸚e**   hand
sich **handeln um**   to concern, deal
with, be a matter of
der **Handschuh, -e**   glove
die **Handtasche, -n**   purse
hängen* (*intrans.*)   to hang
(hängt), hing, ist gehangen
hängen (*trans.*)   to hang
(hängt), hängte, gehängt
hart, härter, härtest-   hard;
severe
häßlich   ugly
hauptsächlich   mainly,
principally
die **Hauptstraße, -n**   main street
das **Haus, ⸚er**   house
das **Häuschen, —**   little house
zu **Hause**   at home
nach **Hause**   home (*motion
towards*)
die **Hausmusik**   music in the
home

die **Heide, -n**   heather; heath
heiß   hot
heißen*   to be called
(heißt), hieß, geheißen
helfen* (+ *dat.*)   to help
(hilft), half, geholfen
das **Hemd, -en**   shirt
der **Hemdsärmel, —**   shirt sleeve
her (*indicates motion
toward speaker*)
herauf   up (here)
herauf · kommen*   to come
up
(kommt . . . herauf),
kam . . . herauf, ist
heraufgekommen
heraus   out (here)
heraus · geben*   to publish
(gibt . . . heraus),
gab . . . heraus,
herausgegeben
heraus · kommen*   to come
out
(kommt . . . heraus),
kam . . . heraus, ist
herausgekommen
der **Herbst, -e**   fall, autumn
herein   in (here)
herein · kommen*   to come in
(kommt . . . herein),
kam . . . herein, ist
hereingekommen
her · kommen*   to come from
(kommt . . . her),
kam . . . her, ist
hergekommen
der **Herr, -n, -en**   gentlemen; Mr.
her · sehen*   to look (here)
(sieht . . . her), sah . . . her,
hergesehen
(Sieh mal her! Look here!**)**

her · stellen   to manufacture
herum · laufen*   to run
  around
  (läuft . . . herum),
  lief . . . herum, ist
  herumgelaufen
herunter   down (here)
herunter · kommen*   to come
  down
  (kommt . . . herunter),
  kam . . . herunter, ist
  heruntergekommen
hervorragend   outstanding
das Heu   hay
heute   today
heute abend   this evening
hier   here (location)
hierher   here (destination)
die Hilfe   help
hin   (indicates motion away
  from speaker)
hinauf   up (there)
hinauf · gehen*   to go up
  (geht . . . hinauf),
  ging . . . hinauf, ist
  hinaufgegangen
hinaus   out (there)
hinaus · gehen*   to leave,
  go out
  (geht . . . hinaus),
  ging . . . hinaus, ist
  hinausgegangen
hinein   in (there)
hinein · gehen*   to go in
  (geht . . . hinein),
  ging . . . hinein, ist
  hineingegangen
hin · fahren*   to drive (there)
  (fährt . . . hin),
  fuhr . . . hin,
  ist hingefahren

hin · legen   to lay (something)
  down
sich hin · legen   to lie down
hin · stellen   to put, put down
hinter   (two-way prep.)
  behind
hinunter   down (there)
hinunter · gehen*   to go down
  (geht . . . hinunter),
  ging . . . hinunter, ist
  hinuntergegangen
die Hitze   heat
hoch, höher, höchst-   high
höchst   highly
hoffen (auf + acc.)   to hope
  (for)
die Hoffnung, -en   hope
hoh- (alternate stem of hoch
  used with adj. endings)
holen   to fetch, get
das Holz   wood
hören   to hear
das Hörspiel, -e   radio play
die Hose, -n   pants
das Hotel, -s   hotel
hübsch   pretty
der Hubschrauber, —   helicopter
der Hund, -e   dog
hundert   hundred
hungrig   hungry
die Hütte, -n   hut

die Idee, -n   idea
ihr   her, their
Ihr   your (polite form)
immer   always
immer noch   still
in   (two-way prep.)   in; into,
  to
indem (conj.)   in that; by
  (do)ing (something); while

der **Ingenieur, -e** engineer
die **Innenstadt** inner city
intelligent intelligent
interessant interesting
interessieren to interest
sich **interessieren (für** + *acc.*) to be interested (in)
sich **irren** to be mistaken, be wrong
(das) **Italien** Italy
der **Italiener, —** Italian
die **Italienerin, -nen** Italian (female)
italienisch Italian

die **Jacke, -n** jacket
das **Jahr, -e** year
jahrelang for years
die **Jahrhundertwende** turn of the century
der **Januar** January
je ... desto the ... the
je mehr desto besser the more the better
jeder, jedes, jede each, every
jedoch however
jetzt now
der **Journalist, -en, -en** journalist
die **Jugend** youth
der **Juli** July
jung, jünger, jüngst- young
der **Junge, -n, -n** boy
der **Juni** June

der **Kaffee** coffee
kalt, kälter, kältest- cold
das **Kammerorchester, —** chamber orchestra
kaputt broken

die **Karte, -en** ticket; postcard; map; card
die **Katze, -n** cat
kauen to chew
kaufen to buy
das **Kaufhaus, ¨er** department store
kaum hardly, scarcely
die **Kaution, -en** security deposit
kein none, not any
der **Keller, —** cellar, basement
der **Kellner, —** waiter
kennen to know, be acquainted with
kennen·lernen to meet, make the acquaintance of
das **Kind, -er** child
die **Kindheit** childhood
das **Kino, -s** movie theater
die **Kirche, -n** church
klagen (über + *acc.*) to complain (about)
klar clear
klassisch classical
das **Klavier, -e** piano
das **Kleid, -er** dress
klein small
klopfen to knock
klug, klüger, klügst- clever, smart
kochen to cook; boil
der **Koffer, —** suitcase
(das) **Köln** Cologne (the city)
kommen* to come (kommt), kam, ist gekommen
die **Kompetenz, -en** competence, authority
der **Kompromiß, -sse** compromise

die **Königin, -nen** queen
die **Konjunktur** (national) economy
können* can, be able to (kann), konnte, gekonnt
kontrollieren to check, inspect
das **Konzert, -e** concert
der **Kopf, ⁼e** head
der **Korrespondent, -en, -en** correspondent
der **Korridor, -e** corridor
kosten to cost
kräftig powerful(ly), with force
das **Krankenhaus, ⁼er** hospital
die **Krankheit, -en** sickness, disease
die **Krawatte, -n** tie
der **Kreidekreis** chalk circle
der **Kreis, -e** circle
der **Krieg, -e** war
kriegen to get
der **Kritiker, —** critic
die **Küche, -n** kitchen; cuisine
die **Kuh, ⁼e** cow
kühl cool
der **Kuli** (*short for* **Kugelschreiber**) ballpoint pen
der **Kunde, -n, -n** customer
der **Kurs, -e course**
kurz, kürzer, kürzest- short

das **Labyrinth, -e** labyrinth
lächeln to smile
lachen to laugh
laden* to load; invite (lädt), lud, geladen
der **Laden, ⁼** store, shop

die **Lampe, -n** lamp
das **Land, ⁼er** country: land
die **Landschaft, -en** landscape
lang, länger, längst,- long
langsam slow
langweilig boring
der **Lärm** noise
lassen* to let, allow; have something done (läßt), ließ gelassen
der **Lastwagen, —** truck
das **Laufen** running
laufen* to run (läuft), lief, ist gelaufen
der **Läufer, —** runner
laut, lauter, lautest- loud
der **Lautsprecher, —** loudspeaker
leben to live
das **Leder, —** leather
legen to lay
der **Lehrer, —** teacher
die **Lehrerin, -nen** teacher (*female*)
leicht easy, easily; light; slight
die **Leidenschaft, -en** passion
leihen to lend
leise soft(ly)
sich **leisten** to afford, spend (*on oneself*)
lernen to learn, study
lesen* to read (liest), las, gelesen
letzt- last
die **Leute** (*pl.*) people
das **Licht, -er** light
die **Liebe, -n** love
lieben to love
lieber preferably
der **Liebhaber, —** lover

das **Lied, -er**   song
liefern   to deliver
liegen*   to lie, recline
(liegt), lag, gelegen
die **Liste, -n**   list
der **Löffel, —**   spoon
das **Lokal, -e**   place (e.g.,
restaurant, bar)
lösen   to solve
los · lassen*   to let loose
(läßt . . . los), ließ . . . los,
losgelassen
die **Lust**   desire

machen   to make, do, take
(e.g., a trip)
das **Mädchen, —**   girl
der **Mai**   May
der **Major, -e**   major
der **Majorsrang**   rank of major
mal   ever; just
das **Mal, -e**   time, occasion
das **Mal [erste]**   the first time
man   one
manch-   many a
der **Mann, ⁻er**   man
der **Mantel, —**   coat
die **Mappe, -n**   bookbag,
briefcase
das **Märchen, —**   fairytale
die **Mark, —**   mark (*currency*)
die **Marke, -n**   brand,
trademark, name brand
der **Markenartikel, —**   brand-
name goods
der **März**   March
die **Maus, ⁻e**   mouse
das **Meer, -e**   sea, ocean
mehr   more
mehrere   several
mein   my

meinen   to think, be of the
opinion; mean
meinetwegen   for my sake;
for all I care
meistens   usually
die **Mensa**   student dining hall
der **Mensch, -en, -en**   man,
human being
sich **merken**   to keep in mind
merken   to notice
das **Messer, —**   knife
die **Methode, -n**   method
die **Metzgerei, -en**   butcher
shop
mieten   to rent
die **Milch**   milk
die **Milchflasche, -n**   milk bottle
der **Minister, —**   minister
die **Minute, -n**   minute
mißverstehen*   to
misunderstand
(mißversteht), mißverstand,
mißverstanden
mit (+ *dat*.)   with
mit · bringen*   to bring
along
(bringt . . . mit),
brachte . . . mit, mitgebracht
miteinander   with each other
mit · kommen*   to come
along
(kommt . . . mit), kam . . .
mit, ist mitgekommen
das **Mitleid**   sympathy
mit · nehmen*   to take along
(nimmt . . . mit), nahm . . .
mit, mitgenommen
der **Mittag, -e**   noon
das **Mittagessen, —**   lunch
mit · teilen   to transmit,
communicate

die **Mitternacht** midnight
der **Mittwoch, -e** Wednesday
ich **möchte** I would like
  modern modern
  mögen* to like; may
  (**mag**), **mochte, gemocht**
  möglich possible
der **Monat, -e** month
  monatelang for months
der **Mond, -e** moon
der **Montag, -e** Monday
  morgen tomorrow
  morgen früh tomorrow
  morning
der **Morgen, —** morning
die **Mücke, -n** gnat, bug
  müde tired
die **Müdigkeit** tiredness
die **Mühe, -n** effort
  München Munich
der **Münchner, —** person from
  Munich
die **Musik** music
der **Musikfreund, -e** music lover
der **Musikunterricht** music
  lessons
  müssen* must, to have to
  (**muß**), **mußte, gemußt**
die **Mutter, ⏜** mother
  Mutti Mom

  nach (+ *dat.*) to; after
der **Nachahmer, —** imitator
  nachdem (*conj.*) after
  nachher (*adv.*) afterwards
  nach · laufen* to run after
  (**läuft . . . nach**), **lief . . .**
  nach, ist nachgelaufen
der **Nachmittag, -e** afternoon
  nachmittags in the
  afternoon

  nächst- next
die **Nacht, ⏜e** night
  nachts nights, at night
der **Nachttisch, -e** night table
  nah(e), näher, nächst- near,
  close
die **Nähe** vicinity
der **Name, -ns, -n** name
die **Nase, -n** nose
die **Nase voll haben*** to have a
  belly full
der **Nebel, —** fog
  neben (*two-way prep.*) next
  to, beside
  nebenan next door
  nehmen* to take
  (**nimmt**), **nahm, genommen**
  nein no
  nennen* to call, name
  (**nennt**), **nannte, genannt**
  nervös nervous
  nett nice
  neu new
  nicht wahr isn't it, aren't
  they, etc.
  nichts nothing
  nie never
  niemand no one
  noch still
  immer noch still
  noch nicht not yet
der **Norweger, —** Norwegian
  norwegisch (*adj.*)
  Norwegian
  notwendig necessary
die **Novelle, -n** novella
der **November** November
  nur only

  ob whether
  oben on top, up there

obwohl although, even
though
oder or
öffnen to open
oft, öfter, öftest- often
öfters often, frequently
ohne (+ *acc*.) without
der Oktober October
der Onkel, — uncle
die Oper, -n opera
operieren to operate on
die Orange, -n orange
das Orchester, — orchestra
die Ordnung order
originell original
das Ostern Easter
(das) Österreich Austria

das Paket, -e package
der Park park
parken to park
das Parlament, -e parliament
die Party, -s party
der Patient, -en, -en patient
das Penizillin penicillin
der Pfadfinder, — Boy Scout
der Pfennig, -e cent (*1/100th
of a mark*)
das Pferd, -e horse
das Pferderennen, — horse race
das Pfingsten Pentecost
pflanzen to plant
die Phase, -n phase
der Philosoph, -en, -en
philosopher
der Physiker, — physicist
die Pistole, -n pistol
der Plan, ̈e plan
die Platte, -n (Schallplatte)
record

der Plattenspieler, — record
player
Platz nehmen* to take a
seat, to sit down
der Platz, ̈e seat; place
plaudern to chat
pleite broke (*financially*)
die Polizei police
der Polizist, -en, -en policeman
der Porsche, -s Porsche
positiv positive
die Post mail; post office
der Präsident, -en, -en president
der Preis, -e price
das Preisgerangel competitive
pricing
das Problem, -e problem
der Professor, -en professor
profitieren to profit
die Prüfung, -en test, exam
der Pulli, -s sweater, pullover
putzen to polish, clean
die Putzfrau, -en cleaning
woman

das Radio, -s radio
der Rand, ̈er edge, border
der Randalierer, — rowdy
rar rare
rasch quick
rasieren to shave
sich rasieren to shave
(oneself)
der Rat advice
raten* (+ *acc. with things*)
(+ *dat. with people*)
to advise
(rät), riet, geraten
das Rathaus, ̈er city hall
rauchen to smoke

die **Rechnung, -en** bill
recht right
recht haben* to be right
einem recht sein* to be all
  right with someone
rechts to the right
rechtzeitig on time
der **Redner, —** speaker
der **Regen, —** rain
die **Regierung, -en** government
regnen to rain
reich rich
die **Reihe, -n** row
  (**an der Reihe sein*** to be
  one's turn)
die **Reise, -n** trip
das **Reisebüro, -s** travel agency
reisen(s) to travel
der **Reisescheck, -s** traveller's
  check
reiten* to ride (a horse)
  (reitet), ritt, ist (hat)
  geritten
rennen* to run
  (rennt), rannte, ist gerannt
die **Reparatur, -en** repair,
  (repair), shop
reparieren to repair
reservieren to reserve
das **Restaurant, -s** restaurant
das **Resultat, -e** result
der **Ring, -e** ring
roh coarse; raw
die **Rolle, -n** role
rollen to roll
der **Roman, -e** novel
die **Romantik** Romanticism
rot red
der **Rotwein, -e** red wine
rufen* to call
  (ruft), rief, gerufen

ruhig quiet
der **Rundfunk** radio station

die **Sache, -n** thing, affair
sagen to say, tell
saisonal seasonal
sammeln to gather, collect
der **Samstag, -e** Saturday
samstags Saturdays
der **Satz, ̈-e** sentence
sauber · machen to clean,
  clean up
saufen* to drink (*of*
  animals); booze
  (säuft), soff, gesoffen
schaden (+ *dat.*) to hurt,
  damage
schaffen to make; to
  accomplish
sich **schämen (über** + *acc.*) to be
  ashamed (of)
scharf, schärfer, schärfst-
  sharp
der **Schauspieler, —** actor
der **Scheck, -s** check
schenken to give (a present)
schicken to send
schieben* to shove, push
  (schiebt), schob, geschoben
das **Schiff, -e** ship
das **Schild, -er** sign
schlafen* to sleep
  (schläft), schlief, geschlafen
schlagen* to hit, beat
  (schlägt), schlug,
  geschlagen
der **Schlagstock, ̈-e** night stick,
  billy
schlank slender
schlecht bad

schließen* to close
(schließt), schloß,
geschlossen
der Schluß, ⁻sse conclusion, end
der Schlüssel, — key
schmuggeln to smuggle
die Schneiderei, -en tailor's
shop
schnell, schneller, schnellst-
fast
der Schnellzug, ⁻e express train
das Schnitzel, — cutlet
die Schokolade chocolate
schon already
schön beautiful
die Schönheit beauty
schreiben* to write
(schreibt), schrieb,
geschrieben
der Schreibtisch, -e desk
das Schreibwarengeschäft, -e
stationery store
der Schritt, -e step
der Schuh, -e shoe
schuld (sein) (to be)
responsible for
schuld an (+ dat.) guilty of,
responsible for
die Schule, -n school
schwach, schwächer,
schwächst- weak
die Schwankung, -en
fluctuation, variation
schwarz black
das Schwarzbrot black bread
(das) Schweden Sweden
die Schweinerei dirty business
die Schweiz Switzerland
der Schweizer, — Swiss
die Schweizerin, -nen Swiss
(female)

schwer heavy, difficult
die Schwester, -n sister
die Schwierigkeit, -en difficulty
das Schwimmen swimming
schwimmen* to swim
(schwimmt), schwamm,
ist, hat geschwommen
die See, -n sea
der See, -n lake
sehen* to see
(sieht), sah, gesehen
sehr very
sein his, its
sein* to be
(ist), war, ist gewesen
seit (+ dat.) since
seitdem (adv.) since then
(conj.) (ever) since
die Seite, -n side
die Sekretärin, -nen secretary
selten (adj.) rare
(adv.) seldom
das Semester, — semester
die Seminararbeit, -en term
paper (for a seminar)
die Sendung, -en program (radio
or television)
der September September
servieren to serve
die Serviette, -n napkin
setzen to set
sich setzen [hin] to sit down
sicher certain(ly), sure(ly)
siebzig seventy
das Silber silver
silbergrau silver-gray
singen* to sing
(singt), sang, gesungen
sitzen* to sit
(sitzt), saß, gesessen
ski · laufen* to ski

(läuft . . . ski), lief . . . ski,
  ist skigelaufen
so so, that way
so ein such a
sobald as soon as
das **Sofa, -s** couch, sofa
sofort immediately
der **Sohn, ⁻e** son
solange as long as
solch- such
sollen to be supposed to, be
  said to; ought to, should
der **Sommer, —** summer
der **Sommeranzug, ⁻e** summer
  suit
das **Sommerfest, -e** summer
  festival
das **Sommerhaus, ⁻er** summer
  house
sondern but (but rather)
der **Sonntag, -e** Sunday
sooft as often as
der **Sopran, -e** soprano
sorgen für to provide for
sowieso anyway, anyhow
der **Spanier, —** Spaniard
die **Spanierin, -nen** Spanish
  woman
sparen to save (*money*)
spät, später, spätest- late
spätestens at the latest
spazieren to stroll, walk
spazieren · gehen* to go for
  a walk
  (geht . . . spazieren),
  ging . . . spazieren, ist
  spazierengegangen
die **Speisekarte, -n** menu
die **Sperre, -n** barrier,
  roadblock
der **Spezialist, -en, -en** specialist

das **Spiel, -e** game
spielen to play
der **Sportfilm, -e** sport film
die **Sprache, -n** language
sprechen* (**über** + *acc.*) to
  speak (about)
  (spricht), sprach,
  gesprochen
der **Sprecher, —** speaker
springen* to jump
  (springt), sprang, ist
  gesprungen
die **Staatsuniversität, -en**
  government-supported
  university
die **Stadt gehen*** [**in**] to go
  downtown
die **Stadt, ⁻e** city
das **Städtchen** little city
der **Stadtplan, ⁻e** map of the city
stark, stärker, stärkst-
  strong
statt (+ *gen.*) instead of
stattdessen instead of that
stehen* to stand
  (steht), stand, gestanden
stehlen* to steal
  (stiehlt), stahl, gestohlen
steigen* to climb
  (steigt), stieg, ist gestiegen
der **Stein, -e** stone
stellen to put, place
stellen [**eine Frage**] to pose
  or ask a question
sterben* to die
  (stirbt), starb, ist gestorben
die **Steuer, -n** tax
die **Stimme, -n** voice
der **Stock, ⁻e** stick; story
  (*building*)
stolz proud

stören to disturb
stoßen* **(gegen** + *acc.*) to
  hit, run into
  (stößt), stieß, gestoßen
der **Strand, ⸚e** beach
die **Straße, -en** street
die **Straßenbahn, -en** streetcar
die **Straßenlaterne, -n** street
  light
  streiten* to quarrel, argue
  (streitet), stritt, gestritten
das **Stück, -e** piece; play
  (**Theaterstück**)
der **Student, -en, en** student
  studieren to study
der **Stuhl, ⸚e** chair
  stumm silently, without a
  word
die **Stunde, -en** hour
  suchen to hunt for
(das) **Südamerika** South America
(das) **Süddeutschland** South
  Germany
die **Suppe, -n** soup

die **Tafel, -n** blackboard
der **Tag, -e** day
  tagelang for days
  tagsüber during the day
die **Taktlosigkeit, -en**
  tactlessness, breach of
  tact
die **Tankstelle, -n** gas station
  Tante Elvira Aunt Elvira
die **Tante, -n** aunt
  tanzen to dance
  tapfer brave
die **Tasse, -n** cup
  tätig active
  tausend thousand

der **Tee** tea
die **Telefonnummer, -n** phone
  number
der **Teller, —** plate
das **Tennis** tennis
der **Tennisplatz, ⸚e** tennis court
der **Tennisschläger, —** tennis
  racket
der **Tennisspieler, —** tennis
  player
der **Tenor, -e** tenor
  teuer expensive
das **Theater, —** theater
das **Theaterstück, -e** play
das **Tier, -e** animal
die **Tinte, -n** ink
der **Tisch, -e** table
die **Tochter, ⸚** daughter
der **Todgeweihte** (*adj. noun*)
  doomed man
  todkrank deathly ill
  toll crazy
die **Tomate, -n** tomato
der **Tote** (*adj. noun*) dead person
  tragen* to carry; wear
  (trägt), trug, getragen
das **Tränengas** tear gas
  trauen (+ *dat.*) to trust
  treffen* to meet
  (trifft), traf, getroffen
die **Treppe, -n** stair(case)
  treten* to step
  (tritt), trat, ist, hat getreten
  treu true, faithful
  trinken* to drink
  (trinkt), trank, getrunken
  trocken dry
  trotz (+ *gen.*) in spite of
  trotzdem nevertheless
die **Tschechoslowakei**
  Czechoslovakia

tun* to do
(tut), tat, getan
der **Tunnel, —** tunnel
die **Tür, -en** door
die **Türkei** Turkey

die **U-Bahn (Untergrundbahn),**
-en subway
UNO United Nations
Organization
über (*two-way prep.*) over,
above; across
überall everywhere
überholen to overtake;
repair
übernachten to spend the
night, stay overnight
überraschen to surprise
der **Überschuß, ⁻sse** surplus
übersetzen to translate
überzeugen to convince
die **Übung, -en** exercise, drill
die **Uhr, -en** watch, clock;
o'clock
um (+ *acc.*) around; at
um . . . zu in order to
um · kommen* to die
(kommt . . . um), kam um,
ist umgekommen
unausgesetzt continual,
uninterrupted
und and
etwas **Undenkbares** something
unthinkable
unerwartet unexpected
der **Unfall, ⁻e** accident
ungewöhnlich unusual
die **Universität, -en** university
unmöglich impossible
unrecht haben* to be wrong

unser our
der **Unsinn** nonsense
unten below
unter (*two-way prep.*) under,
beneath
unterhalten* to entertain
(unterhält), unterhielt,
unterhalten
sich **unterhalten*** to entertain
oneself; converse
unternehmen* to undertake
(unternimmt), unternahm,
unternommen
unterschreiben* to sign
(unterschreibt),
unterschrieb,
unterschrieben
unterstützen to support
die **Untertasse, -n** saucer

der **Vater, ⁻** father
verbringen* to spend (time)
(verbringt), verbrachte,
verbracht
verdienen to earn, deserve
der **Verfasser, —** author
vergessen* to forget
(vergißt), vergaß, vergessen
verkaufen to sell
verkommen* to go to ruin
(verkommt), verkam, ist
verkommen
verlassen* to leave
(verläßt), verließ, verlassen
verletzen to injure
vermögen* to be capable of,
to be able to do (vermag),
vermochte, vermocht
verpassen to miss (e.g., a
bus, an opportunity)

verschieden different
versprechen* to promise
(verspricht), versprach,
versprochen
verstehen* to understand
(versteht), verstand,
verstanden
der **Verteidigungsminister, —**
secretary (minister) of
defense
das **Verwaltungsgebäude, —**
administration building
der **Verwandte** (*adj. noun*)
relative
viel, mehr, meist- much
viele many
vieles many things
viertel (das **Viertel**) quarter
das **Violinkonzert, -e** violin
concerto
voll full
völlig complete(ly)
von (+ *dat.*) from; off of;
of; by
vor (*two-way prep.*) in front
of
vorbei·fahren* to drive by
(fährt . . . vorbei),
fuhr . . . vorbei, ist
vorbeigefahren
vorbei·gehen* to pass, pass
by (geht . . . vorbei),
ging . . . vorbei, ist
vorbeigegangen
vor·bereiten to prepare
vor·finden* to find (there)
(findet . . . vor), fand . . .
vor, vorgefunden
vorher (*adv.*) before,
beforehand
vorig- last

vor·kommen* to happen
(kommt . . . vor), kam . . .
vor, ist vorgekommen
die **Vorlesung, -en** lecture
der **Vormittag, -e** forenoon,
morning
vorne up front
der **Vorschlag, ⁼e** suggestion
die **Vorsicht** (**vor** + *dat.*) care,
caution; Be careful
of . . . !
vorsichtig careful
vor·stellen to introduce
sich **vor·stellen** [**etwas**] to
imagine
wachsen* to grow
(wächst), wuchs, ist
gewachsen
die **Wachstumsrate, -n** growth
rate
der **Wagen, —** car
wählen to elect, choose
wahr true
während (*conj.*) while
(*prep.*) during
wahrscheinlich probably
der **Wald, ⁼er** woods, forest
die **Wand, ⁼e** wall
wandern(s) to hike, wander
wann when
warm, wärmer, wärmst-
warm
warten (**auf** + *acc.*) to wait
(for)
warum why
was what
was für ein what kind of
waschen* to wash
(wäscht), wusch, gewaschen
das **Wasser** water
der **Wecker, —** alarm clock

der **Weg, -e** way, path, road
wegen (+ *gen.*) on account
of, due to
weg · fahren to drive off
(fährt weg), fuhr
weg, ist weggefahren
weg · laufen* to run away
(laüft . . . weg),
lief . . . weg,
ist weggelaufen
weg · nehmen* to take away
(nimmt . . . weg), nahm . . .
weg, weggenommen
weh · tun* to hurt
(tut . . . weh), tat . . . weh,
wehgetan
die **Weihnachten** (*pl.*) Christmas
weil because
der **Wein, -e** wine
weise wise
weit far
weiter · arbeiten to go on
working
weiter · gehen* to walk on,
walk by
(geht . . . weiter), ging . . .
weiter, ist weitergegangen
welcher, welches, welche
which
weltbekannt world-
renowned
der **Weltkrieg, -e** world war
die **Weltmacht, ⸚e** world power
wenig little, few
wenige (*pl.*) few
wenn if; when, whenever
wer who
werden* to become, get
(wird), wurde, ist geworden
werfen* to throw
(wirft), warf, geworfen

das **Werk, -e** work
im Westen in the West
weswegen why, on what
account
das **Wetter** weather
wichtig important
widersprechen* (+ *dat.*) to
contradict
(widerspricht),
widersprach,
widersprochen
wie how; as
wieder again
(das) **Wien** Vienna
Wiener Viennese
das **Wienerschnitzel, —**
wienerschnitzel (breaded
veal cutlet)
wieviel how much
wieviele how many
der **Wille, -ns, -n** will
der **Wind, -e** wind
winken to wave
der **Winter, —** winter
der **Wintermonat, -e** winter
month
wirklich real(ly)
wirtschaften to "run things"
der **Wirtschaftswissenschaftler, —**
economist
das **Wissen** knowledge
wissen* to know (a fact)
(weiß), wußte, gewußt
wo where
die **Woche, -n** week
wochenlang for weeks
woher where from
wohin where (to)
wohl probably
wohlwollend benevolent,
well-meaning

wohnen   to live, reside
die **Wohnung, -en**   apartment
das **Wohnzimmer, —**   living
room
wollen*   to want, want to
(will). wollte, gewollt
das **Wort**   word
die **Worte** (*pl.*)   words (in
context)
die **Wörter** (*pl.*)   words (*not in
context*)
wundern   to surprise
sich **wundern**   to be surprised
die **Würde**   dignity
der **Wutanfall, ¨e**   fit of rage,
tantrum

der **Zahn, ¨e**   tooth
zart   gentle, delicate
zehn   ten
zeigen   to show; point at
die **Zeit, -en**   time
die **Zeitung, -en**   newspaper
zerstören   to destroy
ziehen*   to pull, drag; move
to (zieht), zog, gezogen
die **Zigarette, -n**   cigarette
die **Zigarre, -n**   cigar
der **Zigarrenrauch**   cigar smoke
das **Zimmer, —**   room

zittern   to tremble
zu (+ *dat.*)   to; at; for
zuerst   first
der **Zufall, ¨e**   chance; accident
zufrieden   satisfied
der **Zug, ¨e**   train
zu · hören   to listen
zu · machen   to close
zurück · bringen*   to bring
back, take back
(bringt . . . zurück),
brachte. . . zurück,
zurückgebracht
zurück · kommen*   to come
back (kommt . . . zurück),
kam . . . zurück, ist
zurückgekommen
zusammen   together
zuviel   too much
zu · winken (+ *dat.*)   to wave
(to someone)
zwanzig   twenty
**zwanziger (in den) zwanziger
(Jahren)**   in the 1920s
zweit-   second
zwingen*   to force
(zwingt), zwang,
gezwungen
zwischen (*two-way prep.*)
between

Index